THE
BONDS
OF
LOVE

THE BONDS OF LOVE

*PSYCHOANALYSIS, FEMINISM, AND THE
PROBLEM OF DOMINATION*

Jessica Benjamin

■

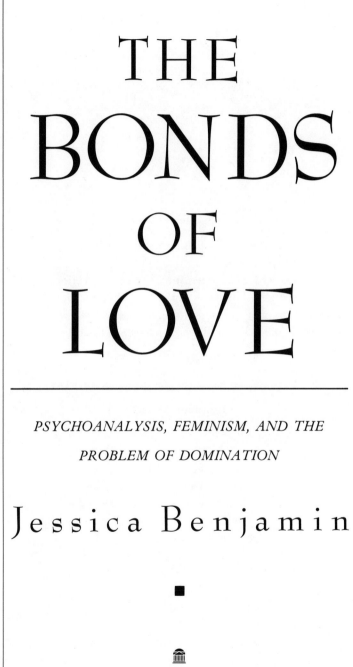

PANTHEON BOOKS NEW YORK

COPYRIGHT © 1988 BY JESSICA BENJAMIN

All rights reserved under International and Pan-American Copyright Conventions. Published in the United States by Pantheon Books, a division of Random House, Inc., New York, and simultaneously in Canada by Random House of Canada Limited, Toronto.

Library of Congress Cataloging-in-Publication Data

Benjamin, Jessica.
The bonds of love.

Bibliography: p.
Includes index.
1. Sex role. 2. Dominance (Psychology)
3. Recognition (Psychology) 4. Interpersonal reactions. 5. Feminism. 6. Psychoanalysis. I. Title.
BF692.2.B46   1988   155.3   87-46057
ISBN 0-394-55133-8
ISBN 0-394-75730-3 (pbk.)

BOOK DESIGN BY GUENET ABRAHAM

Manufactured in the United States of America

First Edition

C O N T E N T S

A C K N O W L E D G M E N T S

I WISH TO acknowledge several institutions that have given me their support during the writing of this book. A National Institute of Mental Health fellowship (F32MH07993) enabled me to study infancy and the mother-infant relationship under the auspices of the Department of Psychiatry, Albert Einstein College of Medicine. There, Dr. Beatrice Beebe of Yeshiva University generously allowed me to participate in her research project and to interview her subjects. The New

York Institute of the Humanities and its founder Richard Sennett offered me an intellectual home and financial support as I developed the themes of this book. As a fellow at the Blanche, Edith, and Irving Laurie New Jersey Chair in Women's Studies at Douglass College, I was able to complete the main draft of this book. I am grateful to the administrative staff for their support, and especially to Carol Gilligan, holder of the chair, for her encouragement and criticism of my work.

A number of friends and colleagues read parts of this manuscript, offering their criticism and suggestions as well as their enthusiasm. My thanks to Donna Bassin, Serafina Bathrick, Beatrice Beebe, Elsa First, Daphne Joslin, Maureen Mahoney, Barbara Ottenhof, Steve Rosenheck, Ellen Ross, and Christine Stansell. I also wish to thank the editors of several anthologies for their comments on earlier versions of some parts of this book: Hester Eisenstein, Mark Kann, Sharon Thompson, Teresa de Lauretis, Kathleen Woodward, and Judith Alpert.

Over the years I have benefited greatly from discussions with and critical readings by Nancy Chodorow, Carol Gilligan, and Evelyn Keller, with whom I share many common assumptions, and whose work has strongly influenced my own.

I have had the good fortune to constantly test my ideas in dialogue with several friends: for over a decade I have discussed feminism with Sibylla Flügge, psychoanalysis with Rita Wohlfarth, and intersubjectivity, recognition, and infant development with Maureen Mahoney.

My small group—Muriel Dimen, Virginia Goldner, and Adrienne Harris—has shared with me the pleasure and the difficulties of the project of joining psychoanalysis and feminism; their stimulation and encouragement, as well as their feedback, have been invaluable.

The major difficulty in writing this book—to do justice to its complex psychoanalytic and philosophical arguments while making it available to the nonspecialist audience—could not have been solved without my editors. Ed Cohen, with his ear for the well-tempered sentence, helped me to render this a coherent text. Sara Bershtel, whose devotion to lucidity is equal to all complexity, edited it with a prodigious fervor, rigor, and fidelity. I am very thankful to them both.

To Emmanuel Ghent, who has been unstintingly generous with his ideas, as well as support and criticism of this work, and who has shared with me his radical yet undogmatic faith in the emotional and intellectual possibilities of psychoanalysis, I am deeply grateful.

My special thanks go to Andy Rabinbach, trusty foe of the Spirit of Gravity, whose irreverent humor and irony have kept me from sinking under the weight of critical consciousness these many years; and whose unideological commitment to the "mission impossible" of dual parenting and dual writing has been constant and indispensable. And to my son Jacob, who in the midst of it all enjoyed himself audibly and unhurriedly.

This book is dedicated to the memory of Herbert Benjamin, inveterate believer in social struggle, and to his grandchildren.

THE
BONDS
OF
LOVE

INTRODUCTION

Men are not gentle creatures who want to be loved,
and who at the most can defend themselves if they
are attacked; they are, on the contrary, creatures
among whose instinctual endowments is to be reck-
oned a powerful share of aggressiveness. As a result,
their neighbor is for them not only a potential
helper or sexual object, but also someone who
tempts them to satisfy their aggressiveness on him,
to exploit his capacity for work without compensation, to use him sexually without his consent, to
seize his possessions, to humiliate him, to cause him
pain, to torture and to kill him. *Homo homini lupus.*
Who, in the face of all his experience of life and
of history, will have the courage to dispute this
assertion?
—Sigmund Freud, *Civilization and Its Discontents*

SINCE THOMAS HOBBES, in his justification of
authority, first analyzed the passions, domination has
been understood as a psychological problem. Echoing
Hobbes's view of the state of nature, Freud locates the

origins of the problem in our lupine proclivities. The injunction to love our neighbor is not a reflection of abiding concern for others, but a testimony to the opposite: our propensity for aggression. While Freud acknowledges that the restrictions of culture are painful, he also believes that they protect us from the dangers of nature, or, put another way, that the rule of authority is preferable to the war of all against all. An unflinching scrutiny of human destructiveness convinces him that the repression demanded by civilization is preferable to the ruthlessness that prevails in the state of nature. Some kind of domination is inevitable; the only question is which kind. In the face of Freud's monumental theory of psychic life and its interaction with culture, who indeed would challenge his conclusion?

But Freud's vision of the conflict between instinct and civilization, each with its own dangers and drawbacks, has actually created an impasse for social thought. In framing the problem of domination in such terms, Freud left no exit: either we accept the necessity of some rational authority to control our dangerous nature, or we maintain naïvely that our better nature is dangerously repressed by the social order. But this opposition between instinct and civilization obscures the central question of how domination actually works. As Foucault puts it: "If power were never anything but repressive, if it never did anything but to say no, do you really think one would be brought to obey it?"[1]

The concept of repression cannot grasp that "power holds good" not by denying our desire but by forming it, converting it into a willing retainer, its servant or representative. It cannot grasp domination as a system that transforms all parts of the psyche. Only when we realize that power is not simply prohibition can we step outside the framework of choosing between repressive authority and unbridled nature.

In truth, Freud's understanding of authority is more complex than this choice suggests. He does take into account what we may call the culture's "erotic" means of binding individuals in spite of their resistance. Obedience to the laws of civilization is first inspired, not by fear or prudence, Freud tells us, but by love, love for those early powerful figures who first demand obedience. Obedience, of course, does not exorcise aggression; it merely directs it against the self. There it becomes a means of self-domination, infusing the voice of conscience with the hostility that cannot be aimed at the "unattackable authority."[2] Freud has thus given us a basis for seeing domination as a problem not so much of human nature as of human relationships—the interaction between the psyche and social life. It is a problem that must be defined not simply in terms of aggression and civilized constraints, but as an extension of the bonds of love.

This book is an analysis of the interplay between love and domination. It conceives domination as a two-way process, a system involving the participation of those who submit to power as well as those who exercise it. Above all, this book seeks to understand how domination is anchored in the hearts of the dominated.

This is not a new question. Dostoevsky's classic discussion of authority, "The Grand Inquisitor," dramatized the psychological force of domination. In it, Christ returns to earth during the Inquisition and confronts the Inquisitor with the Church's debasement of faith: Why has a free act of love been transformed into a practice of submission? The Inquisitor responds that people do not want freedom and truth, which only cause deprivation and suffering; they want miracle, mystery, and authority. The pain that accompanies compliance is preferable to the pain that attends freedom. The awesome nearness of the ultimate power embodied in the Church makes pain tolerable, even a source of inspiration or transcendence. This ability to enlist the hope for redemption is the signature of the power that inspires voluntary submission. We recognize it in a wide range of social phenomena— whether pope or political party—as the power that inspires fear and adoration simultaneously.

Freud offered the most far-reaching perspective on the workings of domination. In accord with his view of the state of nature, Freud imagined the origins of civilization in the primal struggle between father and son. The sons who overthrow the father's authority become afraid of their own aggression and lawlessness and regret the loss of his wonderful power; and so they reinstate law and authority in the father's image. Thus, in a seemingly unbreakable circle, revolt is always followed by guilt and restoration of authority. As Herbert Marcuse noted, in every revolution the hope of abolishing domination has been defeated by the establishment of a new authority—"every revolution has also been a betrayed revolution."[3]

The psychoanalytic inquiry into domination has been reformulated a number of times since Freud, but always in terms of the primary metaphor of the father-son struggle. Some psychoanalytic critics concluded that paternal authority wasn't so bad after all, because the sons inherit the benefits as well as the limits of the law. Others countered this concession to authority, arguing that the lifting of repression could *potentially* dissolve the destructiveness of the instincts. But their opposition to paternal law was based on an embrace of nature that evaded the problem of human destructiveness, and seemed indeed to fly in the face of all we know about life and history.

The historic problem that shaped the inquiry into domination most powerfully was, of course, the appearance of fascist mass movements with their ecstatic submission to the hypnotic leader. Some psychoanalytic social critics argued that it was the failure of rational paternal authority—a "fatherless society"—that stimulated the yearnings for surrender to a powerful leader. Thus the paradigm of the struggle between father and son framed the understanding of domination as a choice between rational-democratic and irrational authority—essentially a choice of the lesser evil.[4]

What is extraordinary about the discussion of authority throughout Freudian thought is that it occurs exclusively in a world of men. The struggle for power takes place between father and son; woman plays no part in it, except as prize or temptation to regression, or as the third point of a triangle. There is no struggle between man and woman in this story; indeed, woman's subordination to man is taken for granted, invisible. Even the most radical of Freudians left strangely untouched psychoanalysis's most profound and unexamined assumption about domination: the subordination of women to men.[5] This assumption does more than just give sanctuary to all the old ideas, conscious and unconscious, about men and women; it also provides, as we will see, the ultimate rationalization for accepting all authority.

This book makes use of feminist criticism and reinterpretation of psychoanalytic theory to consider anew the problem of domination.[6] The contemporary consciousness of women's subjugation has profoundly challenged the acceptance of authority that permeates psychoanalytic thinking. Feminism has provided a fulcrum for raising the Freudian edifice, revealing its foundation to lie in the acceptance of authority and gender relations. Thus what appeared in Freudian thought as the psychological inevitability of domination can now be seen as the result of a complex process of psychic development and not as "bedrock."

The point of departure for this reexamination of the problem of domination is Simone de Beauvoir's insight: that woman functions as man's primary other, his opposite—playing nature to his reason, immanence to his transcendence, primordial oneness to his individuated separateness, and object to his subject.[7] This analysis of gender domination as a complementarity of subject and object, each the mirror image of the other, offers a fresh perspective on the dualism that permeates Western culture. It shows how gender polarity underlies such familiar dualisms as autonomy and dependency, and thus establishes the coordinates for the positions of master and slave.

The fundamental question we must consider is why these positions continue to shape the relationship between the sexes despite our society's formal commitment to equality; what explains their psychological persistence? I believe psychoanalytic theory can help illuminate what it formerly accepted: the genesis of the psychic structure in which one person plays subject and the other must serve as his object. My purpose is to analyze the evolution of this structure and show how it forms the fundamental premise of domination.

I will show how the structure of domination can be traced from the relationship between mother and infant into adult eroticism, from the earliest awareness of the difference between mother and father to the global images of male and female in the culture. We will begin with the conflict between dependence and independence in infant life, and move outward toward the opposites of power and surrender in adult sexual life. We will see how masculinity and femininity become associated with the postures of master and slave—how these postures arise in boys' and girls' different relationships to mother and father, and how they shape the different destinies of male and female children. We will observe the identification of girls as object and boys as subject in the central psychoanalytic model of development, the Oedipus complex, and see how this opposition distorts the very ideal of the individual. Finally, we will follow this ideal into the culture at large, which preserves the structure of domination even while it appears to embrace equality.

The anchoring of this structure so deep in the psyche is what gives domination its appearance of inevitability, makes it seem that a relationship in which both participants are subjects—both empowered and mutually respectful—is impossible. As a theory of unconscious mental processes, psychoanalysis offers a most promising point of entry for analyzing that structure. But it also, as we have seen in Freud's thought, harbors the best rationalization of authority. As a result, we find in psychoanalysis an illustration of our problem as well as a guide to it. This book therefore weaves into the analysis of domination a critique of psychoanalytic thinking about each of the issues we will consider—individual development, gender difference, and authority.*

---

*Since this critique often contrasts "classical" psychoanalytic theory with recent revisions, I have reserved many technical and specialized details for the endnotes for the

To challenge previous psychoanalytic thinking is not, as some feminists believe, merely a matter of arguing that the sexual stereotypes or "biases" in Freudian thought are socially constructed. Nor is it a matter of challenging Freud's view of human nature by arguing that women, unlike men, are "gentle creatures." In adopting the feminist critique of gender polarity, I am aware that it has sometimes tended to reinforce the dualism it criticizes. Every binary split creates a temptation to merely reverse its terms, to elevate what has been devalued and denigrate what has been overvalued. To avoid the tendency toward reversal is not easy—especially given the existing division in which the female is culturally defined as that which is not male. In order to challenge the sexual split which permeates our psychic, cultural, and social life, it is necessary to criticize not only the idealization of the masculine side, but also the reactive valorization of femininity. What is necessary is not to take sides but to remain focused on the dualistic structure itself.

The stakes of this enterprise are high. A sharper perspective on this matter is particularly important to feminist thought today, because a major tendency in feminism has constructed the problem of domination as a drama of female vulnerability victimized by male aggression. Even the more sophisticated feminist thinkers frequently shy away from the analysis of submission, for fear that in admitting woman's participation in the relationship of domination, the onus of responsibility will appear to shift from men to women, and the moral victory from women to men. More generally, this has been a weakness of radical politics: to idealize the oppressed, as if their politics and culture were untouched by the system of domination, as if people did not participate in their own submission. To reduce domination to a simple relation of doer and done-to is to substitute moral outrage for

---

interested reader. I have done so in the belief that psychoanalysis ought to stand with one leg in clinical theory and practice and the other in public intellectual discourse.

analysis. Such a simplification, moreover, reproduces the structure of gender polarity under the guise of attacking it.

In this book I have tried to build on and reframe psychoanalytic theory in order to retell Freud's story of domination in a way that preserves its complexity and ambiguity. It was Freud's conclusion that we could not do without authority (internalized as guilt), and that we could not but suffer under its constraint. No doubt our historical situation readily allows us to question the masculine form of authority—as Freud did not—but this in itself does not immediately resolve the problem of destructiveness or submission. It only starts us on a new approach to grasping the tension between the desire to be free and the desire not to be. To persevere in that approach, it seems to me, requires of theory some of that quality which Keats demanded for poetry— negative capability. The theoretic equivalent of that ability to face mystery and uncertainty "without any irritable reaching after fact and reason" would be the effort to understand the contradictions of fact and reason without any irritable reaching after one side at the expense of the other.

As I have said elsewhere, a theory or a politics that cannot cope with contradiction, that denies the irrational, that tries to sanitize the erotic, fantastic components of human life cannot visualize an authentic end to domination but only vacate the field.

The First
Bond

PSYCHOANALYSIS HAS SHIFTED its focus since Freud, aiming its sights toward ever earlier phases of development in childhood and infancy. This reorientation has had many repercussions: it has given the mother-child dyad an importance in psychic development rivaling the oedipal triangle, and consequently, it has stimulated a new theoretical construction of individual development. This shift from oedipal to preoedipal—that is, from father to mother—can actually be said to have changed the entire frame of psychoanalytic thinking. Where formerly the psyche was conceived as a force field of drives and defenses, now it became an inner drama of ego and objects (as psychoanalysis terms the mental representation of others). Inevitably, the focus on the ego and its inner object relationships led to an increased interest in the idea of the self, and more generally, in the relationship between self and other. The last twenty-five years have seen a flowering of psychoanalytic theories about the early growth of the self in the relationship with the other.[1]

In this chapter I will show how domination originates in a transformation of the relationship between self and other. Briefly stated, domination and submission result from a breakdown of the necessary tension between self-assertion and mutual recognition that allows self and other to meet as sovereign equals.

Assertion and recognition constitute the poles of a delicate balance. This balance is integral to what is called "differentiation": the individual's development as a self that is aware of its distinctness from others. Yet this balance, and with it the differentiation of self and other, is difficult to sustain.[2] In particular, the need for recognition gives rise to a paradox. Recognition is that response from the other which makes meaningful the feelings, intentions, and actions of the self. It allows the self to realize its agency and authorship in a tangible way. But such recognition can only come from an other whom we, in turn, recognize as a person in his or her own right. This struggle to be recognized by an other, and thus confirm our selves, was shown by Hegel to form the core of relationships of domination. But what Hegel formulated at the level of philosophical abstraction can also be discussed in terms of what we now know about the psychological development of the infant. In this chapter we will follow the course of recognition in the earliest encounters of the self with the nurturing other (or others), and see how the inability to sustain paradox in that interaction can, and often does, convert the exchange of recognition into domination and submission.

·   ·   ·

THE BEGINNING OF RECOGNITION

As she cradles her newborn child and looks into its eyes, the first-time mother says, "I believe she knows me. You do know me, don't you? Yes, you do." As she croons to her baby in that soft, high-pitched repetitive voice (the "infantized" speech that scientists confirm is the universal baby talk), she attributes to her infant a knowledge beyond ordinary knowing. To the skeptical observer this knowledge may appear to be no more than projection. For the mother, this peaceful moment after a feeding—often after a mounting storm of cries and body convulsions, the somewhat clumsy effort to get baby's mouth connected to the nipple, the gradual relaxation as baby begins to suck and milk begins to flow, and finally baby's alert, attentive, yet enigmatic look—this moment is indeed one of recognition. She says to her baby, "Hey, stranger, are you really the one I carried around inside of me? Do you know me?" Unlike the observer, she would not be surprised to hear that rigorous experiments show that her baby can already distinguish her from other people, that newborns already prefer the sight, sound, and smell of their mothers.[3]

The mother who feels recognized by her baby is not simply projecting her own feelings into her child—which she assuredly does. She is also linking the newborn's past, inside her, with his future, outside of her, as a separate person.* The baby is a stranger to her, she is not yet sure who this baby is, although she is certain that he or she is already someone, a unique person with his or her own destiny.† Although the

---

*Although I use the word "carried" and refer to research on mother-infant pairs in which the infant was the biological offspring of this mother, I am not suggesting that the experience is radically different in adoption. Adoptive mothers, like biological ones, hold their baby inside their minds before birth, and identify with their own mothers who carried them. It is this mental holding, and the shift to a relationship with a real—outside—baby that I am referring to here.

†Since there is no graceful solution to the problem of what gender pronoun to use for the infant, I shall alternate between masculine and feminine. In those paragraphs where

baby is wholly dependent upon her—and not only on her, but perhaps equally on a father or others—never for a moment does she doubt that this baby brings his own self, his unique personality, to bear on their common life. And she is already grateful for the baby's cooperation and activity—his willingness to be soothed, his acceptance of frustration, his devotion to her milk, his focusing on her face. Later, as baby is able to demonstrate ever more clearly that he does know and prefer her to all others, she will accept this glimmer of recognition as a sign of the mutuality that persists in spite of the tremendous inequality of the parent–child relationship. But perhaps never will she feel more strongly, than in those first days of her baby's life, the intense mixture of his being part of herself, utterly familiar and yet utterly new, unknown, and other.

It may be hard for a mother to accept this paradox, the fact that this baby has come from her and yet is so unknown to her. She may feel frustrated that her child cannot yet tell her who he is, what he knows or doesn't know. Certainly, a new mother has a complex range of feelings, many of which are dismissed or utterly denied by the common sentimentality surrounding motherhood. She may feel bored, unsure of what she should be doing to quiet or please baby, exhausted, anxious about herself and her body, angry that baby demands so much from her, dismayed at the lack of visible gratitude or response, impatient for baby to reveal himself, afraid that her baby is not normal, that he is going to stay like this forever.

Despite such doubts and difficulties, however, most first-time mothers are able to sustain a powerful connection to a newborn child.

I refer to the mother as "she," I will generally avoid confusion by calling the infant "he." In those paragraphs where I refer to the infant alone and therefore the referent for the pronoun is clear, the infant will generally be "she." Although I write about the mother, I mean simply the significant adult, which could equally be a father or any other caregiver well known to the child. But since it is quite relevant to my argument that the principal caregiver in our culture is usually (or is assumed to be) "the mother," this ambiguity will have to remain.

Naturally, some of a mother's ability to mother reflects the nurturance her own parents gave her and the support she receives from other adults. But what sustains her from moment to moment is the relationship she is forming with her infant, the gratification she feels when baby, with all that raw intensity, responds to her.[4] In this early interaction, the mother can already identify the first signs of mutual recognition: "I recognize *you* as my baby who recognizes *me*."

To experience recognition in the fullest, most joyful way, entails the paradox that "you" who are "mine" are also different, new, outside of me. It thus includes the sense of loss that you are no longer inside me, no longer simply my fantasy of you, that we are no longer physically and psychically one, and I can no longer take care of you simply by taking care of myself. I may find it preferable to put this side of reality out of my consciousness—for example, by declaring you the most wonderful baby who ever lived, far superior to all other babies, so that you are my dream child, and taking care of you is as easy as taking care of myself and fulfills my deepest wishes for glory. This is a temptation to which many new parents succumb in some measure.

Still, the process of recognition, charted here through the experience of the new mother, always includes this paradoxical mixture of otherness and togetherness: You belong to me, yet you are not (any longer) part of me. The joy I take in your existence must include *both* my connection to you *and* your independent existence—I recognize that you are real.

INTERSUBJECTIVITY

Recognition is so central to human existence as to often escape notice; or, rather, it appears to us in so many guises that it is seldom grasped as one overarching concept. There are any number of near-synonyms for it: to recognize is to affirm, validate, acknowledge, know, accept, understand, empathize, take in, tolerate, appreciate, see, identify with, find familiar, . . . love. Even the sober expositions of research on infancy, which detail the exchange of infant and caregiver, are full of the language of recognition. What I call *mutual recognition* includes a number of experiences commonly described in the research on mother-infant interaction: emotional attunement, mutual influence, affective mutuality, sharing states of mind. The idea of mutual recognition seems to me an ever more crucial category of early experience. Increasingly, research reveals infants to be active participants who help shape the responses of their environment, and "create" their own objects. Through its focus on interaction, infancy research has gradually widened psychology's angle of observation to include infant *and* parent, the simultaneous presence of two living subjects.[5]

While this may seem rather obvious, psychoanalysis has traditionally expounded theories of infancy that present a far less active exchange between mothers and infants. Until very recently, most psychoanalytic discussions of infancy, early ego development, and early mothering depicted the infant as a passive, withdrawn, even "autistic" creature. This view followed Freud, for whom the ego's initial relation to the outside world was hostile, rejecting its impingement. In Freud's reconstruction, the first relationship (i.e., with mother) was based on oral drive—a physiological dependency, a nonspecific need for someone to reduce tension by providing satisfaction. The caregiver merely appeared as the object of the baby's need, rather than as a specific person with an independent existence. In other words, the baby's relationship to the world was only shaped by the need for food and comfort, as represented by the breast; it did not include any of the curiosity and responsiveness to sight and sound, face and voice, that are incipiently social.[6] Those elements of psychic life that demand a living, responsive other had little place in psychoanalytic thought.

Much of the impetus for change came from research based on nonpsychoanalytic models of development. Piaget's developmental psychology, which saw the infant as active and stimulus-seeking, as constructing its environment by action and interaction, eventually led to a wave of research and theory that challenged the psychoanalytic view of infantile passivity.[7] Equally important was the influence of ethological research that studied animal and human infants in their natural environments, and so identified the growth of attachment, the social connection to others—especially the mother—that we have been describing.[8] From knowing and preferring its mother, the infant proceeds to form a relationship with her that involves a wide range of activities and emotions, many of which are independent of feeding and caregiving.

Basing their work largely on infant observation, the "attachment theorists"—preeminently the British psychoanalyst John Bowlby— argued that sociability was a primary rather than a secondary phenomenon. In the late 1950s, Bowlby explicitly contested the earlier psychoanalytic view that saw the infant's tie to the mother exclusively in terms of his oral investment in her. Bowlby drew on extensive research which showed that separation from parents and deprivation of contact with other adults catastrophically undermined infant emotional and social development.[9] Social stimulation, warmth, and affective interchange, he concluded, are indispensable to human growth from the beginning of life. Research with infants who were securely embedded in a relationship confirmed that attachment to specific persons (not only mothers but fathers, siblings, and caregivers as well) was a crucial milestone of the second six months of life.[10] Bowlby's work coincided with an influential tendency in British psychoanalysis called object relations theory, which put new emphasis on the child's early relationship with others. Together they offered psychoanalysis a new foundation: the assumption that we are fundamentally social beings.[11]

The idea that the infant's capacity and desire to relate to the world is incipiently present at birth and develops all along has important consequences. It obviously demands a revision of Freud's original view of the human subject as a monadic energy system, in favor of a self that is active and requires other selves. But it also contests the view of early infancy in the dominant American psychoanalytic paradigm, ego psychology. Ego psychology's most important theory of infant development, formulated by the child analyst and observer Margaret Mahler in the late 1960s, describes the child's gradual separation and individuation from an initial symbiotic unity with the mother.[12] The problem with this formulation is the idea of separation from oneness; it contains the implicit assumption that we grow *out of* relationships rather than becoming more active and sovereign *within* them, that we start in a state of dual oneness and wind up in a state of singular oneness.

Mahler's work on separation-individuation was, nevertheless, a landmark in the theory of the self. It offered a genealogy of the anxiety and conflict associated with becoming independent, and thus profoundly changed the focus of both clinical practice and psychoanalytic theory. Separation-individuation theory influenced psychoanalytic thinking in its drift toward the object relations approach; it also formulated more concretely the actual interaction between parent and child, admitting the importance of interpersonal dynamics without denying inner unconscious reality. In separation-individuation theory, the self-other relationship almost has its day. However, its theoretical construction of early infancy reiterates the old view of the baby who never looks up from the breast. This baby, who "hatches" like a bird from the egg of symbiosis, is then brought to the world by its mother's ministrations, just as Freud thought the ego was brought into being by the pressure of the outside world.[13]

It was, therefore, a radical challenge to the contemporary American psychoanalytic paradigm of infancy as well as to the classical Freudian view, when psychoanalyst and infancy researcher Daniel Stern contended in the 1980s that the infant is never totally undifferentiated (symbiotic) from the mother, but is primed from the beginning to be interested in and to distinguish itself from the world of others.[14] Once we accept the idea that infants do not begin life as part of an undifferentiated unity, the issue is not only how we separate from oneness, but also how we connect to and recognize others; the issue is not how we become free of the other, but how we actively engage and make ourselves known in relationship to the other.

This view of the self emerged not only from the observation of infants, but also in the consulting rooms where psychoanalysts began to discern the infant cry in the adult voice. The desperate anguish of those who feel dead and empty, unable to connect to themselves or to others, led to the question, What makes a person feel authentic? a question which also led back to the infant. In the words of the British psychoanalyst D. W. Winnicott, the question is, What kind of relationship "enables the infant to begin to exist, to build a personal ego, to ride instincts, and to meet with all the difficulties inherent in life?"[15] This question motivated the "backward" shift of psychoanalytic interest: away from neurosis, oedipal conflicts, and sexual repression, toward the preoedipal conflicts of the ego, disturbances in the sense of self, and the feeling of acute loneliness and emptiness. What psychoanalysts began to look at was how a sense of self is consolidated or disrupted. Their focus was no longer on just the wish that is gratified or repressed, but on the self that is affected by the other's denial or fulfillment of that wish. Each denial or fulfillment could make a child feel either confirmed or thwarted in his sense of agency and self-esteem. The issue of the self's attitude to itself (self-love, self-cohesion, self-esteem) gave rise to the psychoanalytic preoccupation with narcissism as a clinical and a theoretical issue. In the 1970s, Heinz Kohut founded a new direction in American psychoanalysis called self psychology, which reinterpreted psychic development in terms of the self's need to find cohesion and mirroring in the other.[16]

From the study of the self who suffers the lack of recognition, as well as the new perception of the active, social infant who can respond to and differentiate others, emerges what I call the *intersubjective view.* * The intersubjective view maintains that the individual grows in and

---

*The concept of intersubjectivity has its origins in the social theory of Jürgen Habermas (1970), who used the expression "the intersubjectivity of mutual understanding" to designate an individual capacity and a social domain. I have taken the concept as a theoretical standpoint from which to criticize the exclusively intrapsychic conception

through the relationship to other subjects. Most important, this perspective observes that the other whom the self meets is also a self, a subject in his or her own right. It assumes that we are able and need to recognize that other subject as different and yet alike, as an other who is capable of sharing similar mental experience. Thus the idea of intersubjectivity reorients the conception of the psychic world from a subject's relations to its object toward a subject meeting another subject.

The intersubjective view, as distinguished from the intrapsychic, refers to what happens in the field of self and other. Whereas the intrapsychic perspective conceives of the person as a discrete unit with a complex internal structure, intersubjective theory describes capacities that emerge in the interaction between self and others. Thus intersubjective theory, even when describing the self alone, sees its aloneness as a particular point in the spectrum of relationships rather than as the original, "natural state" of the individual. The crucial area we uncover with intrapsychic theory is the unconscious; the crucial element we explore with intersubjective theory is the representation of self and other as distinct but interrelated beings.

I suggest that intrapsychic and intersubjective theory should not be seen in opposition to each other (as they usually are) but as complementary ways of understanding the psyche.[18] To recognize the intersubjective self is not to deny the importance of the intrapsychic: the inner world of fantasy, wish, anxiety, and defense; of bodily symbols

---

of the individual in psychoanalysis. The term was first brought from Habermas's theory to infant psychology by Colin Trevarthen, who documented a "period of primary intersubjectivity, when sharing of intention with others becomes an effective psychological activity." More recently, Daniel Stern has outlined the psychological development of intersubjectivity in infancy, locating intersubjective relatedness as a crucial point in self development when the infant is able to share subjective (especially emotional) experiences. Because intersubjectivity refers both to a capacity and to a theoretical standpoint, I will generally call the capacity recognition, and the theory intersubjectivity.[17]

and images whose connections defy the ordinary rules of logic and language. In the inner world, the subject incorporates and expels, identifies with and repudiates the other, not as a real being, but as a mental object. Freud discovered these processes, which constitute the dynamic unconscious, largely by screening out the real relations with others and focusing on the individual mind.[19] But my point here is not to reverse Freud's decision for the inner world by choosing the outside world; it is, rather, to grasp both realities.* Without the intrapsychic concept of the unconscious, intersubjective theory becomes one-dimensional, for it is only against the background of the mind's private space that the *real* other stands out in relief.

In my view, the concept that unifies intersubjective theories of self development is the need for recognition. A person comes to feel that "I am the doer who does, I am the author of my acts," by being with another person who recognizes her acts, her feelings, her intentions, her existence, her independence. Recognition is the essential response, the constant companion of assertion. The subject declares, "I am, I do," and then waits for the response, "You are, you have done." Recognition is, thus, reflexive; it includes not only the other's confirming response, but also how we find ourselves in that response. We recognize ourselves in the other, and we even recognize ourselves in inanimate things: for the baby, the ability to recognize what she has seen before is as Stern says, "self-affirming as well as world-affirming," enhancing her sense of effective agency: "My mental representation works!"[20]

Psychologists speak of contingent responsiveness—this refers to the baby's pleasure in things that respond directly to the baby's own acts,

---

*Unfortunately it is beyond the scope of this discussion to propose a scheme for synthesizing the two approaches. The problem is that each focuses on different aspects of psychic experience which are too interdependent to be simply severed from one another. I am emphasizing intersubjectivity over intrapsychic theory because the latter is better developed and usually overshadows the former, not because I think one ought to preclude the other.

the mobile that moves when baby jerks the cord tied to her wrist, the bells that ring when she kicks her feet. Contingent responses confirm the baby's activity and effectiveness, and therein lies the pleasure: the baby becomes more involved in making an impact (the kicking has results!) than in the particular sight or sound of the thing.[21] And soon the pleasure derives from both the effect on the object and the reaction of the other subject who applauds. The nine-month-old already looks to the parent's face for the shared delight in a sound. The two-year-old says, "I did it!" showing the peg she has hammered and waiting for the affirmation that she has learned something new, that she has exercised her agency.

Of course not all actions are undertaken in direct relation to a recognizing other. The child runs down the hill and feels the pleasure of her body in motion. She is simply aware of herself and her own action, absorbed in herself and the moment. This experience, like the play with objects, may be based on pleasure in mastery as well as self-expression. Yet we know that such pleasure in one's own assertion requires and is associated with a supportive social context. We know that serious impairment of the sense of mastery and the capacity for pleasure results when the self-other matrix is disrupted, when the life-giving exchange with others is blocked. The ten-month-old may hesitate to crawl away and explore the new toys in the corner if he senses that the mother will withdraw her attention the moment he is not absorbed in her, or if the mother's doubtful look suggests it is not all right to go.[22] As life evolves, assertion and recognition become the vital moves in the dialogue between self and other.

Recognition is not a sequence of events, like the phases of maturation and development, but a constant element through all events and phases. Recognition might be compared to that essential element in photosynthesis, sunlight, which provides the energy for the plant's constant transformation of substance. It includes the diverse responses and activities of the mother that are taken for granted as the background in all discussions of development—beginning with the mother's ability to identify and respond to her infant's physical needs, her "knowing her baby," when he wants to sleep, eat, play alone, or play together. Indeed, within a few months after birth, this so-called background becomes the foreground, the raison d'être, the meaning and the goal of being with others. As we trace the development of the infant, we can see how recognition becomes increasingly an end in itself—first an achievement of harmony, and then an arena of conflict between self and other.

But the need for *mutual* recognition, the necessity of recognizing as well as being recognized by the other—this is what so many theories of the self have missed. The idea of mutual recognition is crucial to the intersubjective view; it implies that we actually have a need to recognize the other as a separate person who is like us yet distinct. This means that the child has a need to see the mother, too, as an independent subject, not simply as the "external world" or an adjunct of his ego.

It must be acknowledged that we have only just begun to think about the mother as a subject in her own right, principally because of contemporary feminism, which made us aware of the disastrous results for women of being reduced to the mere extension of a two-month-old.[23] Psychology in general and psychoanalysis in particular too often partake of this distorted view of the mother, which is so deeply embedded in the culture as a whole.[24] No psychological theory has adequately articulated the mother's independent existence. Thus even the accounts of the mother-infant relationship which do consider parental responsiveness always revert to a view of the mother as the baby's vehicle for growth, an object of the baby's needs.[25] The mother is the baby's first object of attachment, and later, the object of desire. She is provider, interlocutor, caregiver, contingent reinforcer, significant other, empathic understander, mirror. She is also a secure presence to walk away from, a setter of limits, an optimal frustrator, a shockingly real outside otherness. She is external reality—but she is rarely regarded as another subject with a purpose apart from her existence for her child. Often enough, abetted by the image of mothering in childrearing literature and by the real conditions of life with baby, mothers themselves feel they are so confined. Yet the real mother is not simply an object for her child's demands; she is, in fact, another subject whose independent center must be outside her child if she is to grant him the recognition he seeks.[26]

This is no simple enterprise. It is too often assumed that a mother will be able to give her child faith in tackling the world even if she can no longer muster it for herself. And although mothers ordinarily aspire to more for their children than for themselves, there are limits to this trick: a mother who is too depressed by her own isolation cannot get excited about her child learning to walk or talk; a mother who is afraid of people cannot feel relaxed about her child's association with other children; a mother who stifles her own longings, ambitions, and frustrations cannot tune in empathically to her child's joys and failures. The recognition a child seeks is something the mother is able to give only by virtue of her independent identity. Thus self psychology is misleading when it understands the mother's recognition of the child's feelings and accomplishments as maternal mirroring. The mother cannot (and should not) be a mirror; she must not merely reflect back what the child asserts; she must embody something of the not-me; she must be an independent other who responds in her different way.[27] Indeed, as the child increasingly establishes his own independent center of existence, her recognition will be meaningful only to the extent that it reflects her own equally separate subjectivity.

In this sense, notwithstanding the inequality between parent and child, recognition must be mutual and allow for the assertion of each self. Thus I stress that mutual recognition, including the child's ability to recognize the mother as a person in her own right, is as significant a developmental goal as separation. Hence the need for a theory that understands how the capacity for mutuality evolves, a theory based on the premise that from the beginning there are always (at least) two subjects.

MUTUALITY: THE ESSENTIAL TENSION

So far I have tried to convey the idea that differentiation requires, ideally, the reciprocity of self and other, the balance of assertion and recognition. While this may seem obvious, it has not been easy to conceptualize psychological development in terms of mutuality. Most theories of development have emphasized the goal of autonomy more than relatedness to others, leaving unexplored the territory in which subjects meet. Indeed, it is hard to locate the intersubjective dimension through the lens of such theories. Let us look more closely at the dominant psychoanalytic paradigm, ego psychology, and at its most important expression, Mahler's separation-individuation theory, to see the difference intersubjectivity makes.

Mahler's theory, it will be remembered, conceptualized a unilinear trajectory that leads from oneness to separateness, rather than a continual, dynamic, evolving balance of the two.[28] Moving along this unilinear trajectory, the subject presumably extricates himself from the original oneness, the primary narcissism, in which he began. Although Mahler acknowledges that the child grows into a fuller appreciation of the other's independence, her emphasis is on how the self separates, how the baby comes to feel not-one with the mother. Seen in this light, relationship is the ground and separation is the figure;[29] recognition appears as a fuzzy background and individual activity thrusts forward out of it. This has seemed plausible to so many people for many reasons, but especially because of our culture's high valuation of individualism. And, of course, it corresponds to our subjective feeling of being "the center of our own universe" and to our struggle to enhance the intensity of that feeling.

Interestingly enough, when we do succeed in reaching that enhanced state of self-awareness, it is often in a context of sharpened awareness of others—of their unique particularity and independent existence. The reciprocal relationship between self and other can be compared with the optical illusion in which the figure and ground are constantly changing their relation even as their outlines remain clearly distinct—as in Escher's birds, which appear to fly in both directions. What makes his drawings visually difficult is a parallel to what makes the idea of self-other reciprocity conceptually difficult: the drawing asks us to look two ways simultaneously, quite in opposition to our usual sequential orientation. Since it is more difficult to think in terms of simultaneity than in terms of sequence, we begin to conceptualize the movement in terms of a directional trajectory. Then we must try to correct this inaccurate rendering of what we have seen by putting the parts back together in a conceptual whole which encompasses both directions. Although this requires a rather laborious intellectual reconstruction, intuitively, the paradoxical tension of this way and that way "feels right."

In the last fifteen years, infancy research has developed a new model for early experiences of emotional intensity and exchange which emphasizes reciprocity as opposed to instinctual gratification or separation. Already at three to four months, the infant has the capacity to interact in sophisticated facial play whose main motive is social interest. At this age, the baby can already initiate play. She can elicit parental response by laughing and smiling; she can transform a diaper change into a play session. In this play, the reciprocity that two subjects can create, or subvert, is crucial.[30] True, the moving ducks on the mobile respond to the kick of the infant's foot and so "recognize" her, providing her with the vital experience of contingent response that fosters a sense of mastery and agency. But the mother's response is both more attuned (it "matches" the infant) and more unpredictable than the ducks'. The child enjoys a dose of otherness. Let mother not coo in a constant rhythm, let her vary her voice and gestures, mixing novelty with repetition, and the baby will focus longer on her face and show pleasure in return. The combination of resonance and difference that the mother offers can open the way to a recognition that transcends mastery and mechanical response, to a recognition that is based on *mutuality*.

Frame-by-frame analysis of films of mothers and babies interacting reveals the minute adaptation of each partner's facial and gestural response to the other: mutual influence.[31] The mother addresses the baby with the coordinated action of her voice, face, and hands. The infant responds with his whole body, wriggling or alert, mouth agape or smiling broadly. Then they may begin a dance of interaction in which the partners are so attuned that they move together in unison.[32] This early experience of unison is probably the first emotional basis for later feelings of oneness that characterize group activities such as music or dance. Reciprocal attunement to one another's gestures prefigures adult erotic play as well. Play interaction can be as primary a source of the feeling of oneness as nursing or being held. Thus the ultimate gratification of being in attunement with another person can be framed not—or not only—in terms of instinctual satisfaction, but of cooperation and recognition.

The study of early play interaction also reveals that the baby's principal means of regulating her own feelings, her inner state of mind, is to act on her partner outside. Being able to make herself feel better is directly dependent on being able to make the other act in attunement with her feelings. As Stern points out, "The issue at stake is momentous. The infant requires the integrative experience [that her action] successfully restructures the external world"—that what she does changes the other. Since these acts are also charged with emotion, with pleasure or pain, acting on the world also means being able to change one's own feelings "in the desired direction."[33] In the interaction situation, when stimulation becomes too intense, the infant regulates her own arousal by turning her head away. If the partner reads this correctly as a message to lay back, the baby experiences relief of tension without losing the connection and dropping out of the exchange. The baby can control her own level of excitement by directing the other. Now she is able to feel both that the world is responsive and that she is effective. If the baby is not successful, she feels a simultaneous loss of inner and outer control.

We also observe how mutual regulation breaks down and attunement fails: when baby is tired and fussy, when mother is bored and

depressed, or when baby is unresponsive and this makes mother anxious. Then we will see not just the absence of play, but a kind of
anti-play in which the frustration of the search for recognition is
painfully apparent. The unsuccessful interaction is sometimes almost
as finely tuned as the pleasurable one. With each effort of the baby
to withdraw from the mother's stimulation, to avert his gaze, turn his
head, pull his body away, the mother responds by "chasing" after the
baby.[34] It is as if the mother anticipates her baby's withdrawal with
split-second accuracy and can only read his message to give space as
a frustration of her own efforts to be recognized. Just as the baby's
positive response can make the mother feel affirmed in her being, the
baby's unresponsiveness can amount to a terrible destruction of her
self-confidence as a mother. The mother who jiggles, pokes, looms, and
shouts "look at me" to her unresponsive baby creates a negative cycle
of recognition out of her own despair at not being recognized. Here
in the earliest social interaction we see how the search for recognition
can become a power struggle: how assertion becomes aggression.

If we take this unsuccessful interaction as a model, we can see how
the fine balance of mutual recognition goes awry. The child loses the
opportunity for feeling united and attuned, as well as the opportunity
for appreciating (knowing) his mother. He is never able to fully
engage in or fully disentangle himself from this kind of sticky, frustrat-
ing interaction. Neither separateness nor union is possible. Even as he
is retreating he has to carefully monitor his mother's actions to get
away from them: even withdrawal is not simple.[35] Thus the child can
never lose sight of the other, yet never see her clearly; never shut her
out and never let her in. In the ideal balance, a person is able to be
fully self-absorbed or fully receptive to the other, he is able to be alone
or together. In a negative cycle of recognition, a person feels that
aloneness is only possible by obliterating the intrusive other, that
attunement is only possible by surrendering to the other.

While the failure of early mutuality seems to promote a premature
formation of the defensive boundary between inside and outside, the

positive experience of attunement allows the individual to maintain a more permeable boundary and enter more readily into states in which there is a momentary suspension of felt boundaries between inside and outside. The capacity to enter into states in which distinctness and union are reconciled underlies the most intense experience of adult erotic life. In erotic union we can experience that form of mutual recognition in which both partners lose themselves in each other without loss of self; they lose self-consciousness without loss of awareness. Thus early experiences of mutual recognition already prefigure the dynamics of erotic life.

This description of the intersubjective foundation of erotic life offers a different perspective than the Freudian construction of psychosexual phases, for it emphasizes the tension *between interacting individuals* rather than that *within the individual.* Yet, as I have said above, these rival perspectives seem to me not so much mutually exclusive as concerned simply with different issues. The inner psychic world of object representations—the intrapsychic life with which classical psychoanalysis is concerned—does not yet exist at four months; indeed, it awaits the development of the capacity to symbolize in the second year of life. The distinction between inner and outer is only beginning to be developed; inner and outer regulation still overlap. This does not mean that the infant is unable to differentiate self and other in actual practice or to represent them mentally. It means that the infant represents self and other concretely, not through the mediation of symbols that later characterize mental representation.[36]

The mental organization of self and other enters a new phase, Stern theorizes, when the infant begins to be aware of the existence of "other minds." While the infant of four months can participate in a complex social interaction, she does not do so self-consciously. But at seven to nine months, she takes a great leap forward to the discovery that different minds can share the same feelings or intentions. This is where Stern introduces the term *intersubjectivity* proper, to designate the moment at which we know that others exist who feel and think as we do. In my view, however, intersubjective development is best understood as a spectrum, and this moment marks a decisive point along that spectrum at which the infant more consciously recognizes the other as like and different.[37]

Now, when the infant reaches excitedly for a toy, he looks up to see if mother is sharing his excitement; he gets the meaning when she says, "Wow!" The mother shows that she is feeling the same, not by imitating the infant's gesture (he shakes the rattle), but by matching his level of intensity in a different mode (she whoops). This translation into a different form of expression more clearly demonstrates the congruence of *inner* experience than simple, behavioral imitation.[38] Technically the mother is not feeling the exact same feeling as her child: she is not excited by the rattle itself; but she is excited by his excitement, and she wants to communicate that fact. When mother and child play "peekaboo" (a game based on the tension between shared expectancy and surprise), the mother takes similar pleasure in contacting her child's mind. This conscious pleasure in sharing a feeling introduces a new level of mutuality—a sense that inner experience can be joined, that two minds can cooperate in one intention. This conception of emerging intersubjectivity emphasizes how the awareness of the separate other enhances the felt connection with him: this *other* mind can share *my* feeling.

The development toward increasingly mutual and self-conscious recognition, Stern argues, contrasts sharply with Mahler's theory of separation–individuation.[39] That theory focuses on the infant's sense of separateness, but does not show how this sense of separateness simultaneously enhances the capacity for sharing with and appreciating the other. According to Mahler, the infant of ten months is primarily involved in the pleasure of expressing his separate mind by exploring the world. The infant's psychological well-being depends on whether he can use the mother to refuel for his forays into the world, whether he can maintain a certain amount of contact while venturing off on his own, and whether the mother can give her infant the push from the nest rather than responding anxiously to his new independence.[40]

But, as I see it, intersubjective theory expands and complements (without negating) this picture, by focusing on the affective content of the mother-child exchange. The baby who looks back as he crawls off toward the toys in the corner is not merely refueling or checking to see that mother is still there, but is wondering whether mother is *sharing* the feeling of his adventure—the fear, the excitement, or that ambiguous "scarey-wonderful" feeling.[41] The sense of shared feeling about the undertaking is not only a reassurance, but is, itself, a source of pleasurable connection. For the separation-individuation perspective, such emotional attunement may be part of the landscape, but it is absent at the level of theory; the concepts grasp only how mother protects the child's ego from anxiety so that it can separate. Intersubjective theory introduces attunement, or the lack of it, as an important concept.[42] In so doing, it reintroduces the idea of *pleasure,* pleasure in being with the other, which had gotten lost in the transition from drive theory to ego psychology—but redefines it as pleasure in being with the other.

At the same time, the awareness of separate minds and the desire for attunement raises the possibility of a new kind of conflict. Already at one year the infant can experience the conflict between the wish to fulfill his own desire (say, to push the buttons on the stereo), and the wish to remain in accord with his parents' will.[43] Given such inevitable conflict, the desire to remain attuned can be converted into submission to the other's will. At each phase of development, the core conflict between assertion and recognition is recast in terms of the new level at which the child experiences his own agency and the distinctness of the other.

THE PARADOX OF RECOGNITION

The conflict between assertion of self and need for the other was articulated long before modern psychology began to explore the development of self. Hegel analyzed the core of this problem in his discussion of the struggle between "the independence and dependence of self-consciousness" and its culmination in the master-slave relationship.[44] He showed how the self's wish for absolute independence clashes with the self's need for recognition. In Hegel's discussion two hypothetical selves (self-consciousness and the other, who is another self-consciousness) meet. The movement between them is the movement of recognition; each exists only by existing for the other, that is, by being recognized. But for Hegel, it is simply a given that this mutuality, the tension between asserting the self and recognizing the other, *must* break down; it is fated to produce an insoluble conflict. The breakdown of this tension is what leads to domination.*

The need of the self for the other is paradoxical, because the self is trying to establish himself as an absolute, an independent entity, yet he must recognize the other as like himself in order to *be* recognized by him. He must be able to find himself in the other. The self can only be known by his acts—and only if his acts have meaning for the other do they have meaning for him. Yet each time he acts he negates the other, which is to say that if the other is affected then he is no longer *identical* with who he was before. To preserve his identity, the other resists instead of recognizing the self's acts ("Nothing you do or say can affect me, I am who I am").

Hegel creates a conceptual representation of the two-sided interplay of opposites. As each subject attempts to establish his reality, he must take account of the other, who is trying to do the same: "they recognize themselves as mutually recognizing one another."[46] But almost immediately Hegel observes that this abstract reciprocity is not really

---

*The reader may ask, Why does this tension have to break down? The answer is, for Hegel every tension between oppositional elements carries the seeds of its own destruction and transcendence *(Aufhebung)* into another form. That is how life is. Without this process of contradiction and dissolution, there would be no movement, change, or history. We do not need to accept this conclusion in order to draw on Hegel's understanding of this process; but if we wish to argue that tension can be sustained, it behooves us to show how that is possible.[45]

how the subject experiences things. Rather, the subject, first of all, experiences himself as an absolute, and then searches for affirmation of self through the other. The mutuality that is implied by the concept of recognition is a problem for the subject, whose goal is only to be certain of himself. This absoluteness, the sense of being one ("My identity is entirely independent and consistent") and alone ("There is nothing outside of me that I do not control"), is the basis for domination—and the master-slave relationship.[47]

Now we can see how Hegel's notion of the conflict between independence and dependence meshes with the psychoanalytic view. Hegel posits a self that has no intrinsic need for the other, but uses the other only as a vehicle for self-certainty. This monadic, self-interested ego is essentially the one posited in classical psychoanalytic theory. For Hegel, as for classical psychoanalysis, the self begins in a state of "omnipotence" (Everything is an extension of me and my power), which it wants to affirm in its encounter with the other, who, it now sees, is like itself. But it cannot do so, for to affirm itself it must acknowledge the other, and to acknowledge the other would be to deny the absoluteness of the self. The need for recognition entails this fundamental paradox: at the very moment of realizing our own independence, we are dependent upon another to recognize it. At the very moment we come to understand the meaning of "I, myself," we are forced to see the limitations of that self. At the moment when we understand that separate minds can share the same state, we also realize that these minds can disagree.

To see just how close this conceptual picture comes to the psychoanalytic one, let us again look at Mahler's theory of separation-individuation. According to Mahler, the infant moves through three subphases: differentiation,* practicing, and rapprochement. From the first hatching in the differentiation phase (six to eight months), we

---

*This subphase, differentiation, is not to be confused with the larger process of establishing the awareness of self as distinct from the other, which is also called differentiation.

follow the infant, who is able to move around, and so maintain distance and closeness to mother, into the practicing phase (ten to thirteen months). The practicing phase is an elated, euphoric phase of discovery in which the infant is delighted with the world and himself, discovering his own agency as well as the fascinating outside. It has been called "a love affair with the world."[48] The screech of delight at moving about is the hallmark of practicing. But in this phase of new self-assertion the infant still takes himself for granted, and his mother as well. He does not realize that it is mother, not himself, who insures that he does not fall when he stands on the chair to reach for something interesting on the table. He is too excited by *what* he is doing to reflect on the relation of his will and ability to his sovereignty.

But soon this Eden of blissful ignorance comes to an end. At fourteen months or so the infant enters rapprochement, a phase of conflict in which he must begin to reconcile his grandiose aspirations and euphoria with the perceived reality of his limitations and dependency. Although he is now able to do more, the toddler will insist that mother (or father) share everything, validate his new discoveries and independence. He will insist that mother participate in all his deeds. He will tyrannically enforce these demands if he can, in order to assert—and have mother affirm—his will. The toddler is confronting the increased awareness of separateness and, consequently, of vulnerability: he can move away from mother, but mother can also move away from him.[49] To the child, it now appears that his freedom consists in absolute control over his mother. He is ready to be the master in Hegel's account, to be party to a relationship in which the mutuality breaks down into two opposing elements, the one who is recognized and the one whose identity is negated. He is ready, in his innocence, to go for complete control, to insist on his omnipotence.[50]

What is life like for the mother of a toddler who manifests the constant willfulness, the clinging or the tyrannical demands typical of rapprochement? Depending, in part, on how imperious or clinging the child is, the mother may feel extremely put upon ("Her reactions are tinged with feelings of annoyance," Mahler reports).[51] Suddenly the child's demands no longer appear to be merely the logical results of needs that ought to be met with good grace, but, rather, as irrational and willful. The issue is no longer what the child needs, but what he *wants*. Here, of course, is where many a mother-child pair come to grief. A variety of feelings well up in the mother: the distance from her no-longer-perfect child, the wish to retaliate, the temptation to take the easier path of giving in, the fear or resentment of her child's will. What the mother feels during rapprochement and how she works this out will be colored by her ability to deal straightforwardly with aggression and dependence, her sense of herself as entitled to a separate existence, and her confidence in her child's wholeness and ability to survive conflict, loss, and imperfection.

As Freud reminds us, the parents' abandoned expectations of their own perfection are recalled to life in their child, "His Majesty the Baby."[52] The rapprochement crisis is thus also a crisis of parenting. By identifying with her child's disillusionment, and by knowing that he will survive it, the parent is able to respond appropriately; in doing so she has to accept that she cannot make a perfect world for her child (where he can get everything he wants)—and this is the blow to her own narcissism. The self-obliteration of the permissive parent who cannot face this blow does not bring happiness to the child who gets everything he demands. The parent has ceased to function as an other who sets a boundary to the child's will, and the child experiences this as abandonment; the parent co-opts all the child's intentions by agreement, pushing him back into an illusory oneness where he has no agency of his own. The child will rebel against this oneness by insisting on having his way even more absolutely. The child who feels that others are extensions of himself must constantly fear the emptiness and loss of connection that result from his fearful power. Only he exists; the other is effaced, has nothing real to give him. The painful result of success in the battle for omnipotence is that to win is to win nothing: the result is negation, emptiness, isolation.

Alternatively, the parent who cannot tolerate the child's attempt to do things independently will make the child feel that the price of freedom is aloneness, or even, that freedom is not possible. Thus if the child does not want to do without approval, she must give up her will. This usually results in the "choice" to stay close to home and remain compliant. Not only is she constantly in need of a parent's protection and confirmation in lieu of her own agency, but the parent remains omnipotent in her mind.

In both cases the sense of omnipotence survives, projected onto the other or assumed by the self; in neither case can we say that the other is recognized, or, more modestly (given the child's age), that the process of recognition has begun. The ideal "resolution" of the paradox of recognition is for it to continue as a *constant tension,* but this is not envisaged by Hegel, nor is it given much place in psychoanalysis. Mahler, for example, views the resolution of rapprochement as the moment when the child takes the mother inside himself, can separate from her or be angry at her and still know her to be there—as a "constant object."[53] But this does not tell us how the toddler comes to terms with the difficulty that his own freedom depends on the other's freedom, that recognition of independence must be mutual.

The decisive problem remains *recognizing the other.* Establishing *my*self (Hegel's "being for itself") means winning the recognition of the other, and this, in turn, means I must finally acknowledge the other as existing for *him*self and not just for me. The process we call differentiation proceeds through the movement of recognition, its flow from subject to subject, from self to other and back. The nature of this movement is necessarily contradictory, paradoxical. Only by deepening our understanding of this paradox can we broaden our picture of human development to include not only the separation but also the meeting of minds—a picture in which the bird's flight is always in two directions.

DISCOVERING THE OTHER

Even if we assume that life begins with an emergent awareness of self and other, we know that many things will conspire to prevent full attainment of that consciousness. The problem of recognizing the other was addressed directly by Winnicott, and his original, innovative perceptions point the way out of the paradox of recognition. Winnicott, as we have noted, was concerned with what makes a person feel unreal to himself, with the deadness and despair that accompany the sense of unreality, with what he called "the false self."[54] He concluded that one of the most important elements in feeling authentic was the recognition of an outside reality that is not one's own projection, the experience of contacting other minds.

In his essay, "The Use of an Object,"[55] which is, in many ways, a modern echo of Hegel's reflections on recognition, Winnicott presents the idea that in order to be able to "use" the object we first have to "destroy" it. He distinguishes between two dimensions of experience: *relating* to the object and *using* the object. (These terms can be troublesome, for Winnicott uses them in quite the opposite sense than we might in ordinary speech: "using" here does not mean instrumentalizing or demeaning, but being able to creatively benefit from another person; it refers to the experience of "shared reality" in which "the object's independent existence" is vital. "Relating" refers to the experience of "the subject as an isolate," in which the object is merely a "phenomenon of the subject.")[56]

At first, Winnicott says, an object is "related" to, it is part of the subject's mind and not necessarily experienced as real, external, or independent. But there comes a point in the subject's development where this kind of relatedness must give way to an appreciation of the object as an outside entity, not merely something in one's mind. This ability to enter into exchange with the outside object is what Winnicott calls "using" the object. And here he finds "the most irksome of all the early failures that come for mending." When the subject fails to make the transition from "relating" to "using," it means that he has not been able to place the object outside himself, to distinguish it from his mental experience of omnipotent control. He can only "use" the object when he perceives it "as an external phenomenon, not as a projective entity," when he recognizes it *"as an entity in its own right."*[57] (italics added)

Winnicott explains that the recognition of the other involves a paradoxical process in which the object is *in fantasy* always being destroyed.[58] The idea that to place the other outside, in reality, always involves destruction has often been a source of puzzlement. Intuitively, though, one senses that it is quite simple. Winnicott is saying that the object must be destroyed *inside* in order that we know it to have survived *outside;* thus we can recognize it as not subject to our mental control. This relation of destruction and survival is a reformulation of and solution to Hegel's paradox: in the struggle for recognition each subject must stake his life, must struggle to negate the other—and woe if he succeeds. For if I completely negate the other, he does not exist; and if he does not survive, he is *not there* to recognize me. But to find this out, I must *try* to exert this control, *try* to negate his independence. To find out that he exists, I must wish myself absolute and all alone— then, as it were, upon opening my eyes, I may discover that the other is still there.

Destruction, in other words, is an effort to differentiate. In childhood, if things go well, destruction results simply in survival; in adulthood, destruction includes the intention *to discover* if the other will survive. Winnicott's conception of destruction is innocent; it is best understood as a refusal, a negation, the mental experience of "You do not exist for me," whose favorable outcome is pleasure in the other's survival.[59] When I act upon the other it is vital that he be affected, so that I know that I exist—but not completely destroyed, so that I know he also exists.

Winnicott's description of what destruction means in the analytic context is also evocative of early childhood experiences.

> The subject [patient] says to the object [analyst]: "I destroyed you," and the object is there to receive the communication. From now on the subject says: "Hullo object!" "I destroyed you." "I love you." "You have value for me because of your survival of my destruction of you." "While I am loving you I am all the time destroying you in (unconscious) *fantasy.*"[60]

Perhaps this tension between denial and affirmation is another of the many meanings of that favorite toddler game "Peekaboo" or of Freud's observations of the toddler making the spool disappear and reappear (the famous *"fort-da,"* or gone-there, game). Probably destruction in fantasy also underlies the joy in the young toddler's constant repetition of "Hi!" It has something to do with constantly rediscovering that *you* are there.

The wish for absolute assertion of oneself, the demand to have one's way, the negation of the outside—all that Freud understood as aggression and omnipotence—must sometime crash against the reality of an other who reflects back the intransigent assertion that the self displays. The paradox of recognition, the need for acknowledgment that turns us back to dependence on the other, brings about a struggle for control. This struggle can result in the realization that if we fully negate the other, that is, if we assume complete control over him and destroy his identity and will, then we have negated ourselves as well. For then there is no one there to recognize us, no one there for us to desire.

The experience of rapprochement might be reframed in light of Winnicott's understanding of destruction: If I completely destroy the other, she ceases to exist for me; and if she completely destroys me, I cease to exist—that is, I cease to be an autonomous being. So if the mother sets no limits for the child, if she obliterates herself and her own interests and allows herself to be wholly controlled, then she ceases to be a viable other for him. She is destroyed, and not just in fantasy. If she retaliates, attempting to break his will, believing that any compromise will "spoil" him, she will also inculcate the idea that there is room for only one ego in any relationship—he must obliterate his for now, and hope to get it back, with a vengeance, later. Only through the other's survival can the subject move beyond the realm of submission and retaliation to a realm of mutual respect.

Elsa First, a child psychoanalyst influenced by Winnicott, has offered a picture of how the rapprochement struggle for control may yield to mutual respect. Observing toddlers, she suggests how the post-rapprochement child may begin to apprehend mutuality in rela-

tion to the mother's leaving. The toddler's initial role-playing imitation of the departing mother is characterized by the spirit of pure
retaliation and reversal—"I'll do to you what you do to me." But
gradually the child begins to identify with the mother's subjective
experience and realizes that "I could miss you as you miss me," and,
therefore, that "I know that you could wish to have your own life
as I wish to have mine." First shows how, by recognizing such shared
experience, the toddler actually moves from a retaliatory world of
control to a world of mutual understanding and shared feeling. From
the intersubjective standpoint, this movement is crucial. By accepting
the other's independence, the child gains something that replaces control—a renewed sense of connection with the other.[61]

Mutual recognition cannot be achieved through obedience, through
identification with the other's power, or through repression. It requires, finally, contact with the other. The meaning of destruction is
that the subject can engage in an all-out collision with the other, can
hurtle himself against the barriers of otherness in order to feel the shock
of the fresh, cold outside.[62] And he can experience this collision as
hurtful neither to the other nor to himself, as occasioning neither
withdrawal nor retaliation. Thus Winnicott advises parents:

> It is a healthy thing for a baby to get to know the full extent
> of his rage. . . . If he really is determined he can hold his breath
> and go blue in the face, and even have a fit. For a few minutes
> he really intends to destroy or at least to spoil everyone and
> everything, and he does not even mind if he destroys himself in
> the process. Naturally you do what you can to get the child out
> of this state. It can be said, however, that if a baby cries in a state
> of rage and feels as if he has destroyed everyone and everything,
> and yet the people round him remain calm and unhurt, this
> experience greatly strengthens his ability to see that what he feels
> to be true is not necessarily real. . . .[63]

Winnicott's theory of destruction also implies a revision in the psychoanalytic idea of reality—it suggests a "reality principle" that is a

positive source of pleasure, the pleasure of connecting with the outside, and not just a brake on narcissism or aggression. Beyond the sensible ego's bowing to reality is the joy in the other's survival and the recognition of shared reality. Reality is thus *discovered,* rather than *imposed;* and authentic selfhood is not absorbed from without but discovered within. Reality neither wholly creates the self (as the pressure of the external world creates Freud's ego) nor is it wholly created by the self.

Winnicott's view of reality echoes the themes of his earlier work on "transitional objects," things like teddy bears, blankets, even special ways of humming or stroking. The child both creates and discovers these things, without ever having to decide which: "The baby creates the object, but the object was there waiting to be created. . . . We will never challenge the baby to elicit an answer to the question: Did you create that or did you find it?"[64] The object existed objectively, waiting to be found, and yet the infant has created it subjectively, as if it emerged from herself. This paradox is crucial to the evolving sense of reality.

The transitional object is literally a means of passage toward the awareness of otherness, toward establishing a boundary between inside and outside. But it is precisely an intermediate experience in which that boundary has not yet hardened. Out of this initial conception Winnicott created the broader notion of a transitional *realm* in which the child can play and create as if the outside were as malleable as his own fantasy. One could say the baby experiences something like this: "Reality recognizes me so I recognize it—wholly, with faith and trust, with no grudge or self-constraint." Thus the transitional realm allows "the enjoyment and love of reality," and not merely adaptation to it.[65]

The infancy researcher Louis Sander has conceptualized a very early form of transitional experience that he calls "open space."[66] Open space occurs in the first month of life when the mother and infant have achieved sufficient equilibrium to allow for moments of relaxation from internal pressure or external stimulation. In these moments of optimal disengagement, the infant can explore himself and his surroundings, can experience his own initiative and distinguish it from the other's action, for example, by putting thumb into mouth. The baby might lie on his side and move his hands slowly in front of his face, watching them intently—an activity one baby's parents aptly called "doing Tai Chi." In the balance between self and other, disengagement (open space) is as important as engagement. Indeed, as we saw in the antagonistic anti-play between mother and infant, disengagement and engagement form a crucial balance: the opportunity to disengage is the condition of freely engaging, its counterpoint.

What disengagement means here is not simple detachment, but what Winnicott called "being alone in the presence of the other,"[67] that is, in the safety that a nonintrusive other provides. Prior to self-consciousness, this experience will appear to the child as that of the self alone; but later it will be understood as a particular way of being with the other. In these moments of relaxation, Winnicott proposed, when there is no need to react to external stimuli, an impulse can arise from within and feel real. Here begins the sense of authorship, the conviction that one's act originates *inside* and reflects one's own intention. Here, too, begins the capacity for full receptivity and attention to what is outside, the freedom to be interested in the object independent of the pressure of need or anxiety. In this sense, the earliest transitional experience forms a continuum with the most developed capacities for contemplation and creativity, for discovering the outside as an object existing in its own right.[68]

BEYOND INTERNALIZATION

The discovery of the object as a real, external being distinguishes the intersubjective view of differentiation from the more conventional ego psychology of separation-individuation theory. In ego psychology, development occurs through separation and identification—by taking something in from the object, by assimilating the other to the self.* Most of psychoanalytic theory has been formulated in terms of the isolated subject and his internalization of what is outside to develop what is inside. Internalization implies that the other is consumed, incorporated, digested by the subject self. That which is not consumed, what we do not get and cannot take away from others by consumption, seems to elude the concept of internalization. The joy of discovering the other, the agency of the self, and the outsideness of the other—these are at best only fuzzily apprehended by internalization theory. When it defines differentiation as separating oneself from the other rather than as coming together with him, internalization theory describes an instrumental relationship. It implies an autonomous individual defined by his ability to do without the "need-satisfying object." The other seems more and more like a cocoon or a husk that must gradually be shed—one has got what one needs, and now, goodbye.

Let us consider how ego psychology thinks about the matter Winnicott called destruction, the matter of the infant's aggression and the mother's survival. Ego psychology conceives of the establishment of a constant internal object that survives frustration and absences, so that the mother is not internally destroyed when the infant is angry or when she goes away. In this conception, the infant can separate and yet be internally connected, be angry and yet still reclaim his love. This is both an accurate and a useful statement of what is going on from the intrapsychic point of view. What it does not capture, however—and what Winnicott's theory includes—is the intersubjective aspect of destruction, the recognition of the other,

---

*The theory of identification has been central to psychoanalysis since Freud's development of ego psychology in the 1920s. The Oedipus complex now resulted not only in the resolution of the conflict between wish and defense, but also in the consolidation of the tripartite structure of id, ego, and superego. The ego and superego developed through identification with the parental objects. Since those formulations, the theory has been greatly expanded to include the internalization of a whole world of objects.[69]

the joy and urgency of discovering the external, independent reality of another person.

A similar difference appears when we look at how ego psychology understands the phenomenon Winnicott identified as transitional experience.[70] In ego psychology's terms, the infant uses the transitional object (the favorite bear or the beloved blanket) to soothe and comfort himself, as a substitute for the mother's function in regulating tension. He *internalizes* the soothing function of the mother, and this represents a shift "from passivity to increasing activity," doing to himself what was previously done to him by the mother. By means of such internalization, the child progresses toward autonomy; he frees himself "from exclusive dependence on the need-satisfying object." Accordingly, the ego psychologist Marie Tolpin argues that Winnicott was wrong to say that the transitional object is not internalized. In her view, it goes inside just as the mother does, as mental structure.[71] And in the process of clinical work with adults, one can see how this framing of the problem occurs. One sees the way in which certain persons are unable to soothe themselves or regulate their own self-esteem. They act as if the internal "good mother," or her structural equivalent, were missing.

But Winnicott's transitional realm was primarily about creativity and play, about fantasy and reality, not about soothing. And even in regard to soothing, his concepts were getting at something beside internalization, something which is implied by his use of terms like "the holding environment" and "the facilitating environment." I think he was trying to define the area in which the child is able to develop his innate capacities because the people around him facilitate such development.* The ability to soothe oneself is not generated by internalizing the other's function; it is a capacity of the self which the other's response helps to activate. Infants are born with this capacity

---

*Thus the analytic situation itself has come to be understood as a potential transitional space, creating the conditions for the growth of authentic agency through play, rather than merely a context for interpretation, in which the analyst "changes" the patient.[72]

in more or less developed form; some are quite adept from the first day, while others need someone to comfort them in order to fall asleep or stay awake without feeling uncomfortable. Within a few months an infant can also regulate himself through interaction—for example, when he looks away to reduce stimulation.[73] The activation of innate capacities is a very different developmental process from internalization; it presupposes at all times the presence of *two* interacting subjects who each contribute, rather than *one* subject who incorporates the action of the object.

Internalization theory and intersubjective theory are not mutually exclusive. But they are radically different ways of looking at development. Intersubjective theory is concerned not with how we take in enough from the other to be able to go away, but how the other gives us the opportunity to do it ourselves to begin with. This theory attributes all agency neither to the subject with his innate capacities or impulses, nor to the object which stamps the blank slate of the psyche with its imprint. It argues that the other plays an active part in the struggle of the individual to creatively discover and accept reality.

Intersubjective theory also permits us to distinguish two subjects recognizing each other from one subject regulating another. Stern has argued that we should not conflate instances where our main experience is of *being with* the other person with those in which the other simply helps to regulate our physiological tension. He suggests that although psychoanalysis has traditionally seen only certain moments of need gratification as "the cardinal 'magic moments' against which most all else in early infancy is background,"[74] these only represent one kind of relationship to the other. Nursing and going blissfully to sleep, says Stern, is an instance of having one's self dramatically transformed by the other's ministrations. It is quite different from facial play where the essential experience is *with* the other.*

---

*I would add that the nursing experience itself has legitimately been understood quite variously: in terms of oral sexual pleasure, reduction of tension, the sense of efficacy

Of course, the experiences of need gratification and soothing are an indispensable part of gaining a sense of the reliability and responsiveness of the external world—what Erikson called basic trust, and what Stern calls core relatedness. Such experiences contribute in a major way to faith in the other and a sense of one's own agency. But the experience of *being with* the other cannot be reduced to the experience of *being regulated* by an other. Indeed, the model of drive satisfaction has left an entire dimension unaccounted for; and that model has been greatly expanded since Freud. American ego psychology added to it by focusing on the relationship in which regulation occurs, and how that relationship is internalized. Object relations theory modified it by pointing out that the ultimate need is for the whole object, not simply the satisfaction of a drive.[76] But these elaborations still did not conceptualize the elements of activity, reciprocity, and mutual exchange that we now see when we study infants and their interaction with adults. The intrapsychic model thus missed what I consider the essence of differentiation: the paradoxical balance between recognition of the other and assertion of self. It also missed the fact that we have to get beyond internalization theory if we are to break out of the solipsistic omnipotence of the single psyche.

The classic psychoanalytic viewpoint did not see differentiation as a balance, but as a process of disentanglement. Thus it cast experiences of union, merger, and self-other harmony as regressive opposites to

---

resulting from the caregiver's responsiveness, an intense merging or oneness, the "creative illusion" that one has made the breast appear. One might distinguish the element of soothing and relief of hunger from the element of emotional attunement and facial mirroring that follow or accompany relief. Within a few weeks of birth, the infant has sufficient control over physiological tension that hunger may be less pressing than his interest in mother's face. Thus nursing, as a primary metaphor of infancy, encompasses all three kinds of relationships to the other that, according to Stern, appear in psychoanalytic thinking: being transformed by another (as in tension relief), complementarity (as in being held), and mental sharing (as in mutual gaze).[75] The power of the breast metaphor, I believe, has always lain in the multiplicity of meanings it evoked.

differentiation and self-other distinction. Merging was a dangerous form of undifferentiation, a sinking back into the sea of oneness—the "oceanic feeling" that Freud told Romain Rolland he frankly couldn't relate to.[77] The original sense of oneness was seen as absolute, as "limitless narcisissm," and, therefore, regression to it would impede development and prevent separation. In its most extreme version, this view of differentiation pathologized the sensation of love: relaxing the boundaries of the self in communion with others threatened the identity of the isolate self. Yet this oneness was also seen as the ultimate pleasure, eclipsing the pleasure of difference. Oneness was not seen as a state that could coexist with (enhance and be enhanced by) the sense of separateness.[78]

One of the most important insights of intersubjective theory is that sameness and difference exist simultaneously in mutual recognition. This insight allows us to counter the argument that human beings fundamentally desire the impossible absolutes of "oneness" and perfection with the more moderate view that things don't have to be perfect, that, in fact, it is *better* if they are not. It reminds us that in every experience of similarity and subjective sharing, there must be enough difference to create the feeling of reality, that a degree of imperfection "ratifies" the existence of the world.[79]

Experiences of "being with" are predicated on a continually evolving awareness of difference, on a sense of intimacy felt as occurring between "the *two* of us." The fact that self and other are not merged is precisely what makes experiences of merging have such high emotional impact. The externality of the other makes one feel one is truly being "fed," getting nourishment from the outside, rather than supplying everything for oneself.

As infancy research informs us, the intense high feeling of union occurs as much in the active exchange *with* the other as in experiences of being regulated or transformed *by* the other. But psychoanalysis has seen only those interactions in which the infant's state of tension is regulated—feeding and holding—as the prototypical merging experiences. Above all, psychoanalysis has stressed complementarity in interaction over mutuality. The other is represented as the answer, and the self as the need; the other is the breast, and the self is the hunger; or the other is actively holding, and the self is passively being held.[80] This complementarity of activity and passivity forms a dual unity which can be internalized and reversed ("Now I'm the Mommy and you're the baby"). The dual unity form has within it this tendency to remain constant even in reversal, never to equalize but simply invert itself within relationships of dependency. As we will see in chapter 2, the complementary dual unity is the basic structure of domination. And while it is certainly one of the structures of the psyche, it is not the only one. To see it as such is to leave no space for equality.

To transcend the experience of duality, so that both partners are equal, requires a notion of mutuality and sharing. In the intersubjective interaction both partners are active; it is not a reversible union of opposites (a doer and a done-to). The identification with the other person occurs through the sharing of similar states, rather than through reversal. "Being with" breaks down the oppositions between powerful and helpless, active and passive; it counteracts the tendency to objectify and deny recognition to those weaker or different—to the other. It forms the basis of compassion, what Milan Kundera calls "co-feeling,"[81] the ability to share feelings and intentions without demanding control, to experience sameness without obliterating difference.

The intersubjective view certainly doesn't negate all that we have learned from Freud, nor does it erase the many grounds he saw for pessimism. Often enough we see evidence of the striving for omnipotent control, and the hostility to otherness. The intersubjective view, however, suggests that there are aspects of the self, missing from the Freudian account, that can oppose (and help to explain) these tendencies. Perhaps Freud had them in mind when he referred to the instinctual force of Eros, the life force that aims at creating unities, but he never gave Eros a place in psychic structure.[82] It is this missing dimension of the psyche that finally enables us to confront the painful aspect of external reality—its uncontrollable, tenacious otherness—as a condition of freedom rather than of domination.

. . .

In the effort to explore the genesis of domination, we have had to undertake a broad theoretical revision. We have had to recast the psychoanalytic framework to include a largely neglected dimension of experience, the intersubjective dimension in which recognition is so crucial. I have tried to show that the erotic component of infant life is bound up with recognition, and that the struggle for recognition requires the self to relinquish its claim to absoluteness. Yet in the course of differentiation, the recognition process may go awry and the self may resort to asserting omnipotence (either its own or the other's). The breakdown in the fundamental tension between assertion of self and recognition of other that then occurs is, I believe, the best point of entry to understanding the psychology of domination.

The traditional psychoanalytic view of differentiation cannot account for this breakdown, because it only dimly recognizes the existence of that tension. Its model of the mind is based on a well-established dualism of oneness and separateness, difference and sameness. Although in their clinical practice most psychoanalysts would reject these oppositions in favor of a balance between autonomy and connection, the overvaluing of separation is a strong bias in the theory. This is the result of a conception of the individual as a closed system. Within this closed system, the ego invests objects with his desire and takes in these objects to further his autonomy from them. This conception of the individual cannot explain the confrontation with an independent other as a real condition of development and change. It does not comprehend the simultaneous process of transforming and being transformed by the other.

By contrast, intersubjective theory sees the relationship between self and other, with its tension between sameness and difference, as a continual exchange of influence. It focuses, not on a linear movement from oneness to separateness, but on the paradoxical balance between them. What we see in early infancy is not symbiosis, or complete undifferentiation, but, rather, an interest in externality alternating with absorption in internal rhythms; later, there is alternation between the oneness of harmonious attunement and the "two-ness" of disengagement.

But why has the dualistic view of the individual enjoyed plausibility for so long? Why does the idea of the linear movement toward separation, of the construction of the psyche in terms of the internalization of objects ring so true? Perhaps it is because this conception of the individual reflects a powerful experience—whose origins we have discovered in the rapprochement conflict—the experience of paradox as painful, or even intolerable. Perhaps, also, because of a continuing fear that dependency on the other is a threat to independence, that recognition of the other compromises the self. When the conflict between dependence and independence becomes too intense, the psyche gives up the paradox in favor of an opposition. Polarity, the conflict of opposites, replaces the balance within the self. This polarity sets the stage for defining the self in terms of a movement away from dependency.

It also sets the stage for domination. Opposites can no longer be integrated; one side is devalued, the other idealized (splitting). In this chapter we have concentrated on infancy, on the shifts in the balance of assertion and recognition at the earliest moments in the self–other relationship. We have seen how a crisis arises as differentiation proceeds and recognition of otherness confronts the self with a momentous paradox. In the following chapters we shall analyze how this inability to sustain the tension of paradox manifests itself in all forms of domination, and why this occurs.

We shall begin by following the breakdown of tension into its adult form, erotic domination and submission.

CHAPTER TWO

Master and Slave

IN THE POST-FREUDIAN world it is common-
place to assume that the foundations of erotic life lie in
infancy. This means that adult sexual love is not only
shaped by the events dating from that period of intense
intimacy and dependency, it is also an opportunity to
reenact and work out the conflicts that began there.
Where the site of control and abandon is the body, the
demands of the infant self are most visible—and so is the
shift from differentiation to domination. In sadomaso-

chistic fantasies and relationships we can discern the "pure culture" of domination—a dynamic which organizes both domination and submission.

The fantasy of erotic domination embodies both the desire for independence and the desire for recognition. This inquiry intends to understand the process of alienation whereby these desires are transformed into erotic violence and submission. What we shall see, especially in voluntary submission to erotic domination, is a paradox in which the individual tries to achieve freedom through slavery, release through submission to control. Once we understand submission to be the *desire* of the dominated as well as their helpless fate, we may hope to answer the central question, How is domination anchored in the hearts of those who submit to it?

DOMINATION AND DIFFERENTIATION

Domination begins with the attempt to deny dependency. No one can truly extricate himself from dependency on others, from the need for recognition. In the first relationship of dependency, between child and parent, this is an especially painful and paradoxical lesson. A child must come to terms with the fact that he does not magically control the mother, and that what she does for him is subject to her, not his, will. The paradox is that the child not only needs to achieve independence, but he must be recognized as independent—by the very people on whom he has been most dependent.

As we have seen in chapter 1, much can go amiss at this point. If, for example, the child is unable to relinquish the fantasy of omnipotence, he may be tempted to believe that he can become independent without recognizing the other person. ("I will continue to believe that mother is my servant, a genie who fulfills my wishes and does as I command, an extension of my will"). The child may be tempted to believe that the other person is not separate. ("She belongs to me, I control and possess her.") In short, he fails to confront his own dependency on someone outside himself. Alternatively, the child may continue to see the mother as all-powerful, and himself as helpless. In this case, the apparent acceptance of dependency masks the effort to retain control by remaining connected to the mother ("I am good and powerful because I am exactly like my good and powerful mother wishes me to be"). This child does not believe he will ever gain recognition for his own independent self, and so he denies that self.

In my discussion of infancy, I have already demonstrated that the balance *within* the self depends upon mutual recognition *between* self and other. And mutual recognition is perhaps the most vulnerable point in the process of differentiation. In Hegel's notion of recognition, the self requires the opportunity to act and have an effect on the other to affirm his existence. In order to exist for oneself, one has to exist for an other. It would seem there is no way out of this dependency. If I destroy the other, there is no one to recognize me, for if I allow him no independent consciousness, I become enmeshed with a dead, not-conscious being. If the other denies me recognition, my acts have no meaning; if he is so far above me that nothing I do can alter his attitude toward me, I can only submit. My desire and agency can find no outlet, except in the form of obedience.

We might call this the dialectic of control: If I completely control the other, then the other ceases to exist, and if the other completely controls me, then I cease to exist. A condition of our own independent existence is recognizing the other. True independence means sustaining the essential tension of these contradictory impulses; that is, both asserting the self and recognizing the other. Domination is the consequence of refusing this condition.

In mutual recognition the subject accepts the premise that others are separate but nonetheless share like feelings and intentions. The subject is compensated for his loss of sovereignty by the pleasure of sharing, the communion with another subject. But for Hegel, as for Freud, the breakdown of essential tension is inevitable. The hypothetical self presented by Hegel and Freud does not *want* to recognize the other, does not perceive him as a person just like himself. He gives up omnipotence only when he has no other choice. His need for the other—in Freud, physiological, in Hegel, existential—seems to place him in the other's power, as if dependency were the equivalent of surrender. When the subject abandons the project of absolute independence or control, he does so unwillingly, with a persistent, if unconscious, wish to fulfill the old omnipotence fantasy.[1] This is a far cry from actually appreciating the other as a being in his or her own right.

Since the subject cannot accept his dependency on someone he cannot control, the solution is to subjugate and enslave the other—to make him give that recognition without recognizing him in return. The primary consequence of the inability to reconcile dependence with independence, then, is the transformation of need for the other into domination of him.

For Freud and Hegel this is precisely what happens in the "state of nature." In Freud's terms, aggression and the desire for mastery—necessary derivatives of the death instinct—are part of our nature. Without the restraint of civilization, whoever is more powerful will subjugate the other. The wish to restore early omnipotence, or to realize the fantasy of control, never ceases to motivate the individual. In Hegel's terms, self-consciousness wants to be absolute. It wants to be recognized by the other in order to place itself in the world and make itself the whole world. The I wants to prove itself at the expense of the other; it wants to think itself the only one; it abjures dependency. Since each self raises the same claim, the two must struggle to the death for recognition. For Hegel this struggle does not culminate in the survival of each for the other, in mutual recognition. Rather, the stronger makes the other his slave.

But this viewpoint would imply that submission is simply the hard lot of the weak.[2] And indeed, the question of why the oppressed submit is never fully explained. Yet the question of submission is implicitly raised by Hegel and Freud, who see that the slave must grant power of recognition to the master. To understand this side of the relationship of domination, we must turn to an account written from the point of view of one who submits.

THE FANTASY OF EROTIC DOMINATION

Sadomasochistic fantasy, the most common form of erotic domination, replicates quite faithfully the themes of the master-slave relationship. Here subjugation takes the form of transgressing against the other's body, violating his physical boundaries. The act of violation of the body becomes a way of representing the struggle to the death for recognition. Ritual violation is a form of risking the psychological, if not the physical, self.

I have based my analysis of sadomasochistic fantasy on a single, powerful study of the erotic imagination, Pauline Réage's *Story of O*. Réage's tale is a web in which the issues of dependency and domination are inextricably intertwined, in which the conflict between the desire for autonomy and the desire for recognition can only be resolved by total renunciation of self. It illustrates powerfully the principle that the root of domination lies in the breakdown of tension between self and other.

Perhaps the greatest objection to this work by feminists has been directed against its depiction of O's voluntary submission. For them, the account of O's masochism is not an allegory of the desire for recognition, but simply the story of a victimized woman, too weak or brainwashed or hopeless to resist her degradation.[3] Such a viewpoint cannot, of course, explain what satisfaction is sought and found in submission, what psychological motivations lead to oppression, humiliation, and subservience. It denies the unpleasant fact that people really do consent to relationships of domination, and that fantasies of domination play a vigorous part in the mental lives of many who do not actually do so.

Story of O confronts us boldly with the idea that people often submit not merely out of fear, but in complicity with their own deepest desires. Told from the point of view of the woman who submits, and representing, as it does, the fantasy life of a gifted woman writer,[4] the story compels the reader to accept the authenticity of the desire for submission. But the narrative also makes clear that the desire for submission represents a peculiar transposition of the desire for recognition. O's physical humiliation and abuse represent a search for an elusive spiritual or psychological satisfaction. Her masochism is a search for recognition through an other who is powerful enough to bestow this recognition. This other has the power for which the self longs, and through his recognition she gains it, though vicariously.

At the beginning of *Story of O,* the heroine is, without warning, brought by her lover to Roissy Castle, an establishment organized by men for the ritual violation and subjugation of women. There she is given specific instructions:

> You are here to serve your masters. . . . At the first word or sign from anyone you will drop whatever you are doing and ready yourself for what is really your one and only duty: to lend yourself. Your hands are not your own, nor are your breasts, nor most especially, any of your orifices, which we may explore or penetrate at will. . . . You have lost all right to privacy or concealment . . . you must never look any of us in the face. If the costume we wear . . . leaves our sex exposed, it is not for the sake of convenience . . . but for the sake of insolence, so your eyes will be directed there upon it and nowhere else so that you may learn that there resides your master. . . . [Your] being whipped . . . is less for our pleasure than for your enlightenment. . . . Both this flogging and the chain attached to the ring of your collar . . . are intended less to make you suffer, scream or shed tears than to make you feel, through this suffering, that you are not free but fettered, and to teach you that you are totally dedicated to something outside yourself.[5]

A great deal is contained in these several lines. First, O is to lose all subjectivity, all possibility of using her body for action; she is to be merely a thing. Second, she is to be continually violated, even when she is not actually being used. The main transgression of her boundaries consists of her having to be always available and open. Third, her masters are to be recognized by her in an indirect form. The penis represents their desire, and through this indirect representation they will maintain their sovereignty. By interposing it between her and them they establish a subjectivity that is distanced, independent of her recognition. Indeed, they claim that their abuse of her is more for her "enlightenment" than their pleasure, so that even in using her they do not appear to need her. Their acts are carefully controlled: each act has a goal that expresses their rational intentions. Their sadistic pleasure consists not in direct enjoyment of her pain, but in the knowledge of their power over her—the fact that their power is visible, that it is manifested by outward signs, that it leaves marks.

Why must they find enjoyment more in their command than in her service, and why must it be distanced, that is, symbolized by the penis? Because in order to maintain their separate subjectivity, they must scrupulously deny their dependency on her. Otherwise they would suffer the fate of Hegel's master, who, in becoming dependent on his slave, gradually loses subjectivity to him. A further danger for the master is that the subject always becomes the object he consumes. By negating her will, they turn her into an object. And when her objectification is complete, when she has no more will, they can no longer use her without becoming filled with her thing-like nature. Thus they must perform their violation rationally and ritually in order to maintain their boundaries and to make her will—not only her body—the object of their will.

Finally, the symbolization of male mastery through the penis emphasizes the difference between them and her. It signifies the denial of commonality that gives them the right to violate her. Each act the master takes against O establishes his separateness, his difference from her. He continually places himself outside her by saying, in effect, "I am not you." The rational function (calculation, objectivity, and control) is linked to this distance. The penis symbolizes the master's resistance to being absorbed by the thing he is controlling: however interdependent the master and slave may become, the difference between them will be sustained.

The story is driven forward by the dialectic of control. Since a slave who is completely dominated loses the quality of being able to give recognition, the struggle to possess her must be prolonged. O must be enslaved piece by piece; new levels of resistance must be found, so that she can be vanquished anew—She must acquiesce in ever deeper humiliation, pain, and bondage, and she must will her submission ever anew, each time her masters ask her, "O, do you consent?" The narrative moves through these ever deeper levels of submission, tracing the impact of each fresh negation of her will, each new defeat of her resistance.

The culmination of the dialectic, the point when O has submitted and René, her lover, has exhausted the possibilities of violating her, would, logically, present a narrative problem. But before the problem can arise, before René becomes bored with O's submission and she is used up and discarded, a new source of tension is introduced. One day René presents O to Sir Stephen, his older (and more powerful) step-brother, to whom she is to be "given." Unlike René, Sir Stephen does not love O. He is described as having a "will of ice and iron, which would not be swayed by desire," and he demands that she obey him without loving him, and without his loving her.[6] Yet this more complete surrender of her person and acceptance of her object status further arouses O's desire, makes her wish to matter in some way, to "exist for him." Sir Stephen finds new ways of intensifying O's bondage: he employs her to entice another woman; he sends her to another castle, Samois, where O will abuse and be abused by other women; and he makes her "more interesting" by having her branded and her anus enlarged. These measures make Sir Stephen's form of mastery even more rational, calculating, and self-controlled than René's—more fully independent of his slave.

Furthermore, the fact that René looks up to Sir Stephen as to a father suggests that he is the loved authority not only for O, but also for René. He is the person in whose eyes René wants to be recognized; giving Sir Stephen his lover is a form of "obeisance," and René is obviously "pleased that [Sir Stephen] deigned to take pleasure in something he had given him." Indeed, O realizes that the two men share something "mysterious . . . more acute, more intense than amorous communion" from which she is excluded, even though she is the medium for it. René's delivery of O to Sir Stephen is a way of surrendering himself sexually to the more powerful man. "What each of them would look for in her would be the other's mark, the trace of the other's passage." Indeed, for René, Sir Stephen's possession of O sanctifies her, leaving "the mark of a god."[7]

René's relationship with Sir Stephen calls for a reinterpretation of the story up to this point: we now see that the objectification of the woman is inspired both by the need to assert difference from her, and by the desire to gain prestige in the father's eyes. Thus René begins to relinquish his love for O, the tender and compassionate identification that moved him when she first surrendered, for the sake of his identification and alliance with the father. We might say that the desire for recognition by the father wholly overtakes the love of the mother; it becomes another motive for domination. (This shift in allegiance shows how the roots of domination lie not only in the preoedipal drama of mother and child, but also in the oedipal triad, as chapter 4 will discuss in detail). O's unimportance to either man by comparison with their bond to each other becomes a further aspect of her humiliation and negation.

Despite the narrative's attempt to create more dramatic tension, the story eventually becomes heavy with O's inexorable loss of subjectivity. Playing the complementary part to her masters, O relinquishes all sense of difference and separateness in order to remain—at all costs—connected to them. O's deepest fears of abandonment and separation emerge as her tie to René is gradually dissolved by her bondage to Sir Stephen. Briefly left alone, she begins to believe she has lost René's love; she feels that her life is absolutely void. She thinks, paraphrasing a Protestant text she had seen as a child, "It is a fearful thing to be cast out of the hands of the living God." O is the lost soul who can only be restored to grace by putting herself in the hands of the ideal, omnipotent other.

As the story continues, O's desire for connection increasingly assumes the symbolic and ritual character of a devotion: now it is her task to live according to her new lover's will, to serve him whether he is present or not. Her lover is like a god, and her need for him can only be satisfied by obedience, which allows her to transcend herself by becoming an instrument of his supreme will. In this way, O's story, with its themes of devotion and transcendence, is suggestive of the surrender of the saints. The torture and outrage to which she submits is a kind of martyrdom, seeming "to her the very redemption of her sins."[8] O's great longing is to be *known,* and in this respect she is like any lover, for the secret of love is to be known as oneself. But her desire to be known is like that of the sinner who wants to be known by God. Sir Stephen thrills her because he knows her instantly; he knows her to be bad, wanton, reveling in her debasement. However, this knowing can only go so far, because there is progressively less of O the subject left to be known.

Story of O concludes with a note that proposes two possible endings to the story. In the first, Sir Stephen returns O to Roissy and abandons her there. In the second, O, "seeing that Sir Stephen was about to leave her, said she would prefer to die. Sir Stephen gave her his consent." This is her final gesture of heroism, her last opportunity to express her lover's will. The gesture is in keeping with O's paradoxical hope that in complete surrender she will find her elusive self. For this hope is the other side of O's devotional servitude: in performing the tasks her masters set her, O seeks affirmation of herself. O is actually willing to risk complete annihilation of her person in order to continue to be the object of her lover's desire—to be recognized.

O's fear of loss and abandonment points to an important aspect of the question of pain. The problem of masochism has been oversimplified ever since Freud's paradoxical assertion that the masochist takes pleasure in pain.[9] But current psychoanalytic theory appreciates that pain is a route to pleasure only when it involves submission to an idealized figure. As O demonstrates, the masochist's pleasure cannot be understood as a direct, unmediated enjoyment of pain: "She liked the idea of torture, but when she was being tortured herself she would have betrayed the whole world to escape it, and yet when it was over she was happy to have gone through it."[10] The pain of violation serves to protect the self by substituting physical pain for the psychic pain of loss and abandonment. In being hurt by the other, O feels she is being reached, she is able to experience another living presence.* O's pleasure, so to speak, lies in her sense of her own survival and her connection to her powerful lover. Thus as long as O can transpose her fear of loss into submission, as long as she remains the object and manifestation of his power, she is safe.

The experience of pain has yet another dimension. In Freud's terms, pain is the point at which stimuli become too intense for the body or ego to bear. Conversely, pleasure requires a certain control or mastery of stimuli. Thus Freud suggested that the erotization of pain allows a sense of mastery by converting pain into pleasure.[12] But this is true only for the master: O's loss of self is *his* gain, O's pain is *his* pleasure. For the slave, intense pain causes the violent rupture of the self, a profound experience of fragmentation and chaos.[13] It's true that O now welcomes this loss of self-coherence, but only under a specific condition: that her sacrifice actually creates the master's power, produces his coherent self, in which she can take refuge. Thus in losing her own self, she is gaining access, however circumscribed, to a more powerful one.

---

*As Masud Khan has pointed out, Freud lacked a conception of psychic pain, since it is the property of the self, for which he also lacked a concept. Khan discusses the importance of finding a witness for one's psychic pain, a witnessing that allows the person to achieve a deep sense of self. He also describes the case of a woman for whom the immersion in a compelling sadomasochistic relationship seemed to be the alternative to psychic breakdown. This form of pain substituted for a deep depression based on very early abandonment and loss.[11]

The relationship of domination is asymmetrical. It can be reversed, as when O takes on the role of torturer, but it can never become reciprocal or equal. Identification plays an important part in this reversible relationship, but always with the stipulation that the masochist gains her identity through the master's power, even as he actively negates his identity with her. Inflicting pain is the master's way of maintaining his separate identity. In her pain, O's body "moves" her masters, but chiefly because it displays the marks they have left. Of course, their "emotion" is always checked, and is finally diminished as she becomes increasingly a dehumanized object, as her thing-like nature makes her pain mute. Nonetheless, her submission to their will embodies the ultimate recognition of their power. Submission becomes the "pure" form of recognition, even as violation becomes the "pure" form of assertion. The assertion of one individual (the master) is transformed into domination; the other's (the slave's) recognition becomes submission. Thus the basic tension of forces *within* the individual becomes a dynamic *between* individuals.

DOMINATION, DEATH, AND DISCONTENT

The relationship of domination is fueled by the same desire for recognition that we find in love—but why does it takes this form? Even if we accept that O is seeking recognition, we still want to know why her search culminates in submission, instead of in a relationship of mutuality. Why this complementarity between the all-powerful and the powerless instead of the equal power of two subjects?

We already have some sense of how Freud and Hegel have approached these questions. Their answers, as I have pointed out, assume the inevitable human aspiration to omnipotence and they begin and end in the same place, in the no-exit of domination, in the closed system of opposites: doer and done-to, master and slave. It is true that Hegel's discussion of recognition implies an ideal of mutuality in which both subjects partake of the contradictory elements of negation and recognition. But the polarization of these two "moments" is a necessary part of his dialectic, and therefore each subject winds up embodying only one side of the tension. In psychoanalytic terms, this breakdown of wholeness is understood as "splitting."* Wholeness can only exist by maintaining contradiction, but this is not easy. In splitting, the two sides are represented as opposite and distinct tendencies, so that they are available to the subject only as alternatives. The subject can play only one side at a time, projecting the opposite side onto the other. In other words, in the subject's mind, self and other are represented not as equally balanced wholes, but as split into halves. But is the splitting assumed by Hegel inevitable? Is the breakdown of tension inescapable?

George Bataille has directly applied the Hegelian dialectic to erotic violation. His work enables us to look more closely at *Story of O,* to see how splitting and breakdown assume an erotic form. Individual existence for Bataille is a state of separation and isolation: we are as islands, connected yet separated by a sea of death. Eroticism is the perilous crossing of that sea. It opens the way out of isolation by exposing us to "death . . . the denial of our individual lives."[15] The body stands for boundaries: discontinuity, individuality, and life. Consequently the violation of the body is a transgression of the boundary between life and death, even as it breaks through our discontinuity from the other. This break, this crossing of boundaries, is for Bataille the secret of *all*

---

*The psychoanalytic concept of splitting, like that of repression, has a narrow, technical use as well as a broader metapsychological and metaphoric meaning. Just as repression became a paradigm for a larger cultural process, so might splitting be suggestive not only for individual psychic processes but also for supraindividual ones. Technically, splitting refers to a defense against aggression, an effort to protect the "good" object by splitting off its "bad" aspects that have incurred aggression. But in its broader sense, splitting means any breakdown of the whole, in which parts of self or other are split off and projected elsewhere. In both uses it indicates a polarization, in which opposites—especially good and bad—can no longer be integrated; in which one side is devalued, the other idealized, and each is projected onto different objects.[14]

eroticism; and it assumes its starkest expression in erotic violation. It should be noted, however, that the break must never *really* dissolve the boundaries—else death results. Excitement resides in the *risk* of death, not in death itself. And it is erotic complementarity that offers a way to simultaneously break through and preserve the boundaries: in the opposition between violator and violated, one person maintains his boundary and the other allows her boundary to be broken. One remains rational and in control, while the other loses her self. Put another way, complementarity protects the self. Were both partners to give up control, the dissolution of self would be total. The violated partner would have no controlling partner to identify with; she could not "safely" abandon herself. When both partners dissolve the boundary, both experience a fundamental sense of breakdown, a kind of primary, existential anxiety; instead of connection to a defined other, there is a terrifying void. Thus the desire to inflict or receive pain, even as it seeks to break through boundaries, is also an effort to find them.[16]

As we have seen in *Story of O,* the control, order, and boundary that the master provides are essential to the erotic experience of submission. Indeed, it is the master's rational, calculating, even instrumentalizing attitude that excites submission; it is the image of his exquisite control that makes for his thrilling machismo. The pleasure, for both partners, is in his mastery. His intentions, with their sacramental formality, take on the purposefulness of a higher order. The sadist's disinterestedness, the fact that he does it "less for [his] pleasure than for [the masochist's] enlightenment," offers containment and protection. This protective power constitutes the all-important aspect of authority, without which the fantasy is not satisfying.* This authority is what inspires love and transforms violence into an opportunity for voluntary submission.

---

*A woman who had once been involved in a sadomasochistic relationship complained of her partner that "he was bumbling, he never hurt me where or how I wanted to be hurt." Indeed, a good sadist is hard to find: he has to intuit his victim's hidden desires, protect the illusion of oneness and mastery that stem from his knowing what she wants.[17]

Although the elements of self-control, intentionality, and authority are meant to uphold the difference between violator and violated, control, as we have seen, tends to become self-defeating. The fact that each partner represents only one pole in a split unity creates the major difficulty in sustaining tension. The continual problem in relations of domination, says Bataille in his commentary on Hegel, is "that the slave by accepting defeat . . . has lost the quality without which he is unable to *recognize* the conqueror so as to satisfy him. The slave is unable to give the master the *satisfaction* without which the master can no longer rest."[18] The master's denial of the other's subjectivity leaves him faced with isolation as the only alternative to being engulfed by the dehumanized other. In either case, the master is actually alone, because the person he is with is no person at all. And likewise, for her part, the slave fears that the master will abandon her to aloneness when he tires of being with someone who is not a person.

Eventually the other's unreality becomes too powerful; the sadist is in danger of becoming the will-less thing he consumes unless he separates himself completely. And the masochist increasingly feels that she does not exist, that she is without will or desire, that she has no life apart from the other. Indeed, once the tension between subjugation and resistance dissolves, death or abandonment is the inevitable end of the story, and, as we have seen, *Story of O* is deliberately left open to both conclusions. This ambiguity is appropriate because for the masochist the intolerable end is abandonment, while for the sadist it is the death (or murder) of the other, whom he destroys. A parallel dynamic, in which complementarity replaces reciprocity, is a frequent undertow in "ordinary" intimate relationships: one gives, the other refuses to accept; one pursues, the other loses interest; one criticizes, the other feels annihilated. For both partners, the sense of connection is lost: extreme self-sufficiency leads to detachment from the other; extreme dependency vitiates the separate reality of the other.

Metaphorically, then, and sometimes literally, the sadomasochistic relationship tends toward death, or, at any rate, toward deadness, numbness, the exhaustion of sensation. This end is ironic because such a relationship is initiated in order to reintroduce tension—to counteract numbness with pain, to break encasement through violation. Bataille implies that we need the split unity of master and slave in order to maintain the boundaries that erotic union—the "little death" of the self—threatens to dissolve. But, as we see, split unity culminates in disconnection. The exhaustion of satisfaction that occurs when all resistance is vanquished, all tension is lost, means that the relationship has come full circle, returned to the emptiness from which it was an effort to escape.

But why is loss of tension the beginning and inevitable end of this story? Freud's theory of the instincts offers us one interpretation. Indeed, his whole explanation of the discontents of civilization hinges on his interpretation of loss of tension.[19] Freud believed that only the idea of a death drive that impels us toward complete absence of tension could explain the prevalence of destruction and aggression in human life. Projecting the death drive outward in the form of aggression or mastery was our main protection against succumbing to it. Here, as I see it, is Freud's effort to explain domination, his parallel to the master-slave paradox.

Domination, for Freud, is inevitable since otherwise the death instinct, that primary drive toward nothingness (complete loss of tension), would turn inward and destroy life itself. But fortunately aggression must contend with its "immortal adversary," the life instinct, Eros. Eros, in general, and sexuality, in particular, neutralize or bind aggression. Freud writes that the life and death instincts almost never appear in isolation, but "are alloyed with each other . . . and so become unrecognizable." The best place to observe and analyze this merger is erotic life: sadism and masochism are "manifestations of the destructive instinct . . . strongly alloyed with erotism."[20] Indeed, erotic domination, Freud continues, may be the prime place to apprehend the alliance of Eros and the death instinct:

It is in sadism, where the death instinct twists the erotic aim in its own sense, and yet at the same time fully satisfies the erotic urge, that we succeed in obtaining the clearest insight into its nature, and its relation to Eros. But even where it emerges without any sexual purpose, in the blindest fury of destructiveness, we cannot fail to recognize that the satisfaction of the [death] instinct . . . [presents] the ego with a fulfillment of the latter's old wishes for omnipotence.[21]

When aggression is projected outward and harnessed by civilization, it winds up doing *outside* what it would otherwise do *inside:* reducing the world, objectifying it, subjugating it. If we translate this process back into Hegel's terms, this means that the self refuses the claim of the outside world (the other) to limit his absoluteness. He asserts omnipotence. Omnipotence, we might then say, is the manifestation of Freud's death instinct. When the destructive instinct is projected outward, the problem of omnipotence is not solved, but merely relocated. Nor does the fusion of the death instinct with Eros solve the problem. For even the alloy of destruction and Eros, as the cycle of escape from and return to deadness in erotic domination illustrates, brings us back to the death drive's original aim: the reduction of all tension.

Omnipotence and loss of tension actually refer to the same phenomenon. Omnipotence, whether in the form of merging or aggression, means the complete assimilation of the other and the self. It corresponds to the zero point of tension between self and other. Domination, as Freud sees it, is both an expression of omnipotence (or death)—the complete absence of tension—and an effort to protect the self from it: to create tension, to break up this assimilation of or by the other that allows nothing to exist *outside*. Yet it comes full circle, and leaves the self encapsulated in a closed system—the omnipotent mind—at least until the other fights back.

Let us now see what happens when we examine the cycle of omnipotence, from one point of zero tension to the other, in terms of intersubjective theory. In this view, the circular movement from numbness to exhaustion which characterizes domination is a manifestation not of the death instinct toward zero tension, but of the break-down of recognition between self and other. Domination presumes a subject already caught in omnipotence, unable to make "live" contact with outside reality, to experience the other person's subjectivity. But this apparent first cause is itself the result of an earlier breakdown between self and other—which, though pervasive, is not inevitable. Insofar as domination is an alienated form of differentiation, an effort to recreate tension through distance, idealization, and objectification, it is destined to repeat the original breakdown unless and until the other makes a difference.

DESTRUCTION AND SURVIVAL

Winnicott's idea of destruction is about the difference the other can make. Destruction, after all, is a way of differentiating the self—the attempt to place the other outside one's fantasy and experience him as external reality. I suggest that erotic domination expresses a basic differentiating tendency that has undergone a transformation. As we have seen, the fate of this tendency depends on whether it is met with the other's capitulation/retaliation or survival. In intersubjective terms, violation is the attempt to push the other outside the self, to attack the other's separate reality in order finally to discover it. The adult sadist, for example, is searching for a surviving other, but his search is already prejudiced by his childhood disappointment with an other who did not survive. Likewise, the adult masochist continues to find an other who survives, just as she did in childhood, but again loses herself in the bargain.

The controlled practice of sadomasochism portrays a classic drama of destruction and survival. The thrill of transgression and the sense of complete freedom for the sadist depend on the masochist's survival. When the masochist endures his unremitting attack and remains intact, the sadist experiences this as love. By alleviating his fear (guilt) that his aggression will annihilate her, she creates for him the first condition of freedom. By the same token, the masochist experiences as love the sharing of psychic pain, the opportunity to give over to pain in the presence of a trusted other who comprehends the suffering he inflicts. Hence the love and gratitude that can accompany the ritual of domination when it is contained and limited.[22]

In a child's development the initial destruction can be seen simply as part of assertion: the desire to affect (negate) others, to be recognized. When destruction fails, the aggression goes inside and fuels the sense of omnipotence.[23] Originally, there is a kind of innocence to the project of destruction. In Freud's theory of sadism—developed before he introduced the death instinct[24]—the infant at first ruthlessly attacks and devours the world with no sense of consequences. At this stage of primary sadism the child does not know about inflicting hurt; he simply expects to have his cake and eat it too. Only when the child internalizes his aggression and moves into the masochistic position can he imagine the pain that might come to the other. Then "real" sadism, the desire to hurt and reduce the other as one has been hurt oneself, comes into being. In short, aggression, internalized as masochism, reappears as sadism.* Through this internalization comes the ability to

---

*Jean Laplanche, the French psychoanalyst, has elaborated on Freud's model of the movement from primary sadism to masochism to sadism proper. He suggests that the movement of internalization turns aggression into sexual fantasy; that is, in turning inward, aggression is "alloyed" with sexuality. Whether the fantasy is active or passive, the act of "fantasmatization" is decisive; indeed, it actually constitutes sexuality and the unconscious. Sexuality, by which Laplanche means the realm of sexual fantasy, is the opposite of Eros, a kind of "frenetic anti-life."[25] Eros, if we recall Freud's usage, is directed outward, toward the other—hence the opposite of the inward-turning aggression that is sexuality. It follows from Laplanche's argument that the true opposition of instincts is not between Eros and death, but Eros and aggression, the latter often appearing in the guise of sexuality. This comes close to the intersubjective opposition between negating and recognizing the other. Indeed, Laplanche's idea of the internalization of aggression as sexual fantasy is comparable to Winnicott's idea that when destruction cannot be directed toward the other, the subject remains caught in mental omnipotence. His idea of the opposition between Eros and sexuality suggests something

play both roles in fantasy, to experience vicariously the other's part, and so enjoy the act of violation.

In much of early life, destruction is properly directed toward the other, and is internalized when the other cannot "catch" it, and survive. Ordinarily, some failure to survive is inevitable; for that matter, so is the internalization of aggression. When the parent fails to survive attack—to withstand the destruction without retaliating *or* retreating—the child turns its aggression inward and develops what we know as rage. But when things go well this rage often dissipates through a movement in the relationship, a shift back to mutual understanding that enables the child once again to feel the presence of the other. (For example, the child accepts the frustration but communicates the fantasy of retaliation to the parent who has frustrated him, as in, "Here is a bulldozer coming to knock down the house.")

When the child experiences the parent as caving in, he continues to attack, in fantasy or reality, seeking a boundary for his reactive rage. The child who has been indulged, allowed to abuse his mother (or both parents), and given no limits to his fantasy of omnipotence, is the typical "sadistic" child. ("I can't control him," says the parent, and then repeats for the fifth time "Michael, if you don't behave you'll have to leave the table and go up to your room.") For him, the real object, the one who cannot be destroyed, never comes into view. For him, agency and assertion are not integrated in the context of mutuality and respect for the other but in the context of control and retaliation. The sadist-child is *cognitively* aware of the difference between self and other, but *emotionally* this awareness is hollow and does not counteract the desire to control the other.

When the parent caves in, the child experiences his expanding elation, grandiosity, and self-absorption as flying off into space—he

---

similar to Winnicott's distinction between having an interaction with the outside other and relating to the object as one's mental product—a two-person versus a one-person experience.

finds no limits, no otherness. The world now seems empty of all human life, there is no one to connect with, "the world is all me." As the analyst Sheldon Bach describes it, when the self feels absolute, a loss of differentiation occurs in which "the subject and object are one; the [person] has eaten up reality."[26] What the child feels is something like this: When the other crumbles under the impact of my act, then my act seems to drop off the edge of the world into emptiness, and I feel that I will soon follow. In this void begins the loss of tension or boundaries, a by-product of losing the other.

Survival means that the parent can tolerate deflating the child's grandiosity enough—but just enough—to let him know that he can go only so far and no further, that someone else's needs and reality set a limit to his mental feats. The parent must feel separate and secure enough to be able to tolerate the thwarted child's anger without giving in. Otherwise the parent is destroyed in the child's eyes. The child involved in the process of destruction is like Icarus flying too near the sun. When the parent sets limits, she is actually protecting the child from the dissolution that occurs when the absolute self has its way. Of course, as we will see in our discussion of masochism, the child who is never allowed to destroy can never assume the power to fly or discover his limits.

The conversion from assertion to aggression, from interaction to mental control, works in tandem. When things are not resolved "outside," between self and other, the interaction is transferred into the world of fantasy; this includes identifying with the one we harm. The drama of reversible violator and victim displaces the tension of interaction with the other. This drama now occurs within the omnipotence of mental life, the encapsulated sphere of the intrapsychic. In successful destruction (when the other survives), the distinction between mental acts and what happens out there in "reality" becomes more than a cognitive awareness; it becomes a felt experience. The distinction between my fantasy of you and you as a real person is the very essence of connection.

The underlying theme of sadism is the attempt to break through to the other. The desire to be discovered underlies its counterpart, namely, masochism. Emmanuel Ghent has called this desire the wish for surrender, for which submission is the "ever-ready look-alike."[27] Like the sadist's aggression, the masochist's submission is ambiguous, conflating the repetition of an old frustration and the wish for something new. Ghent suggests that it is a wish to break out of what Winnicott called the "false self." The false self is the compliant, adaptive self that has staved off chaos by accepting the other's direction and control, that has maintained connection to the object by renouncing exploration, aggression, separateness.

This compliance is associated with another kind of failed childhood destruction, one in which the self has not survived. The "masochistic" child has endured not caving in but retaliation, in the form of either punishment or withdrawal. He destroys the other only in fantasy; he will never take a full swing at the parent to test if she will survive. His rage is turned inward and apparently spares the other, yet the loss of a viable external other overshadows the struggle to differentiate. The masochist despairs of ever holding the attention or winning the recognition of the other, of being securely held in the other's mind.

Contemporary Freudian ego psychology has often understood submission as a failure to separate and as an inhibition of aggression. But, as Ghent suggests, framing masochism as the desire for self-discovery in the space provided by the other allows us to recognize the wish as well as the defense. The masochist's self is "false" because, lacking this space, he has not been able to realize the desire and agency that come from within. He has not experienced his impulses and acts as his own, arising without direction from outside. This experience is what he longs for, although he may not know it.[28]

Masochism can be seen, therefore, not only as a strategy for escaping aloneness, but also as a search for aloneness *with* the other: by letting the other remain in control, the masochist hopes to find a "safe" open space in which to abandon the protective false self and allow the nascent, hidden self to emerge. Within this space, he seeks an opportunity for Winnicott's transitional experience free of the self-consciousness and adaptation that inhibit him. The masochist's wish to be reached, penetrated, found, released—a wish that can be expressed in the metaphor of violence as well as in metaphors of redemption—is the other side of the sadist's wish to discover the other. The masochist's wish to experience his authentic, inner reality in the company of an other parallels the sadist's wish to get outside the self into a shared reality.

These dynamics, then, are not merely the stuff of domination; they are also what make mutuality possible. They allow us to maintain connection so that we are not shut off from the world in the monadic capsule of the mind. Mental omnipotence signifies the absence of this connection, a breakdown of differentiation in which self is assimilated to other or other is assimilated to self. Internalization then replaces interaction or exchange with the outside.

The state of omnipotence, with its absence of tension, gives birth to domination. In the absence of a differentiated sense of self and other, the vital sharing between separate minds is replaced by almost exclusively complementary relationships. In infancy, the complementary interaction, in which the parent facilitates a positive change in the infant's states, is often a prelude to intersubjective sharing. The other must often do something to regulate, soothe, and make the self receptive for such exchange. But increasingly the relationship should shift in emphasis from regulation to the true exchange of recognition itself. What we see in domination is a relationship in which complementarity has completely eclipsed mutuality, so that the underlying wish to interact with someone truly outside, with an equivalent center of desire, does not emerge.

This dynamic of destruction and survival is the central pattern of erotic union. In erotic union, the other receives and recognizes the subject's acts including his acts of destruction. Eros is certainly not free of all that we associate with aggression, assertion, mastery, and domination. But what makes sexuality erotic is the survival of the other with and despite destruction. What distinguishes Eros from perversion is not freedom from fantasies of power and surrender, for Eros does not purge sexual fantasy—it plays with it. The idea of destruction reminds us that the element of aggression is necessary in erotic life; it is the element of *survival,* the difference the other can make, which distinguishes erotic union, which plays with the fantasy of domination, from real domination.

As I suggested earlier, in erotic union losing oneself and being wholly there occur together, as if without contradiction. The sense of losing oneself creatively, of becoming absorbed in the other is often only a hairsbreadth away from self-absorption.[29] In erotic union, the fundamental experience of attunement—that separate individuals can share the same feeling—is affirmed. Erotic domination, on the other hand, exemplifies the fatality of dissolving paradox into polarity (splitting) even as it shows it to be the endpoint of a complex process, and not simply the original human condition.

DOMINATION AND THE SEXUAL DIFFERENCE

It might seem that the association of domination and gender is obvious: men, after all, have everywhere dominated women, and one would expect this to color erotic relationships as well. Yet, even if we accepted this logic, we would still want to understand how the subjugation of women takes hold in the psyche and shapes the pattern of domination. Furthermore, it is increasingly apparent that the roles of master and slave are not intrinsically or exclusively male and female respectively; as the original "masochist" of *Venus in Furs* (Leopold von Sacher-Masoch) reminds us, the opposite is often true: the actual practice of sadomasochism frequently reverses heterosexual patterns. And, for that matter, sadomasochism is just as likely to occur in homosexual relationships. The question we are addressing, therefore, is not why are men sadists and women masochists, since this need not be the case; but rather, how have sadism and masochism become associated with masculinity and femininity?

The deep structure of gender complementarity has persisted despite the increased flexibility of contemporary sex roles. To understand the origins of male mastery and female submission, we must look at the characteristic course taken by each gender in the early differentiation process. Since women have almost everywhere been the primary caretakers of small children, both boys and girls have differentiated in relation to a woman—the mother.* When we look to the typical course of male differentiation, we see at once that this creates a special difficulty for boys. While all children identify with their first loved one, boys must dissolve this identification and define themselves as the different sex. Initially all infants feel themselves to be like their mothers. But boys discover that they cannot grow up to *become* her; they can only *have* her. This discovery leads to a break in identification for boys which girls are spared. Male children achieve their masculinity by denying their original identification or oneness with their mothers.[30]

Robert Stoller's work on the development and disruption of gender identity has offered much insight into this process. He has proposed that male identity is a secondary phenomenon, since it is achieved by overcoming a primary identification with the mother. This position, so contrary to Freud's assumption that children of both sexes begin as "little men," has wide ramifications. For the boy to become masculine, writes Stoller, "he must separate himself in the outside world from his mother's female body and in his inside world from his own already formed primary identification with femaleness and femininity. This great task is often not completed. . . ."[31]

The boy develops his gender and identity by means of establishing discontinuity and difference from the person to whom he is most

---

*Despite women's universal role as primary caretakers of small children, there is great variation in the organization of childrearing. Only in Western middle-class families do we see the typical pattern of babies attended by one lone mother. Thus our theory, unless amended, might strictly apply to such families. On the other hand, patterns of childrearing have been changing—in favor of paternal participation—in these families.

attached. This process of disidentification[32] explains the repudiation of the mother that underlies conventional masculine identity formation, and results in a kind of "fault line" running through the male achievement of individuality.

The tendency of erotic love to become erotic domination can be seen as a casualty of this characteristically male form of establishing separation. The need to sever the identification with the mother in order to be confirmed both as a separate person and as a male person—and for the boy these are hard to distinguish—often prevents the boy from recognizing his mother. She is not seen as an independent person (another subject), but as something other—as nature, as an instrument or object, as less than human. The premise of his independence is to say, "I am nothing like she who cares for me." An objectifying attitude comes to replace the earlier interactions of infancy in which mutual recognition and proud assertion could still coexist. Male identity, as Nancy Chodorow points out, emphasizes only one side of the balance of differentiation—difference over sharing, separation over connection, boundaries over communion, self-sufficiency over dependency.[33]

In breaking the identification with and dependency on mother, the boy is in danger of losing his capacity for mutual recognition altogether. The emotional attunement and bodily harmony that characterized his infantile exchange with mother now threaten his identity. He is, of course, able cognitively to accept the principle that the other is separate, but without the experience of empathy and shared feeling that can unite separate subjectivities. Instead, the other, especially the female other, is related to as object. When this relationship with the other as object is generalized, rationality substitutes for affective exchange with the other.[34] This rationality bypasses real recognition of the other's subjectivity. The process might be called "false differentiation."

Violation is an elaboration of this one-sided, or "false," differentiation, asserting absolute difference from its object, an object we can now see as representing the mother.[35] A fantasy of maternal power, of being reabsorbed, underlies this curious method of asserting difference. The danger that violation is meant to oppose—the ultimate loss of tension—is easily equated with the return to oneness with the mother, and can now be evoked by any profound experience of dependency or communion (emotional or physical), such as erotic love. The only defense against losing difference lies in reversing the power relationship so that the master now controls the other, while still proclaiming his boundaries intact.*

Erotic domination represents an intensification of male anxiety and defense in relation to the mother. The repudiated maternal body persists as the object to be done to and violated, to be separated from, to have power over, to denigrate.[36] Thus, on a visit to Sir Stephen's villa in the South, O thinks how fortunate it is that they are far from the sea, for the sea smells like dung *(mer = sea; mère = mother)*. O further complies in the denigration of what is specifically female in her sexuality when Sir Stephen uses her "as a boy," that is, denies her feminine organs. The anal allusions degrade what woman has to offer, her bodily difference from man.

It is precisely this objectification, combined with maintaining absolute difference and control, that informs the master's transgression. The vulnerability of a masculinity that is forged in the crucible of femininity, the "great task" of separation that is so seldom completed, lays the groundwork for the later objectification of women. The mother stands as the prototype of the undifferentiated object. She serves men as their other, their counterpart, the side of themselves they repress.[37]

The view of mother as object resounds throughout our culture. In general psychoanalytic discourse, the child relates to the mother as to

---

*Of course, as we have seen, the infant is never literally one with mother, but this early identification is retroactively called (represented intrapsychically as) "oneness," i.e., the absence of a fundamental difference. The defense against oneness develops according to a principle of reversal: I will do to you what I perceive you are doing to me. If I perceive your love as stifling my subjectivity, I will—again, through love—deny yours. Thus, as complementarity is no longer tempered by commonality, "oneness" appears even more absolute and threatening.

an object of his drives, and correspondingly devalues her independent subjectivity. Independence from the mother as object rather than recognition of her as subject constitutes the essence of individuation. And these assumptions are part of a larger problem: to the extent that until recently "man" and "individual" were synonymous, the male experience of differentiation has stamped the image of individuality. The image of the other that predominates in Western thought is not that of a vitally real presence but a cognitively perceived object. In this sense "false" differentiation has been a constant component of the Western version of individuation. Recognizing the other has been the exceptional moment, a moment of rare innocence, the recovery of a lost paradise.

The complement to the male refusal to recognize the other is woman's own acceptance of her lack of subjectivity, her willingness to offer recognition without expecting it in return. (The classic maternal ideal of motherhood—a paragon of self-abnegation—is only a beautification of this lack.) The female difficulty in differentiation can be described almost as the mirror image of the male's: not the denial of the other, but the denial of the self. Thus the fact of women's mothering not only explains masculine sadism, it also reveals a "fault line" in female development that leads to masochism. Whereas the boy's early difficulty seems to occur in making the switch to a masculine identification, the girl requires no such shift in identification away from her mother. This makes her identity less problematic, but it is a disadvantage in that she possesses no obvious way of disidentifying from her mother, no hallmark of separateness. The feminine tendency therefore is not to emphasize but to underplay independence.

As Chodorow has argued, mothers tend to identify more strongly with their daughters; whereas they push their sons out of the nest, they have greater difficulty separating from daughters.[38] Thus it is more likely that girls would fear separateness and tend to sustain the tie to mother through compliance and self-denial. If not acute, this tendency would be unremarkable. But the girl's relationship to the mother, emphasizing merging and continuity at the expense of individuality and independence, provides fertile ground for submission.

Submission, as we saw in *Story of O,* is often motivated by the fear of separation and abandonment; masochism reflects the inability to express one's own desire and agency. In submission, even the fulfillment of desire is made to appear as the expression of the other's will. The masochist abrogates her will because the exercise of independence is experienced as dangerous. To the extent that the mother has sacrificed her own independence, the girl's attempt at independence would represent an assertion of power for which she has no basis in identification. (As we shall see in chapter 3, the girl may identify with her father, but this has its own difficulties.) The girl's sense of self is shaped by the realization that her mother's source of power resides in her self-sacrifice. For the girl the agony of asserting difference is that she will destroy (internally) her mother, who is not only an object of love but also a mainstay of identity. Thus she protects the all-good, all-powerful maternal object, at the price of compliance. She becomes unable to distinguish what she wants from what mother wants. The fear of separation and difference has been transposed into submission.

Sadomasochism gives this fear objective form. In erotic submission, fear of the master's power takes the place of the deeper fear—of the separation that feels like death. The deepest anxiety can be controlled through "the discipline of service and obedience."[39] In submission, the masochist also protects the other from damage by taking the fault and the injury upon herself. At the same time, she is able to "enjoy" the sadist's attack. His assertion of subjectivity and difference is like a breath of the inaccessible outdoors. He embodies activity and difference for her. The vicarious quality of her enjoyment recapitulates the vicarious pleasure of the self-sacrificing mother with whom she identifies. Thus, submission for women allows a reenactment of their early identificatory relationship to the mother; it is a replication of the maternal attitude itself.

This cyclical mechanism allows us to untangle the fateful association that has dogged psychoanalytic debate since Freud's concept of "feminine masochism" was elaborated by Marie Bonaparte and Helene Deutsch to include the notion that masochism is an inevitable component of female sexuality, childbearing, and motherhood.[40] Undeniably, femininity and motherhood as we know them have been tainted with submission, self-abnegation, and helplessness. This is true even when submission works to conceal or deny the power that women as mothers do exercise.

And this fact, that women participate in their own submission, has often embarrassed critics of psychoanalytic theory. Some feminist critics, who feel that women have unjustly borne the burden of their victimization, have insisted that women are simply unwilling conscripts in an erotic fantasy formed by and for men—victims of the male pornographic imagination. Susan Griffin, for example, argues that the subjugation of women can be equated with the repression of nature.[41] But, in fact, women are not the embodiment of nature, although they have long been captives of that metaphor. Indeed, in accepting that equation, women once again participate in their own subjugation. Women, like men, are by "nature" social, and it is the repression of their sociability and social agency—the repression of the social, intersubjective side of the self—that is at issue. The equation *woman = motherhood = nature* is a symptom, not a cure. Embracing this equation, feminists have become caught in a contradiction: exalting women's maternal "nature" while disclaiming women's masochistic "nature."

Arguing from a different standpoint, the psychologist Paula Caplan has renewed the battle against the psychoanalytic position that women are "innately" masochistic. Caplan attacks the idea of "pleasure in pain" in great detail, but, unfortunately, sidesteps the issue of submission. Her explanation for masochism is that what is "called masochistic has tended to be the very essence of trained femininity in Western culture."[42] Her argument implies that social learning of a cultural myth about womanhood suffices to explain the presence of masochistic fantasies in women, or that the association of femininity with masochism is the result merely of a perjorative view of maternal nurturance and altruism. Caplan is right that the association of femininity with masochism persists in the culture; but the explanation for that persistence cannot be sought in social learning.[43]

From a psychoanalytic point of view, it is unsatisfactory to merely attribute the pervasiveness of submission fantasies in erotic life to cultural labeling or the derogation of women. The alternative to a biological explanation of masochism must be sought not only in culture, but in the interaction of culture and psychological processes. Cultural myths and labels, while undoubtedly destructive, still do not explain how the "essence of trained femininity" gets into women's heads and is there converted into pleasurable fantasies of erotic submission. To begin to explain it, we must start with the way in which the mother's lack of subjectivity, as perceived by both male and female children, creates an internal propensity toward feminine masochism and male sadism. Labeling is a result, not a cause, of that propensity.

Notwithstanding the persistence of these gender associations, it is safe to say that the mainstream of psychoanalytic thought today rejects the idea of feminine masochism. (Caplan has a hard time actually finding recent psychoanalytic proponents.) The analysis of submission as a defensive strategy of the self has become far more popular than Freud's notion of femininity in explaining masochism. If anything, we are faced with the opposite problem: with a few exceptions (notably, in Stoller), these problems of the self have largely been constructed as though gender played no role whatever. Nowhere do we find the explanation that gender polarity plays a role in fostering the breakdown in the balance of differentiation. Yet clearly, the splitting that is so typical in sadomasochism is in large part a problem of gender. The defensive masculine stance promotes a dualism, a polarization of subject and object. The assignment of subject status to male and object status to female follows from the seemingly unavoidable fact that the boy must struggle free with all the violence of a second birth from the woman who bore him. In this second birth, the fantasy of omnipotence and erotic domination begins.

At the same time, and ironically, the fantasy of erotic dominance and submission expresses the deep longing for wholeness. But as long as the shape of the whole is not informed by mutuality, this longing only leads to an unequal complementarity in which one person plays master, the other slave. And even when men and women reverse their roles, as they often do, the sense of "playing the other" is never lost. Gender continues, consciously and unconsciously, to represent only one part of a polarized whole, one aspect of the self-other relationship. One person ("the woman") is not allowed to play the subject; one person ("the man") arrogates subjectivity only to himself. Again, the groundwork for this division is laid in the mother's renunciation of her own will, in her consequent lack of subjectivity for her children, and particularly in the male child's repudiation of his commonality with her.

It would seem obvious that this lack of maternal subjectivity is a great, if not the greatest, impediment to the experience of successful destruction and survival by both male and female children. Only a mother who feels entitled to be a person in her own right can ever be seen as such by her child, and only such a mother can appreciate and set limits to the inevitable aggression and anxiety that accompany a child's growing independence. Only someone who fully achieves subjectivity can survive destruction and permit full differentiation. This fact has been remarkably elusive. It seems intolerable to the narcissism of adults and children alike that the limits a mother sets should not merely be an occasional dose of medicine corresponding to the child's needs, but might actually proceed from the mother's assertion of her own separate selfhood. The possibility of balancing the recognition of the child's needs with the assertion of one's own has scarcely been put forward as an ideal.

It is thus necessary to reconceive the ideal—and the reality—of motherhood in order to realign the process of differentiation, to mitigate the splitting into complementarity. The structure of individuation which permeates our culture, and which privileges separation over dependence, cannot simply be countered by its mirror opposite.

Rather, it must be criticized in light of a vision of a balance in which neither pole dominates the other, in which paradox is sustained.

This vision is important to a feminist critique of society especially now that male and female roles are no longer as binding as they once were. Today women in some sectors of society may adopt the same emphatic autonomy, the same "false" differentiation at the expense of real recognition and attunement, that has heretofore characterized the ideal of masculine individuality. The stereotype of the "career woman" is that she is able to be as detached and impersonal "as a man." But this individuation based on denying the need for others is hardly liberation.

Story of O supports our suspicion that this kind of individuation, rather than dissolving domination, fosters it. O's story is no simple housewife's tale; it is rather that of the "new woman" who emerged in this century. O, herself a fashion photographer, is as much a producer of objectification as its victim. Thus O is not so different from the masochist of a more recent novel, Pat Califia's *Jessie,* a thoroughly independent woman, who describes erotic violation as finally releasing her from "the bubble of the self, the prison of the mind."[44] To repeat, erotic domination, for both sides, draws its appeal in part from its offer to break the encasement of the isolated self, to explode the numbness that comes of "false" differentiation. It is a reaction to the predicament of solitary confinement—being unable to get through to the other, or be gotten through to—which is our particularly modern form of bondage. The castle of Roissy marshals the old forms of bondage—the ritual trappings of male dominion and female submission—as if they could redeem us from the sterility of modern rationality. So in our era of sexual equality and liberation, the fantasy of erotic domination returns like the repressed. But this return does not signal an end to confinement, only a further twisting in the chains, a testimony to the persistence of splitting and gender polarity in our structure of individuality.

To uncover this persistence is to confront the original sin of denying recognition to the other, and to rediscover the lost tension between self and other. This tension, a fragile balance, to be sure, can only be sustained through the lived experience of recognition, the meeting of separate minds. I have argued that the longing for recognition lies beneath the sensationalism of power and powerlessness, that the un-recognizable forms often taken by our desire are the result of a complicated but ultimately understandable process—a process which explains how our deepest desires for freedom and communion become implicated in control and submission. From such desires the bonds of love are forged.

CHAPTER THREE

Woman's
Desire

THE DISCUSSION OF erotic domination has shown how the breakdown of the tension between assertion and recognition becomes associated with the polarization of gender identity. Male and female each adopt one side of an interlocking whole. This one-sided character of differentiation evolves in response to the mother's lack of subjectivity, with which the girl identifies and the boy disidentifies.

This chapter will focus on woman's lack of subjectivity, particularly sexual subjectivity, and on the consequences of the traditional sexual complementarity: man expresses desire and woman is the object of it. We will explore why woman's missing desire so often takes the form of adoring the man who possesses it, why women seem to have a propensity for what we may call "ideal love"—a love in which the woman submits to and adores an other who is what she cannot be. To do this, we will have to turn back to the Freudian world of the father, where women are defined by the lack of what men possess: the very emblem and embodiment of desire, the phallus. In Freudian theory the phallus simultaneously signifies power, difference, and desire; and as bearer of the phallus, the father represents separation from the mother. Moreover, the father's power and the male monopoly of desire are constantly justified on the grounds that they are the only route to individuality.

Naturally, I question this justification; but a convincing argument against it requires us simultaneously to acknowledge and criticize the father's power. As we reconstruct how the initial relationship to the father informs desire, we will also deconstruct classical psychoanalytic theory, in particular, the idea that woman's destiny—her lack of subjectivity—is determined by her lack of a penis. As I will demonstrate, it is not anatomy, but the totality of a girl's relationship with the father, in a context of gender polarity and unequal responsibility for childrearing, that explains woman's perceived "lack." Finally, I will suggest a possible alternate mode of representation to challenge the hegemony of the phallus as the sole embodiment of desire.

THE PROBLEM OF WOMAN'S DESIRE

Perhaps no phrase of Freud's has been quoted more often than "What does woman want?" To my mind, this question implies another: *"Do women want?"* or better yet, "Does woman *have* a desire?" By this revision I mean to shift attention from the object of desire, *what* is wanted, to the subject, *she who desires*. The problem that Freud laid before us with all too painful clarity was the elusiveness of woman's sexual agency. He proposed, in fact, that femininity is constructed through the acceptance of sexual passivity. According to Freud's theory of feminine development, the little girl starts out originally as a "little man." She loves her mother actively until she discovers, in the oedipal phase, that she and mother both lack the phallus. She becomes feminine only when she turns from the mother to her father, from activity to passivity, in the hope of receiving his phallus; her effort to get the missing phallus leads her into the position of being the father's object.[1]

For Freud, woman's renunciation of sexual agency and her acceptance of object status are the very hallmark of the feminine. And though we may refuse his definition, we are nevertheless obliged to confront the painful fact that even today, femininity continues to be identified with passivity, with being the object of someone else's desire, with having no active desire of one's own.[2]

At times we are shocked by how much the reality of woman's condition differs from what we, in our minds, have long since determined it should be. Even the more modest demands for equality that we take for granted have not been realized. So it was when two psychologists, one of them the mother of a newborn boy, strolled by the hospital nursery to peer through the glass at the other newborns. Of course each bassinette had a pink or blue label proclaiming the swaddled baby's sex, which would otherwise be indecipherable (what confusion might that bring!). But astonishment overcame them when they looked at the first pink label. Expecting to find the counterpart to the blue one, which proudly announced, "I'm a boy!" they found instead, "It's a girl!" Further examination forced them to confirm what they at first refused to believe: all the boys were "I" and all the girls were "It." The infant girl was already presented to the world not as a potential "I," but as an object, "It." The sexual difference was already interpreted in terms of complementary and unequal roles, subject and object. The aspect of will, desire, and activity—all that we might conjure up with a subject who is an "I"—was assigned to the male gender alone.

Freud cautioned against the easy equations of femininity with passivity, and masculinity with activity, yet he did in the end conclude that the circuitous path to femininity culminates in the acceptance of passivity. If our received idea of femininity excludes activity—that to be a woman is to be unable to say, "I want that"—is it any wonder that many have agreed that the phallus stands not just for male desire, but *all* desire? Thus Juliet Mitchell, who accepts Freud's understanding of feminine passivity and male desire, proposes that we must logically also accept the singularity of the phallus in representing desire.* Only by acknowledging the power of the phallus, she argues, can we finally uncover the origins of woman's submission, the deep psychic roots of patriarchy.

Admittedly we have no female image or symbol to counterbalance the monopoly of the phallus in representing desire. Though the image of woman is associated with motherhood and fertility, the mother is not articulated as a sexual subject, one who actively desires something for herself—quite the contrary. The mother is a profoundly desexualized figure. And we must suspect that this desexualization is part of her more general lack of subjectivity in society as a whole. Just as the mother's power is not her own, but is intended to serve her child, so, in a larger sense, woman does not have the freedom to do as she wills; she is not the subject of her own desire. Her power may include control over others, but not over her own destiny. We have only to think of the all-sacrificing, all-perfect, and all-knowing Agnes who waits patiently while David Copperfield marries foolishly, is widowed, and

---

*For the mother the phallus represents her lack, what she desires for her completion; for the father it represents what he has and is and does. Thus it stands for both male and female desire.[3]

finally chooses her to be the angel-mother who will oversee his domestic bliss. Woman is to accept the abrogation of her own will, to surrender the autonomy of her body in childbirth and lactation, to live for another. Her own sexual feelings, with their incipient threat of selfishness, passion, and uncontrollability, are a disturbing possibility that even psychoanalysis seldom contemplates.

In any case, once sexuality is cut loose from reproduction, a goal the era of sexual liberation has urged upon our imagination, womanhood can no longer be equated with motherhood. But the alternative image of the femme fatale does not signify an active subjectivity either. The "sexy" woman—an image that intimidates women whether or not they strive to conform to it—is sexy, but as object, not as subject. She expresses not so much *her* desire as her pleasure in being desired; what she enjoys is her capacity to evoke desire in the other, to attract. Her power does not reside in her own passion, but in her acute desirability. Neither the power of the mother nor that of the sexy woman can, as in the case of the father, be described as the power of a sexual subject.

If woman has no desire of her own, she must rely on that of a man, with potentially disastrous consequences for her psychic life. For Freud, woman is doomed to envy the embodiment of desire that will forever elude her, since only a man can possess it. Desire in woman thus appears as envy—perhaps only as envy. And indeed, we know that many women enter into love relationships with men in order to acquire vicariously something they have not got within themselves. Others try to protect their autonomy by resisting passionate involvement with men: because their sexuality is bound up with the fantasy of submission to an ideal male figure, it undermines their sense of a separate self. As Jane Lazarre describes in *On Loving Men:* "There is a connection for me between the ability to feel autonomous, to feel confidently creative, and a fear of certain kinds of love. The love, especially when it includes passionate sexuality, undermines my ability to be myself, pulls me away from open channels, reawakens in me a desire to succumb to the ferocious power of my father's needs."[4] Insofar as a woman's desire pulls her toward surrender and self-denial, she often chooses to curb it altogether.

Let us acknowledge the partial truth of Freud's gloomy view. The equation of masculinity with desire, femininity with object of desire does reflect the existing situation; it is not simply a biased view.[5] Woman's sexual agency is often inhibited and her desire is often expressed by choosing subordination. But this situation is not inevitable; it has come into being through forces that we intend to understand and counteract. We do not need to deny the contribution of "nature" or anatomy in shaping the conditions of femininity; we have only to argue that the psychological integration of biological reality is largely the work of culture—of social arrangements that we *can* change or direct.

Contemporary psychoanalytic feminists have gone some distance toward uncovering the work of culture underlying the feminine condition. They have argued that the cultural institution of women's mothering is the key factor in gender development. In opposition to Freud, they argue that girls achieve their gender identity not by repudiating an initial masculinity, but—since children inevitably identify with their first caregivers—by identifying with their mothers.[6] The feminist position relies on the theory of core gender identity which shows that children consolidate a fixed unalterable sense of gender in the first two years of life, well before the onset of the oedipal complications Freud described. It also shows that maternal identification is the initial orientation for children of both sexes. As we saw in the preceding chapter, girls sustain the primary identification with the mother while boys must switch to an identification with the father.[7] This analysis of early gender identity has, in America at least, largely replaced Freud's view that maternal identification is not truly feminine, that only the penis wish and the passive love of the father are feminine. It has also led to the revaluation of the mother, whose influence Freud neglected.[8]

The idea that little girls develop their femininity through direct identification with the mother is quite persuasive and well documented. But it does not address the other problem that penis envy was meant to explain—the absence of woman's desire. Certainly the little girl whose femininity is formed in the image of a desexualized mother may well feel this lack of an emblem of desire. But this only shifts the problem back a generation. To what, then, do we attribute the mother's lack of sexual subjectivity? Where does absence of desire originate? Why does femininity appear linked to passivity? And why do men appear to have exclusive rights to sexual agency, so that women seek their desire in men, hoping to have it be recognized through the agency of an other?

The emphasis in contemporary feminism on the identity women gain from their mothers tends to gloss over the problem of desire.[9] One strand of feminist politics holds that we can only avoid sexual objectification and passivity by giving up on sex altogether. This rejection began with attacks on pornography, but it often extended to an excoriation of all heterosexual activity and many forms of homosexual activity, until not much was left uncondemned. In the effort to extricate women from the status of sexual object, feminism runs the risk of leaving all sexuality behind.[10]

The puritanical tendencies within the feminist movement are often linked to a tendency to elevate the desexualized mother whose hallmark is not desire but nurturance. The "gentler sex" is thus exalted by the proponents of an essential feminine nature. The result is a simple reversal of idealization, from father to mother; it is a position that ends up glorifying the sexual deprivation to which women have been subjected. In reclaiming the mother's importance, there is a tendency to give unwitting support to this reactive idealization of the feminine.[11] Certainly it is important to revalue what has been women's domain; but feminist theory cannot be satisfied with a simple reversal that leaves the terms of the sexual polarity intact. For the same reason, it cannot be satisfied simply with conquering men's territory for women. The task is more complex: it is to transcend the opposition of the two spheres by formulating a less polarized relationship between them.

The idealization of motherhood, which can be found in both anti-feminist and feminist cultural politics, is an attempt to redeem woman's sphere of influence, the power of the apron strings.[12] However, it pursues this end by idealizing woman's desexualization and lack of agency. This attitude toward sexuality preserves the old gender system, so that freedom and desire remain an unchallenged male domain, leaving women to be righteous but de-eroticized, intimate and caring, but pleasureless. And it fails to understand the underlying force of desire that ratifies male power, the adoration that helps to create it ever anew.

PENIS ENVY—THE CAUSE

But what are the unconscious sources of that desire? Whence comes that adoration of male power? Let us look more closely at that persistent challenge to the feminist argument—penis envy.

For Freud, as we have seen, the little girl begins as a "little man," and only becomes feminine when she turns from the mother to the father in search of a penis. Actually, Freud offers several explanations for why the little girl drops her mother in favor of her father: the little girl turns to love of her father as a refuge from her penis-less state, now wishing to be the passive object who can receive his phallus; she turns to her father because she has no knowledge of her own organ, the vagina, or of its potential for active sexual gratification; she rejects her mother in anger and disappointment for not having supplied her with the essential organ. In any case, she enters her oedipal conflict, propelled by the great discovery of the "lack" she shares with her mother. The mother becomes the depriving (even castrating) figure, and the father, the figure of desire.[13]

The early critics of penis envy, like Karen Horney, questioned the need of so complicated a process to explain the change. Would not the little girl feel an inner impulse toward heterosexuality, toward loving her father, even without the wish to get the phallus vicariously for herself? Horney disputed the idea that true femininity develops only through penis envy; that the narcissistic rather than erotic motive is the only basis for woman's sexuality; that woman is only motivated to get the phallus, not to give or express something of her own.[14]

All of these issues were debated at some length in the twenties, and were then taken up again in the second wave of feminism. For the moment, let us focus on Mitchell's response to Horney's challenge. It fails, she says, because it counters the theory of penis envy with the claim that femininity and heterosexuality do not need to be explained, that they are innate. This view denies Freud's fundamental insight that women are made, not born, that femininity is a complex creation of unconscious mental life. The assumption of innate femininity takes us away from the psychological and cultural roots of our sexual life, and ironically (for Horney was concerned above all with the influence of culture on the psyche) returns us to biology.[15]

Mitchell, I believe, is right to say that we must acknowledge the power of the phallus and its hold on the unconscious. She has argued well that male power cannot be divorced from its roots in the prerogative of the father and his sexual dominion over women. But Mitchell is misled by her idealization of Freud. By following him so faithfully, Mitchell, too, winds up equating the father's power with his possession of the phallus—the lone instrument of separation, the thing that comes between mother and child, forcing the child out into the world and forbidding the stagnation of incest.[16] Thus for Mitchell, as for Freud, it is inevitable that woman should covet this emblem of power and desire, that she should reject her mother in favor of her father. As Mitchell sums up, "She makes the shift from mother-love to father-love because she has to, and then with pain and protest. She has to, because she is without the phallus. No phallus, no power—except those winning ways of getting one."[17] But Mitchell cannot tell us, as Freud could not, why the phallus and the father have this exclusive power, this monopoly on desire, subjectivity, and individuation. She forecloses the possibility of answering this question by seeing the oedipal world, the world in which the mother "has no absolute strength" and the "father is truly powerful," as the whole world.[18]

But we have already elucidated why the oedipal world is not the whole world. We have seen that differentiation of self and other begins in infancy and evolves in preoedipal conflicts; so does the assumption of gender identity—long before the oedipal "switch" from mother to father. Current psychoanalytic thought gives far more attention to preoedipal life than Mitchell's analysis would indicate: and there the mother's power and its impact on the child appear in a different light.[19]

To take just one example, the French analyst Janine Chasseguet-Smirgel has demonstrated that Freud's description of woman as castrated and powerless—a catalogue of lacks—is the exact opposite of the little child's unconscious image of the mother. While the little boy may consciously represent the mother as castrated, clinical evidence reveals that unconsciously the boy sees this mother as extremely powerful.[20] She does not appear lacking a sexual organ; rather her vagina is known and feared for its potential to re-engulf the boy, whose little penis would be far too small to satisfy it. (As an illustration of this fear, consider a three-year-old boy who, shortly after inquiring in detail about his mother's genitals and how babies are born, became panic-stricken at the end of his bath when the plug was pulled: he now feared that he or his toys could be sucked down the drain.) The girl, too, sees her mother as powerful and her wish for her father's penis signifies the desire to "beat back the maternal power."[21]

The meaning of the penis as a symbol of revolt and separation derives, then, from the fantasy of maternal power, not maternal lack.* For psychoanalysts like Chasseguet-Smirgel who have moved away

---

*Chasseguet-Smirgel and her colleagues have stressed the child's conflict with the intrusive, controlling mother of the anal period.[22] Certainly the mother they have in mind, the mother of discipline, cleanliness, and toilet training, who subjects the child's body to her rule, necessarily arouses revolt (however unconscious). I have observed that

from the strict oedipal view, the father is not powerful simply because he *has* a phallus, but because he (with his phallus) represents freedom from dependency on the powerful mother of early infancy. In the preoedipal world, the father and his phallus are powerful because of their ability to stand for separation from the mother. The phallus, then, is not *intrinsically* the symbol of desire, but *becomes* so because of the child's search for a pathway to individuation.[23] The difference is simply between attributing the power to the phallus and attributing it to the father—the symbol of power versus the actual bearer of power.

In Mitchell's view, the father is still, as it were, attached to the phallus, which, *in itself*, represents sexual power and the ability to enforce separation. In the other view, conversely, the symbolic power of the phallus develops as an extension of the father's power; the phallus is not a thing in itself which the girl envies the moment she realizes she hasn't got one. This is the position I wish to elaborate. I recognize, of course, the phenomenon that Freud called penis envy, but I interpret it as an expression of the girl's effort to identify with the father as a way of establishing the separateness that is threatened by identifying with her mother.

Chasseguet-Smirgel's idea that the phallus serves to "beat back the mother" grasps the double nature of the father's power to represent difference: it is a defense against the mother's fearful power *and* it is an expression of the child's innate striving to individuate. But there is one problem with this idea: it implies that the establishment of independence from the mother has a predominantly hostile and defensive coloring. This antagonistic picture obscures the positive side of

---

women preoccupied with the penis wish frequently describe their mother as controlling, physically intrusive, and sexually restrictive. In American psychoanalytic writing we less frequently encounter an anally controlling mother than a "narcissistic" mother, who impedes separation because she fantasizes the daughter as an extension of herself—an orally controlling mother, shall we say, indulgent, overinvolved, but oblivious.

becoming independent in the relationship with mother—becoming a more active partner in (affectionate) interaction with her.[24] The striving to individuate is not just an expression of hostility toward dependency; it also expresses love of the world. Whether hostility or love predominates depends largely on the circumstances in which the child grows up.

The fantasy of dangerous maternal omnipotence may well be intensified by specific conditions of mothering (widespread in much of Western society) that trap mother and child in an emotional hothouse and make it difficult for either one of them to accomplish separation.[25] This is the context in which the father and his phallus become a weapon for the embattled self struggling to differentiate. But as we have seen in the analysis of erotic domination, using fire to fight fire—using the fantasy of one omnipotent parent (or organ) to subdue the other one—does not solve the real problem of differentiation, which is to break out of omnipotence altogether. We must find a form of differentiation that does not involve exchanging one master for another.

Chasseguet-Smirgel, having identified the deep unconscious roots of phallic power in fear and envy of the mother, believes she has hit bedrock. But feminist critics draw a different conclusion about the relationship between paternal and maternal power. They do not accept the inevitability of defensive differentiation; rather, they see the necessity of challenging the existing gender arrangements.

CHOOSING THE FATHER

Once we take the view that the father—not the phallus—is the locus of power, we may scrutinize more critically the daughter's relationship to him.

Let us consider the experience of a woman who was a "father's daughter," who as a child used her identification with her father to achieve liberation from a controlling and intrusive, although demeaned, mother. Lucy was a successful professional woman, a lawyer like her father, and the eldest of three girls. She sought help in dealing with the painful end of a long marriage to an older man who she felt had completely controlled her. She consciously saw her submission as an extension of her relationship to her father, whom she adored yet vaguely resented. In Lucy's recollections, which are quite vivid, the antithesis stands out between her father, the active, desiring subject, and her mother, the restrictive prohibitor of desire.

In one session Lucy discussed a dream of having something rubbery between her legs which she must squeeze when she has to put on the brakes while driving in a car. She associates to images of both father and mother. First she thinks of the rubbery thing as a penis, then as a diaphragm. She mentions a childhood dream in which she was attacked by a man with a knife. Then she associates to the recollections that she has often brought up of her mother interfering with her masturbation. She then returns, on the theme of humiliation, to remember how her father would tease her while swimming, ducking her head and splashing her until she was in tears and enraged. He would persist just a little too long, until she was upset, and then laugh at her. She recalls how he would mock her mother until, in silent protest, she left the room. She then veers back to a memory of her mother expressing disgust at the behavior of two teenagers caught having sex in the park. Then she thinks of pressing her legs together to control her urine flow, as her mother had taught her, and thinks again of the rubbery thing, this time as the rubber panties a child wears over diapers to keep them from leaking. Here is a not uncommon female constellation, involving resentment of maternal prohibition complicated by a fear of paternal intrusion.*

---

*This is, of course, a classic oedipal constellation; what I am emphasizing, however, is the preoedipal roots of this configuration: the girl repudiates her mother and identifies with her father in the interest of escaping maternal control, but this preoedipal solution leaves her without maternal protection from the threatening genital fantasies inspired by the oedipal father.

In her first description of her problems, Lucy had talked about her difficulty with being female, her sense of exclusion from the female bonds in her family, her preference for male friends, and her sense of being like her father, whom she loved a great deal. Her mother had told her two things about her infancy: that when she was still in the crib Lucy would masturbate frequently and her mother would stop her from doing it; and that when her mother tried to hold her she would squirm away. She could remember being severely reprimanded by her mother when she found her at the end of a nap with her hands between her legs. Reflecting on these recollections she said, "Maybe that's where I got the idea of not wanting to be a girl." The central point of this statement, I think, was that she did not wish to be like her mother, who rejected sexuality and desire in favor of control and self-control: she did not wish to be her, to be close to her and therefore controlled by her. If she were a boy and could disidentify with mother, she would not have to repress her sexuality, she could have her pleasure and autonomy. A boy who experiences humiliation by his mother will turn to his father and strive to be like him—free of mother's control. By wishing to be a boy, Lucy was pursuing a similar strategy.

The child's struggle for autonomy takes place within the realm of the body and its pleasures. Thus, the mother who does not experience her own will and body as sources of pleasure, who does not enjoy her own agency and desire, cannot recognize her daughter's sexuality. But in turning away from such a mother to her father, the girl is often faced with the dilemma that he will "hold her down," force her to submit, humiliate her with her femininity, demean her. She fears he will treat her as she has seen him treat her mother. Virginia Woolf has described such a daughter's passionate struggle with her father in *To the Lighthouse*:

> For no one attracted her more; his hands were beautiful, and his feet, and his voice, and his words . . . his saying straight out before every one, we perish, each alone, and his remoteness. . . . But what remained intolerable, she thought . . . was that crass blind-

ness and tyranny of his which had poisoned her childhood and raised bitter storms, so that even now she woke in the night trembling with rage and remembered some command of his; some insolence: "Do this," "Do that," his dominance: his "Submit to me."[26]

Lucy's core fear was the fear of violation and intrusion, a fear that was expressed in vigilant attempts to maintain her privacy in her family and a preoccupation with "finding a space" for herself in adult life. Both her mother's control and intrusion, and her father's seduction and domination, appeared to coalesce in this fear. And yet, the basic direction that Lucy had chosen throughout her life was to reject her mother in favor of her father, as an object not only of love but of identification. He was the one with the exuberance, the agency, the excitement, and the desire that Lucy was trying to protect in herself from humiliation and prohibition. His recognition of her as his favorite child, his letting her be like him, was crucial.

Lucy had unequivocally made the choice to beat back maternal power with paternal power, to find liberation in the father. But to do this she was always having to struggle against her father—his command of and contempt for her, her mother, and women in general. Lucy's choice had led her to a common daughter's dilemma: How to be a subject in relation to her father (or any man like her father)? How to be like her father and still be a woman? Her identification of femininity with submission, exemplified by her mother, had prevailed in her marriage and left her confused about her identity afterward. Lucy's dilemma suggests how problematic it is for a woman to identify with her father as a mode of separation when the father–mother relationship is one of inequality, when the mother is not a subject herself, but is nevertheless a power over her daughter. This use of the father is a solution that is part of the problem. It leads to that recurrent split between autonomy and sexuality that is so visible in the lives and the politics of women today.

Despite the drawbacks, however, there is no doubt that Lucy drew a certain strength from paternal identification. Under the circumstances, she chose the parent who would provide her with a sense of personal power. But again, if we understand this choice only as an attempt to beat back the mother, we still do not have the whole story about desire. We still need to understand what is so erotic about this paternal power. Let us turn to that point in life when the father becomes the image of liberation from maternal power, when he becomes the one who recognizes and embodies desire.

THE MIRROR OF DESIRE

Recent research and theory now concur that gender identity develops in the second year of life and is well established by the third—much earlier than Freud thought.[27] The child's awareness of the difference between mother and father, now reformulated as gender difference, coincides fatefully with rapprochement. It is this conjunction which shapes the symbolic role of the father and his phallus.

Briefly, this is what I propose: what Freud called penis envy, the little girl's masculine orientation, really reflects the wish of the toddler—of either sex—to identify with the father, who is perceived as representing the outside world. Psychoanalysis has recognized the importance of the boy's early love for the father in forming his sense of agency and desire; but it has not assigned a parallel importance to the girl's. This early love of the father is an "ideal love": the child idealizes the father because the father is the magical mirror that reflects the self as it wants to be—the ideal in which the child wants to recognize himself.[28] Under certain conditions, this idealization can become the basis for adult ideal love, the submission to a powerful other who seemingly embodies the agency and desire one lacks in oneself.

The idealized father solves the paradox of the rapprochement phase, the paradox of the child needing to be recognized as independent by the very person he depends upon. The father's power derives not only from the fact that he is big, but also that he represents a solution to the child's inner conflict. As we saw in our discussion of recognition in chapter 1, rapprochement is a vital transition point in psychic life.* It can be seen as the great fall from grace, when the conflict between self-assertion and separation anxiety brings forth an essential ambivalence.[29] In rapprochement the child first experiences his own activity and will in the context of the parents' greater power and his own limitations. This power relationship—and the realization of his own helplessness—comes as a shock, a blow to the child's narcissism. The child's self-esteem must be repaired by the confirmation that the child *can* do real things in the real world. The child also seeks to repair it through identification, a particular kind of oneness with the person who embodies the power one now feels lacking.

But—note well—in my view this identification is more than just a compensation for a perceived loss. The child is also becoming *conscious* of will and agency, of being the one who desires. The child wants more than simple satisfaction of need. Rather, each want expresses the desire to be recognized as a subject: above and beyond the thing itself that is wanted, the child wants recognition of her will, of her desire, of her act. Nothing is more characteristic of this phase than the reiteration of the word "want." Where the fourteen-month-old said "banana" or "cracker" and pointed, the twenty-month-old says "Want that!" uninterested in naming the object itself. Recognition of this wanting is now the essential meaning of getting what you asked for. The child's tendency to feel that her ego is on the line every time she asks for some paltry thing often mystifies the parent. But this insistence only becomes stronger in each new phase of self-assertion.

---

*Because of the many issues that converge at this point this phase is gradually assuming the theoretical status of a "rapprochement complex," vying in theoretical importance with the Oedipus complex. When, in rapprochement, the father first begins to represent freedom, separation, and desire, this is not simply an earlier version of the Oedipus complex. The father here is not a restrictive authority, not a limit to the child's desire, but rather a model for it, whereas the oedipal father is both.

When the child has a tantrum over which shoes she will wear, the urgency stems from the need to be an agent who can realize her own plans, intentions, and mental images. The rapprochement phase, then, inaugurates the first in a long series of struggles to achieve a sense of agency, to be recognized in one's desire.

This understanding of rapprochement offers a great insight into the problem of woman's desire. What is really wanted at this point in life is recognition of one's desire; what is wanted is recognition that one is a subject, an agent who can will things and make them happen. And at this very point, where desire becomes an issue, the realizations of gender difference first begin to take hold in the psyche. Now each parent may represent one side of the mental conflict between independence and dependence. And the child will articulate this difference between them symbolically—especially the father's difference from the mother. Here begins the child's relationship with the father that has been adduced to explain the power of the phallus It is a relationship that—in theory as well as practice—continues to be dramatically different for boys and girls.

Long before this symbolic consciousness of gender begins, the father is experienced in his total physical and emotional behavior as the exciting, stimulating, separate other. Fathers' play with infants differs from mothers': it is more stimulating and novel, less soothing and accurately tuned.[30] Fathers often introduce a higher level of arousal in early interaction—jiggling, bouncing, whooping. The father's novelty and complexity, as opposed to the mother's smoother, more contained play, have been characterized as an aggressive mode of behavior that "fosters differentiation and individuation."[31] Fathers, whether it is because of their greater sense of bodily separateness, or their identification with their own fathers, tend toward such exciting play. Thus, from the beginning, fathers represent what is outside and different—they mediate the wider world.

Playfulness is, of course, not absent in mothers, but it is more often eclipsed by their function as regulator. Mothers are more likely to be found quieting, soothing, nursing, stabilizing, containing, and *holding* the infant. Still, it has been observed that whatever her style of play, when the mother is the parent who comes and goes, she is the "curious-making" outside parent.[32] We shall have to await the results of current changes in parenting to see what happens when the father is the primary parent and these elements are reshuffled: for example, when the father stays home but his play is aggressive and novel, when the mother is the outside parent, yet soothing and holding. Perhaps parents will ultimately integrate the aspects of holding and excitement. At present, however, the division between the exciting, outside father and the holding, inside mother is still embedded in the culture.

No matter what theory you read, the father is always the way into the world. In some contemporary delivery rooms, the father is literally encouraged to cut the umbilical cord. He is the liberator, the proverbial knight in shining armor. The devaluation of the mother that inevitably accompanies the idealization of the father, however, gives the father's role as liberator a special twist for women. It means that their necessary identification with their mothers, with existing femininity, is likely to subvert their struggle for independence.

The asymmetry of the father's role for boy and girl toddlers, the fact that little girls cannot as readily utilize the father in their separation from the mother or defend against feelings of helplessness, has, with few exceptions, been accepted as inevitable in psychoanalytic literature.[33] The observation that little girls in rapprochement become more depressed and lose more of their exploratory enthusiasm than boys, is noted by Mahler as a fact of life. According to Mahler, the boy succeeds in escaping the depressive mood of rapprochement by virtue of his "greater motor-mindedness," his pleasure in active, aggressive strivings.[34] In light of little boys' well-known fascination with motor vehicles, we might call this the tendency to *vroom vroom vroom* their way through rapprochement. But this activity is a symptom, not the cause of the boy's success in denying helplessness or the little girl's depressed confrontation with it.

Feminist theorists explain this difference by noting the mother's greater identification with the daughter, and her greater willingness to bolster the son's than the daughter's independence.[35] This is doubtless true; but it is equally important to observe that boys resolve the conflict of independence by turning to someone else. This other is conventionally the father, though most any male substitute or symbol will do as the other object of identification. Ernest Abelin, who observed the toddlers in Mahler's study, argued that the father plays this role more for the boy than for the girl. Recognition of himself in the father is what enables the boy to deny helplessness, to feel he is powerful, to protect himself from the loss of the grandiosity he enjoyed in the practicing phase.[36] When the boy is not actively playing daddy, he flies about, announcing his new name—Superman.

Paternal recognition thus has a defensive aspect; with it the child denies dependency and dissociates himself from his previous maternal tie. The father's entry is a kind of *deus ex machina* that solves the insoluble conflict of rapprochement, the conflict between the desire to hold onto mother, and the desire to fly away. The child wants to solve this problem by becoming independent without the experience of loss. And the "solution" to this dilemma is to split—to assign the contradictory strivings to different parents. Schematically, the mother can become the object of desire, the father the subject of desire in whom one recognizes oneself.[37] Separation-individuation thus becomes a gender issue, and recognition and independence are now organized within the frame of gender.

This is the point where the distinction between subject and object, the I and the It, acquires meaning. Abelin postulates that in this phase, excitement is no longer felt as emanating from the object ("It is so attractive"). Desire is now a property of the self, one's own inner desire ("I desire it").[38] And the father now becomes the symbolic figure representing the I who "owns" desire, desire for the mother.*

---

*Although this account of the father's role gives greater weight to object relations than to the genital difference, it still assumes a heterosexual, two-parent family. What about the fact that a large proportion of the children in our society do not grow up under

In the boy's mind, the magical father with whom he identifies possesses the omnipotence that he would like to have. Recognition through identification is now substituted for the more conflictual need to be recognized directly by the primary parent on whom he feels dependent. The boy can enjoy the fantasy that he is being the father toward the mother, and not her helpless baby; he can now see himself as part of a triangle, rather than a dyad; he becomes conscious of himself as acting like father toward mother. And the mother has only to confirm his fantasy, acknowledge his identification, see him as her "little man." She has only to say, as did one mother to her two-year-old, "You and Daddy are as alike as two peas in a pod," to which the boy fervently replied, "Say it again, Mommy!"

The images of separation and desire are thus joined in the father, or more accurately, in his ideal. Presumably, the father has been experienced by both boys and girls as the original representative of excitement and otherness. Now, as the child begins to feel the wish and the excitement as his or her own *inner desire,* he or she looks for recognition from this exciting other. While the child doubtless seeks recognition from both parents at this time, the exciting father is the one the child wishes to be *like.* Desire is intrinsically linked, at this point, to the striving for freedom, for autonomy, but this striving is

---

the conditions presumed by this account? They do not live with mommy and daddy in stereotypical families with a conventional sexual division of labor. I have not forgotten this objection; but I think that differences in psychic development that result from the specific social arrangements of personal life have to be understood against the background of the dominant culture and its gender structure, as represented by an abstract model of personal and sexual life. The figures of mother and father are cultural ideals, but they need not be played by "biological" mothers and fathers, or even by women and men. The father of rapprochement is such an ideal. The male child uses this ideal symbolically to represent separation and agency, whether the father is personally present or not. One could say that the figure of the father is accompanied by a mental notation, such as "present" or "absent," which will have importance in the relationship between the individual's father and the one that is generally recognized in the culture as The Father.[39]

realized in the context of a powerful connection. The wish to be like the father, the identificatory impulse, is not merely a defensive attempt to defeat the mother—it is also the basis for a *new kind of love*. [40] I suggest we call this *identificatory love*.

Identification now plays a central role in recognition and desire. "Being like" is the chief means by which a child of this age can acknowledge the subjectivity of another person, as the well-noted phenomenon of parallel play implies. The element of pleasure in an other is gained through likeness—"We are both drinking juice from blue cups." For the toddler, "being like" is perhaps second only to physical intimacy in emotional importance. The father's subjectivity is appreciated through likeness—"I am being Daddy." Loving someone because they are different—object love—has not yet come view. Loving someone who is the source of goodness is already well established—"I love you; you give me food." But the first form of loving someone as a subject, as an admired agent, is this kind of identificatory love. [41]

In the boy's story, identificatory love is the matrix of crucial psychic structures during rapprochement. The strong mutual attraction between father and son allows for recognition and identification, a special erotic relationship. [42] In rapprochement, the little boy's "love affair with the world" (of the earlier practicing stage) turns into a homoerotic love affair with the father, who *represents* the world. The boy's identificatory love for the father, his wish to be recognized as like him, is the erotic engine behind separation. The boy is in love with his ideal, and through his ideal he begins to see himself as a subject of desire. Through this homoerotic love he creates his masculine identity and maintains his narcissism in the face of helplessness.*

---

*I emphasize that this ideal, the homoerotic love of the father, is not the equivalent of the "negative Oedipus complex," as Freud called it, in which the boy identifies with the mother and passively desires the father. This love, which takes the father as "like" object in support of activity, corresponds to Freud's description of the boy's preoedipal

I regard the identificatory, homoerotic bond between toddler son and father as the prototype of ideal love—a love in which the person seeks to find in the other an ideal image of himself. In rapprochement, the child who is beginning to confront his own helplessness can comfort himself with the belief in parental omnipotence.[44] In this parental power, he will seek to recognize the power of his own desire; and he will elaborate it in the internally constructed ideal. The father-son love affair is the model for later ideal love, just as the conflict of rapprochement between independence and helplessness is the model conflict that such ideal love is usually called upon to solve. And underlying both identificatory love and ideal love is the same desire for recognition.

THE MISSING FATHER

The little boy's identificatory love for his father is the psychological foundation of the idealization of male power and autonomous individuality. This idealization remains untainted by submission as long as the wonderful, exciting father says, "Yes, you are like me." The route to becoming the I who desires leads through identification with him. Thus, I believe, for women, the "missing father" is the key to their missing desire, and to its return in the form of masochism. By reconstructing the way in which the father is missing for the girl, we begin to uncover an explanation for woman's "lack" that goes beyond penis envy.

The psychoanalytic discussion of the father–daughter relationship has been notably thin compared to that of boys and their fathers.[45] The common psychoanalytic line on sexual difference is that the boy has

---

love for the father in *Group Psychology and the Analysis of the Ego.*[43] For Freud, this love serves to explain the mass identification with and the surrender to the ideal leader. As we shall see, woman's search for identificatory love likewise often leads to submission.

one love object (the mother) and the girl has two (must shift from mother to father). But at times it appears as if the boy has two and the girl has none.[46] When we turn to the little girl's story, we find no coherent explanation of the elements of gender, individuation, and paternal identification. Either the father's importance to the girl is ignored (as in maternal identification theory) or he is no more to her than the possessor of the penis she wants (as in classical theory).

Roiphe and Galenson have been the leading contemporary exponents of the idea that toddler girls suffer from penis envy.[47] They claim to notice the same signs of depression in eighteen-month-old girls that Mahler noted—subdued mood, withdrawal, decline in curiosity and responsiveness toward others—but they attribute it to the new genital awareness rather than to separation issues. The girls they observed attempted to emulate their fathers, appropriated his objects ("stealing" his pens—which, they failed to observe, boys do as well), and variously expressed the wish for a penis. Roiphe and Galenson conclude that Freud was right, penis envy does structure femininity. The evidence, they argue, points to an "early genital phase" in which girls suffer from feelings of castration, a further proof that the genital drive is the main force behind gender development.[48] I am willing to credit their evidence that toddler girls display considerable interest in father and penis, just as earlier critics of Freud did not deny that penis envy was readily observable.[49] But *why* do girls want the penis? And is their awareness of lack the main cause of girls' depression? There is no question that the symbol is important, and that it will go on to be more so. But what does it represent?

I interpret the desire for the penis as evidence that little girls are seeking the same thing as little boys, namely, identification with the father of separation, the representative of the outside world.[50] What Galenson and Roiphe see as evidence of a castration reaction I see as a roadblock in the toddler girl's separation from mother and identification with father. But to see the situation this way one must first assume that girls do, in fact, need their fathers, an idea that escapes Galenson and Roiphe altogether. Why not assume that girls are seek-

ing to identify with their fathers and thereby find recognition of their
own desire? Little girls in this phase express the wish for a penis, I
suggest, for the same reason that boys cherish theirs—because they see
it as the emblem of the father who will help them individuate. Like
boys, in their anxiety over separating from mother they are looking
for an attachment figure who will represent their move away from
infant dependency to the great outside. This figure is the father, and
his difference is symbolized and guaranteed by his different genitals.

One consequence of female mothering is that fathers often prefer
their boy infants; and, as infants respond in turn to parental cues, boy
infants tend to form an intense bond with their fathers.[51] The father
recognizes himself in his son, sees him as the ideal boy he would have
been; so identificatory love plays its part on the parent's side from the
beginning. The father's own disidentification with his mother, and his
continuing need to assert difference from women, make it difficult for
him to recognize his daughter as he does his son.[52] He is more likely
to see her as a sweet adorable thing, a nascent sex object.

Consequently we see that little girls often cannot or may not use
their connection with the father, in either its defensive or constructive
aspects (that is, to deny helplessness or to forge a sense of separate
selfhood). The father's withdrawal pushes the girl back to her mother;
the consequent turning inward of her aspirations for independence and
her anger at nonrecognition explain her depressive response to the
rapprochement conflict. Thus little girls are confronted more directly
by the difficulty of separating from mother and their own helplessness.
Unprotected by the phallic sign of gender difference, unsupported by
an alternate relationship, they relinquish their entitlement to desire. It
is tempting to counter this deflation by emphasizing the girl's capacity
for sociability or for future motherhood, a rationalization that has
some truth.[53] But alas, we know that many girls are left with a lifelong
admiration for individuals who get away with their sense of omnipotence intact; and they express their admiration in relationships of overt
or unconscious submission. They grow to idealize the man who has
what they can never possess—power and desire.

Although the psychoanalytic theory of female development has not yet recognized the importance of the missing father, clinicians have begun to realize the girl's equal need to identify with her father and the consequences if he is unavailable for such identification. Galenson and Roiphe actually come rather close to uncovering the real issue. They cite a case in which a little girl was deeply depressed by her father's unavailability; they conclude that "the missing element . . . was not simply his phallus; it was in great part the excitement and erotic nature of their relationship, which had earlier been attached to the father *in toto* and now was identified as emanating from his phallus in particular."[54] This change of focus from the exciting father in general to his phallus in particular is precisely what happens when the father himself is "missing"—that is, when he is absent, not involved, or offers seduction rather than identification. The girl struggles to create the identification with him out of whole cloth: and the symbol thus takes the place of the concrete relationship of recognition that she misses.[55]

I conclude that the little girl's "lack" is the gap left in her subjectivity by the missing father, and that this is what the theory of penis envy presumed to explain. The fact that girls, like boys, seek a relationship of identificatory love with the father also affects our explanation of another aspect of female development that puzzled Freud. Repeatedly he came back to the question of why the little girl "switches" to her father in the oedipal phase, a shift Freud could only explain as the girl's narcissistic desire to gain the penis for herself. It is now possible to transpose this explanation as follows: the preoedipal girl's identificatory love becomes the basis for later heterosexual love; when the girl realizes she cannot *be* the father, she wants to *have* him. Thus we can agree with Irene Fast's theory of gender differentiation, which suggests that boys and girls alike (ideally) go through a phase in which they play out their identification with the opposite sex, after which they are able to renounce it and recognize it as the prerogative of the other.[56] This recognition, coupled with the preceding identification, enables the child to feel heterosexual love, love of what is different.

If the renunciation takes place too soon, however, without full identification, it is compromised by repudiation or idealization.

This point has particular relevance for girls; since, as we know, the
girl's identification with the father is typically refused, her love is
commonly tainted by envy and submission. We know that on the level
of daily life, when the desire to identify goes unanswered, envy takes
its place. Envy is often a signal of thwarted identification. The longing
for the missing phallus, the envy that has been attributed to women,
is really the longing for just such a homoerotic bond as boys may
achieve, just such an identificatory love. This is why there are so many
stories of woman's love being directed toward a hero such as she herself
would be—the wish for disciplehood, serving an idol, submission to
an ideal.

This desire for a homoerotic bond may also illuminate the female
masochistic fantasy which Freud found among many of his patients.
In this fantasy, reported by Freud in his famous essay "A Child Is
Being Beaten," the woman witnesses or overhears a child being pun-
ished by a father. Invariably, the child, with whom she identifies, turns
out to be a boy.[57] In my view, it is the woman's wish *to be like* the
powerful father, and to be recognized by him as *like,* that the fantasy
simultaneously punishes and gratifies. The more common variety of
adult ideal love, a woman's adulation for the heroic man who rejects
love for freedom, can also be traced back to this phase of life, and to
the disappointments a girl usually suffers.

But would it be possible for the girl to make what is *not hers*
represent her own desire? Could an identification with the father allow
her to make desire and agency her own? The girl's wish to identify
with the father, even if satisfied, leads to myriad problems under the
present gender system. As long as the mother is not articulated as a
sexual agent, identification with the father's agency and desire will
appear fraudulent and stolen; furthermore, it conflicts with the cultural
image of woman as sexual object and with the girl's maternal identification. It will not jibe with what she knows about her position in her
father's eyes. And once the relationship between father and daughter

is sexualized, attachment to him becomes a barrier, rather than an impetus, to the girl's autonomy.[58]

It is possible, however, that in a context of different gender arrangements, the girl's identification with the father and symbolic appropriation of the phallus might well be constructive. To envision such an alteration we must reject the assumptions underlying the psychoanalytic account of early gender development. These are: that mothers cannot offer their daughters what fathers offer their sons, a figure of separation and agency; that little girls do not need such a figure because they might just as well remain identified with the mother of early attachment and merging; and that fathers cannot offer their daughters what they offer their sons. These assumptions are, at best, no more than descriptions of our culture. I believe that, given substantial alteration in gender expectations and parenting, both parents can be figures of separation *and* attachment for their children; that both boys *and* girls can make use of identifications with both parents, without being confused about their gender identity.

These assertions are unfortunately still controversial. Their premise is that in the preoedipal phase gender and the associated identifications are quite fluid. There is still room for oscillation between mother and father.[59] Female and male identifications are not yet perceived as mutually exclusive, and little boys are still concerned with establishing an identification with mother, as little girls are with father. As toddlers begin to realize their difference from mother, they often seek reassurance through similarities. Indeed, whether the child emphasizes similarity or difference will often depend upon what the mother emphasizes. The child's desire is to have both: mother *and* father, sameness *and* difference. Thus if the mother emphasizes attachment, the child will strive for difference and insist on wearing father's clothes; if she urges separateness, the child may insist on his similarity to her and wear her clothes.

In my view, toddler boys and girls are struggling equally to maintain identification with both sexes, to keep both parents available as objects of attachment and recognition. Optimally the identification with both parents allows the child to assimilate much of what belongs to the other—identification is not yet limited by identity. In this phase, gender identification is much less rigid than the oedipal organization that comes after it: cross-sex identification can coexist with same-sex identification; sexual identifications have not yet hardened into polarities.

I am not suggesting that gender can or should be eliminated, but that along with a conviction of gender identity, individuals ideally should integrate and express both male and female aspects of selfhood (as culturally defined). This integration already takes place in the constant alternation of identifications in early childhood and can subsequently become a basis for understanding the other as well as the self. When this crossover is permitted at the appropriate time, individuals do not grow up confused about their gender identity; rather, they can be flexible in their expression of it. In the individual's mind the gendered self-representation coexists with a genderless or even opposite-gendered self-representation. Thus a person could alternately experience herself as "I, a woman; I, a genderless subject; I, like-a-man." A person who can maintain this flexibility can accept all parts of herself, and of the other.*

What, then, hampers the crossing over and alternation of gender identifications? Why is the border closed between the genders? Feminist theory concludes that the derogation of the female side of the polarity leads to a hardening of the opposition between male and female individuality as they are now constructed. The taboo on maternal sexual agency, the defensive mode of separation where the father is used to beat back the mother, the idealization of the father in

---

*In other words, the core sense of belonging to one sex or the other is not compromised by cross-sex identifications and behaviors. The wish to be and do what the other sex does is not pathological, nor necessarily a denial of one's own identity. The choice of love object, heterosexual or homosexual, is not the determining aspect of gender identity, an idea that psychoanalytic theory does not always admit.

identificatory love, and the confirmation that dependence and independence are mutually exclusive poles rather than a unified tension—all
serve to devalue femininity. As we shall see in chapter 4, the idealization of the father and the devaluation of the mother constitute a
profound split that has infused the culture at large, and shaped our very
notion of individuality.

The problem of woman's desire has led us to the missing father. But
to restore this father means to challenge the whole gender structure
in which mother and father have mutually exclusive roles. Although
I have stressed the girl's need for her father, this father can be used
satisfactorily only by a girl who also draws a sense of self from her
mother. The "real" solution to the dilemma of woman's desire must
include a mother who is articulated as a sexual *subject,* one who
expresses her own desire.[60] When mother and father (in reality and as
cultural ideals) are not equal, the parental identifications will necessarily oppose each other. As we have seen, the toddler's experience of a
split between a holding mother and an exciting father begins as a way
of resolving the conflict between dependence and independence. This
split can be repaired only when each parent sustains sexual cross-
identification and provides an example of integration rather than
complementarity.[61] Under such conditions, the child's tendency to
split the paradoxical elements of differentiation would not be reinforced by the gender arrangements. The parental relationship would
stand for integration and the sustaining of tension, rather than its
breakdown into inequality and one-sidedness. It would offer children
an ideal of separation and difference that is not defensive, a way out
of the sexual power relationship in which one side is devalued and
subordinated to the other.

WOMAN'S QUEST FOR IDEAL LOVE

The failure to appreciate the importance of identificatory love in the
father-daughter tie has led to many psychoanalytic misunderstandings

of women. In the original Freudian account, the girl's paternal identification and her sense of agency were not positive contributions to
her attainment of womanhood, but obstacles to be removed. Her active
longing to be like the father was, when it remained influential, a
neurotic masculinity complex.[62] It had to be superseded by the passive
longing for the father—for his phallus, and his baby. The fragility of
this passive sexual identity, which is without its own sense of agency
and sovereignty, is all too clear to us. Furthermore, the conflict between the identificatory love that enhances agency and the object love
that encourages passivity is replayed over and over in women's efforts
to reconcile autonomous activity and heterosexual love.

In fact, the girl's need for identificatory love in the rapprochment
phase has been obscured by the father's reappearance in the oedipal
relationship. But this later relationship to the father involves very
different aspirations. In rapprochement, the girl's wish is to be recognized as like the father and to share his subjectivity, will, and desire;
in the oedipal phase, the girl's wish is to be united with the father as
love object. Too often, in psychoanalysis identificatory love has been
mistaken for oedipal love.

We are not yet sure what would happen in oedipal love if the girl
has already formed a strong identification with father as well as with
mother, has been recognized by both parents as like. Nor do we know
what it would mean for the girl to perceive her mother as a sexual
subject who desires her father, or to perceive her as the active, exciting
agent in relation to a man or another woman. We do know that as
things now stand the identification with mother and father—the strivings for femininity and sexual agency—often clash irreconcilably. At
times one is even tempted to define femininity by this irreconcilable
conflict.

The thwarting of an early identificatory love with the exciting
outside is damaging to any child's sense of agency, in particular to the
sense of sexual agency. Such early disappointment may well lead to
relationships of subordination or passivity—with or without sexual
enjoyment. Unfortunately, this solution has the cast of normalcy for

women. But we must note that women seek a form of reparation in these relationships. They are drawn to ideal love as a second chance, an opportunity to attain, at long last, a father–daughter identification in which their own desire and subjectivity can finally be recognized and realized.

In some cases, a woman's search for her own desire may take the form of extreme self-abnegation. *Story of O* describes O's satisfaction in complete self-annihilation. But even in the more common form of masochism—adult ideal love—woman loses herself in the identification with the powerful other who embodies the missing desire and agency.

Simone de Beauvoir analyzed this function of ideal love in great detail. Here she quotes a patient of Pierre Janet, the nineteenth-century physician of nervous illness, who expressed this mixture of self-abnegation and wish for transcendence quite eloquently:

> All my foolish acts and all the good things I have done have the same cause: an aspiration for a perfect and ideal love in which I can give myself completely, entrust my being to another, God, man, or woman, so superior to me that I will no longer need to think what to do in life or to watch over myself. . . . How I envy the ideal love of Mary Magdalene and Jesus: to be the ardent disciple of an adored and worthy master; to live and die for him, my idol. . . .[63]

De Beauvoir comments that "Many examples have already shown us that this dream of annihilation is in fact an avid will to exist. . . . When woman gives herself completely to her idol, she hopes that he will give her at once possession of herself and of the universe he represents."[64]

The belief that the man will provide access to a world that is otherwise closed to her is one of the great motives in ideal love. It is not difficult for women to give up the narcissism of the absolute self, but to find another path to the world, they often look for a man whose will they imagine to be untrammeled. So George Eliot describes the fate of Dorothea in *Middlemarch:*

> We are all of us born in moral stupidity, taking the world as an udder to feed our supreme selves: Dorothea had early begun to emerge from that stupidity, but yet it had been easier for her to imagine how she would devote herself to Mr Casaubon, and become wise and strong in his strength and wisdom, than to conceive . . . that he had an equivalent centre of self, whence the lights and shadows must always fall with a certain difference.[65]

Dorothea is described as a would-be Saint Theresa, whose "ideal nature" demanded "some illimitable satisfaction, . . . the rapturous consciousness of life beyond self." Lacking the social means to such transcendence, Eliot says, the ardor of such women is dissipated, alternating "between a vague ideal and the common yearning of womanhood."[66]

Thus in ideal love, as in other forms of masochism, acts of self-abnegation are in fact meant to secure access to the glory and power of the other. Often, when we look for the roots of this ideal love, we find the idealized father and a replaying of the thwarted early relationship of identification and recognition. Often, too, we find that the parental constellation reveals a split between the missing father of excitement and the present, but devalued, mother. Take the predicament of a young woman photographer, Elaine, who was obsessed with a man who had left her, and whom she couldn't get over. Elaine saw her lover explicitly as her ideal. She understood that he was the person she wished to be—creative, adventurous, unconventional. Through the many projects they worked on together, she was able to experience him as the vehicle for a "love affair with the world." Now, in her daydreams, they travel to exotic and dangerous places for their work. He, like an older brother, takes the lead, and she insists on doing everything he does. She rejects the trappings of femininity, dresses like

a boy, performs feats and has adventures with him. Here, the homoerotic identification emerges with particular clarity. In her mind she
is still proving herself to her lover, still trying to live up to the
independence she thinks he embodies. Her lover was vital to her, she
often said, because of "something to do with freedom. He was the only
one who recognized my true self. He made me feel alive."

Elaine perceives her aspirations and ambitions as thwarted by both
parents, each in a sex-stereotypical way. Her mother, who had many
children, was weak and ineffectual, wholly without ambition for
herself or her children, and especially unable to help or support them
when it came to "anything we did *outside.*" Her father was very much
removed from the family—distant, angry, judgmental, and impatient
with children and wife, involved in his work and frustrated with his
lack of success. Although Elaine reports that now he is occasionally
proud of her work, she is more often wounded by her father's refusal,
in adulthood as in childhood, to acknowledge her accomplishments.

Elaine believes that her mother was valuable to her children when
they were little, as a source of comfort and soothing, but that she was
discouraging and devoid of any excitement or spark—which is what
Elaine thinks most important in life. When she identifies with her
mother or sister she feels weak or ill, and despises herself. Moreover
she is terrified by the depths of self-abasement her sister reached in her
own attempts to please or provoke her father. As a result, Elaine refuses
to invest the therapist with the power to help her, readily admitting
she fears it would mean devotion to an idol. At the same time she
expresses contempt for any soothing or comforting, dismissing it as the
debilitating sympathy her mother used to offer. In both cases, she is
afraid of losing her will altogether.

Elaine's memories suggest that her mother offered support in a way
that discouraged separation: she withdrew her attention as soon as her
children began to crawl away from her, returning it only when they
had fallen or acutely needed her care. In this case the mother's anxiety
about separation led not to intrusive hovering but to a withdrawal of
holding the moment the child ventured away. Her care did not extend

into the wide world; her care, in fact, demanded renunciation of it. Thus Elaine became the sort of child who, by the period of rapprochement, becomes clinging and fearful in overall mood, making only occasional disastrous forays out of the mother's orbit.

I suggest that such a person hopes in a masochistic relationship to overcome her clinging helplessness and separation anxiety even as she simultaneously expresses and gives way to it. Such a person is likely to seek a "heroic" sadist to submit to, someone who represents the liberating father rather than the engulfing mother. This ideal love solves the problems posed by the frustration of desire and agency, the rage at nonrecognition, by offering an avenue of escape and providing a figure of identification.

Elaine's assertion of masculine peership with her ideal lover, with its thrill of homoerotic attraction, shows how male gender identity and the search for one's own desire converge. The failure of the idealized father of rapprochement to provide a recognizing response is often a pivotal issue in a girl's self formation. This idealized figure is maintained internally even though the real father may increasingly reveal his faults and weaknesses to the child, because he remains the symbol of the means of escape and self-realization. But attention to the father-daughter relationship should not cause us to ignore the implications of the mother-daughter dyad, or to de-emphasize the importance of the mother. Elaine is a woman who feels profoundly damaged as a person, in part because of her mother's helplessness and ineffectuality which, in her own eyes (and in the eyes of her internalized father), she cannot overcome. Her tremendous rage at her mother for being unable to withstand the attack she would like to visit upon her reinforces Elaine's sense of powerlessness. The maternal "omnipotence" she is fleeing is actually the mother's weakness and inability to survive and struggle. Identification with this helpless mother is particularly insupportable. Unleashed activity, aggression, desire, would threaten not merely separation but also maternal destruction. Over and over Elaine complains that her mother goes to pieces, becomes vague and helpless, at the slightest confrontation.

Elaine is suffering from a lack of maternal holding as much as from a lack of paternal recognition. She regards both her anger and desire as highly disturbing, even monstrous, and would willingly surrender them to a powerful male who could "hold" them. As we saw, the rationally controlling and sadistic other is wonderful by virtue of his ability to withstand destruction. In the most common fantasy of ideal love, the one so frequently found in mass-market romances, a woman can only unleash her desire in the hands of a man whom she imagines to be more powerful, who does not depend upon her for his strength. Such a man, who desires but does not need her, satisfies the element missing from *both* mother and father, the ability to survive attack and still be there. In this sense the ideal lover actually provides a dual solution, containment *and* excitement, the holding environment and the road to freedom—the joint features of both the ideal mother and father.

The need for an object who is truly outside and survives attack is crucial to the fantasy of ideal love. The boundedness and limits within which one can surrender, and in which one can experience abandonment and creativity, are sought in the ideal lover. The search for more benevolent authority figures also reveals the need for such reparative experiences. Elaine's description of the "good teacher," for example, is a case in point. The good teacher is one who provides you with structure *and* allows you the freedom to immerse yourself in your own imagination, to explore, even make mistakes, until you can finally express your own vision. She adds that when you have got it right, the teacher recognizes that rightness with you. It is worth noting that Elaine's image of desirable authority is not the (oedipal) authority of judgment, with its possibility of condemnation. The controlled abandon that is associated with creative expression is only possible in an atmosphere in which understanding has been purified of judgment.[67]

Elaine's account of the good teacher seems to fit with Winnicott's description of the holding environment as a context for the child's transitional experiences, the beginnings of play and creativity, where the flow of recognition helps the child find what is in him- or herself, rather than vicariously in the other. This finding it in the self much more closely approximates the direct recognition a child needs ("You did it all by yourself!") than does the alienated search for recognition through submission in ideal love. As in the transference to the therapist, the relationship with the teacher may allow for a discreet opportunity to reproduce a holding environment, to create open, transitional space where play and self-exploration are possible.

The longing for a holding environment and open space reminds us that there is a mother who is not fled but sought. She is the holding mother who can support excitement and outside exploration, who can contain the child's anger and frustration, and survive the storms of assertion and separation. The search for the subject of desire—the ideal father—is part of a broader search for the constellation that provides not only the missing father but a reconciliation with the mother who acknowledges this desire (a crucial preview of oedipal tension and resolution). In Elaine's history we see the need to escape a mother who engulfs—albeit with weakness and passivity rather than with intrusive control. But this need to escape is constantly at war with the need to turn back to the mother and complete the struggle for recognition— the struggle to the death for the life of the self.

In part, all of this refers simply to the mother's ability to deal with the child's aggression, to let the child struggle with her. (Often what interferes with this struggle is the fantasy of "mother's good daughter," who will never leave mother, who will never hurt her, who will never be selfish or greedy.) The mother who can absorb and appreciate, and still set limits to the child's excitement and aggression, is the other subject who is sought in the recognition struggle. She is the one the child wants to get through to; getting through to her allows escape from the bubble of the isolate self. For women, then, failures in the struggle for recognition cannot be fully repaired by using a male identification to revolt against the mother. Women must, in addition, confront the paradoxical requirement to simultaneously separate from and identify with the mother.

Let me summarize the discussion so far. Starting with the psychoanalytic feminist perspective on early gender development, we have reappraised the significance of preoedipal experience. By shifting our focus from the oedipal to the preoedipal stage, we were able to explain the "masculine" aspirations of girl toddlers—their tendency to identify with their fathers as well as with their mothers—as a legitimate avenue of psychic development. While masculinity no longer appears to be the original orientation of both children, it does remain associated with strivings toward difference—toward the outside world, toward separateness—which are just as important to the girl's sense of agency as to the boy's. For girls as well as boys, the homoerotic identification with the father informs the image of autonomy. Thus we have traced the experience of recognition into a new development, that of identificatory love.

But when identificatory love is thwarted in childhood, it becomes associated with unattainable yearning and with self-abasement. Opportunities for assertion and recognition later in life often do not suffice to undo this tendency toward submission. What this means is that when identificatory love succeeds in toddlerhood, accompanied by the pleasure of mutual recognition, then identification can serve as a vehicle for developing one's own agency and desire. But when identificatory love is not satisfied within this context of mutual recognition—as it frequently is not for girls—it later emerges as ideal love, the wish for a vicarious substitute for one's own agency. It takes the passive form of accepting the other's will and desire as one's own; from there it is just a step to surrender to the other's will. Thus we see in ideal love a "perversion" of identification, a deformation of identificatory love into submission.

Behind ideal love we have seen the problematic early identification with the father. But this identification is only part of a whole complex that also includes the need for a mother who survives the rapprochement struggle. The problem of woman's desire points again to the special difficulties of resolving the paradox of recognition, all of which stem from the gender division: the fact that the mother is not the active subject of desire for the child and that the father is that subject, the liberator. For the daughter, the constellation of a mother lacking subjectivity and a father who possesses it presents an especially difficult choice. Even when the daughter receives her father's blessing—even *with* his recognition—resolving the identification with each parent is a difficult task. She must try where her mother failed: to synthesize subjectivity and femininity.

The gender division that now exists does not allow for reconciliation of agency and desire with femininity. Any vision of change must challenge the fundamental structure of heterosexuality in which the father supplies the missing excitement, "beats back the maternal power," and denies the mother's subjectivity because it is too dangerous.[68] But the intractability of this structure suggests that the organization of parenting alone is not the sole foundation of the gender division. After all, the idealization of the father as the representative of the outside world seems to operate as powerfully (or nearly so) even when the real parents do not reinforce it. It remains active as a shared longing, joined to the cultural representation of desire. As long as the father stands for subjectivity and desire at the level of culture, woman's desire will always have to contend with his monopoly and the devaluation of femininity it implies. In effect, the father's image subsumes that of the feared mother: once we see St. George with his sword drawn, no one has to paint us a picture of the dragon. We are therefore left to wonder whether there is not another way of representing desire, untouched by that sword.

A DESIRE OF ONE'S OWN

Let us return to the symbolic significance of the phallus, its power to represent desire and liberation. We have seen that the phallus acquires its power as a defensive reaction to maternal power and as an element of excitement that contrasts with her holding and containment. But the question remains: What alternative to the phallus is there? Mitchell argues that there is none, and that until patriarchy is overcome there is no other way to represent desire, difference, or separation. Is she right, or can we discern the rudiments of another way of representing desire—woman's desire—even in the midst of patriarchal culture?

One response is to offer a female representation of desire derived from the image of woman's organs, a representation at the same symbolic level as the phallus. But this strategy faces two problems: first, we have already seen that such representation actually derives its force from the total gestalt of the parent bearing those organs. If the maternal figure is a source of fear, that fearfulness will color her organs as well. Reasserting the symbolic value of the female organs is simply a reversal of the previous denigration; it defies but does not resolve the problem. Woman's sexual subjectivity is expressed through her body, of course; and so it is in women's interest to reclaim and know their bodies.[69] But we are talking about representation, and in a culture in which the representation of the body is organized and dominated by the phallus, woman's body necessarily becomes the *object* of the phallus. As we know, woman's body is endlessly objectified in all the visual media. The element of agency will not be restored to woman by aestheticizing her body—that has already been done in spades.

The second problem is that the symbolic level of the psyche already seems to be occupied by the phallus. The symbolic unconscious discovered by psychoanalysis represents life chiefly as a process of bodies doing to or being done to by other bodies, and the phallus is the principal doer (or done to, in the case of castration anxiety). Thus, for example, the phallus symbolizes both difference from the mother and desire for reunion with her. And, similarly, castration symbolizes the absence of all power and desire. In this world, woman's body, too, is defined in relation to the phallus, and is not represented by its own symbolic structure; thus, for example, the active mother is "phallic," or women are characterized by their absence of phallic or masculine structures.

Simply finding a female counterpart to the phallic symbol does not work; it is necessary to find an alternative psychic register. Here I suggest we return to the concept of intersubjectivity to see how it might lead to a different representation of desire. The phallic mode of representation really corresponds to what we have called the intrapsychic mode, which includes the whole constellation of using the father as a vehicle for separation, and internalizing him as the representative of agency and desire. Once phallic representation has developed, it organizes the processes of internalization and identification that make up intrapsychic life—life within. The intersubjective dimension, on the other hand, refers to experience *between and within* individuals, rather than just *within*. It refers to the sense of self and other that evolves through the consciousness that separate minds can share the same feelings and intentions, through mutual recognition. Its viewpoint encompasses not simply what we take in from the outside but also what we bring to and develop through the interaction with others—our innate capacities for activity and receptivity toward the world. This sense of self later meshes with symbolic structures, but it is not, as internalization theory would have it, created by them. And since this experience of self is not identical with the well-known symbolic structures, we may speculate that it has its own way of being elaborated in the mind.

The mode of representing events intrapsychically is not adequate to convey intersubjective experience. It does not articulate the idea of recognition, nor does it distinguish between real and imagined, or inside and outside. It does not distinguish between *you* as an independently existing subject, and *you* as a fantasy extension of my wishes and desires; between *I* as independently existing and desiring, and *I* as the incorporator of your wishes, agency, and desire; between my withdrawal into private fantasy and our sharing a mutual fantasy and so recognizing one another in it. In the intrapsychic mode—the level of subject-object experience—the other's actual independent subjectivity is not relevant. So if we are going to discover woman's independent

desire—a desire that does not have to be represented by the phallus—
we should consider the intersubjective mode where two subjects meet,
where not only man but also woman can be subject.

Since there is no systematic theory of this alternative to the phallic
order I must simply propose an exploration. My premise is that
recognition of the other is the decisive aspect of differentiation. In
recognition, someone who is different and outside shares a similar
feeling; different minds and bodies attune. In erotic union this attunement can be so intense that self and other feel as if momentarily
"inside" each other, as part of a whole. Receptivity and self-expression, the sense of losing the self in the other and the sense of being
truly known for oneself all coalesce. In my view, the simultaneous
desire for loss of self and for wholeness (or oneness) with the other,
often described as the ultimate point of erotic union, is really a form
of the desire for recognition. In getting pleasure *with* the other and
taking pleasure *in* the other, we engage in mutual recognition.

Understanding desire as the desire for recognition changes our view
of the erotic experience. It enables us to describe a mode of representing desire unique to intersubjectivity which, in turn, offers a new
perspective on woman's desire.

I suggest that the intersubjective mode of desire is expressed in
spatial rather than symbolic representation.[70] Winnicott frequently
described the relationship between self and other in spatial metaphors:
the space that holds us and the space in which we create. Intersubjective
space, if we translate into Winnicott's terms, begins with the holding
environment between mother and baby and expands into the transitional area, the child's area of play, creativity, and fantasy.[71] The
transitional space is suffused with the mother's protection and one's
own freedom to imagine, discover, and create.

As we saw in chapter 1, this transitional space (especially its earliest
manifestation, what Sander called "open space") permits the important
experience of being and playing alone in the unobtrusive but reassur-
ing presence of the other. In the relaxation of this space it is possible
to know one's impulses (drives) as coming from within, to know them

as one's own desire.* Winnicott often quoted a line of poetry from Tagore to express the quality of the holding environment and the child's transitional area: "On the seashore of endless worlds children play."[72] The image suggests a place that forms a boundary and yet opens up into unbounded possibility; it evokes a particular kind of holding, a feeling of safety without confinement. As we saw in the face-to-face interactions of mother and infant, the early representation of self and other evolves in part through a play of distance and closeness, a shifting of spatial boundaries between two bodies. When this play is successful, it is as if both partners are following the same score. The "dance" becomes the mediating element between the two subjects, the movement in the space between them. It is this quality of "in-between" that so often recurs in the spatial metaphor.

Spatial representation and feminine experience were, of course, linked by Erik Erikson in the idea that girls are preoccupied with "inner space."[73] But Erikson understood inner space simply as the receptive and passive half of a phallic dual unity. Viewed this way, reclaiming inner space comes uncomfortably close to accepting anatomical destiny. If feminists are not to ignore the importance of the body in shaping our mental representations, they must read such metaphors differently. Winnicott offered the beginning of such a different reading.

In a brief discussion he once suggested that the two psychic modes corresponded to gender lines, that the classic intrapsychic view of oral and anal stages "arises out of consideration of the pure male element," whereas the "pure female element has nothing to do with drive." It has rather to do with *"being,"* which forms the basis of "self-discovery

---

*Ideally, in the psychoanalytic process, analysand and analyst are able to create a transitional space, in which the line between fantasy and reality blurs and the analysand can explore his own inside. The analytic relationship then becomes a version of the space within which desire can emerge freely, can be felt not as borrowed through identification but as authentically one's own.

. . . the capacity to develop an inside, to be a container."[74] For Winnicott the idea of containment implies not passivity, but the ability to hold oneself, to bear one's feelings without losing or fragmenting oneself—an ability crucial to introspection and self-discovery. This "inside" is the internal version of the safe transitional space (open space) that allows us to feel that our impulses come from within and so are authentically our own. Being able to let go (to rely on the other's holding) is usually seen as the active side of sexual subjectivity, while holding is seen as passive. But this is not entirely true: for the sense of authorship is dependent upon having an inside (holding oneself); without it, desire becomes depersonalized, mere drive. One is "driven," not responsive to the other or to oneself. The ability to hold oneself gives to every act its authority, its purposefulness in regard to the other, its authenticity for the self.

Feminist psychoanalysts have begun to reconceive inner space in just these terms. Thus Donna Bassin, who sees inner space as a metaphor of equal importance to "phallic activity and its representations,"[75] emphasizes holding and self-exploration as the *active* sides of receptivity, as something women might do for themselves. Bassin's argument focuses on the spatial images women poets often employ to express the sources of creativity. But these images can also be used to convey the genesis of sexual desire.

I have found that the spatial metaphor repeatedly comes into play when women try to attain a sense of their sexual subjectivity. For example, a woman who was beginning to detach herself from her enthrallment to a seductive father began to dream of rooms. She began to look forward to traveling alone, to the feeling of containment and freedom as she flew in an airplane, to being alone and anonymous in her hotel room. Here, she imagined, she would find a kind of aloneness that would allow her to look into herself.

The significance of the spatial metaphor for a woman is likely to be in just this discovery of her *own, inner* desire, without fear of impingement, intrusion, or violation. Of course, as we saw in chapter 2, erotic violation may satisfy the wish to be known, to be penetrated, as a way of being discovered. Certainly, woman's desire to be known and to find her own inner space can be, and often is, symbolically apprehended in terms of penetration. But it can also be expressed as the wish for an open space into which the interior self may emerge, like Venus from the sea.

Gilligan and Stern have observed that many adolescent women are preoccupied with solitude. They discuss the themes of solitude and desire in their relation to the myth of Psyche; they cite the Apuleius version of the myth, which describes the young woman's sexual awakening and self-discovery.[76] Psyche is carried by the wind and laid in a bed of flowers; there she is left, gradually to awaken in a state of benign aloneness. By contrast, in her former state, when she was universally adulated for her beauty, Psyche felt as if she were dead. It is only when she is freed from this idealization and objectification that Psyche can experience a true sexual awakening, first alone, and later in her desire to see and recognize her lover, Eros. The idea that sexual desire arises in a state of aloneness—open space—may seem a paradox. But as we have seen, this state offers the opportunity to discover what is authentic in the self.

The idea of open space is important for understanding not only the genesis of woman's sexual desire, but also her experience of sexual pleasure. Let us consider the well-known difference between male and female sexual pleasure. A contemporary psychoanalyst, Noel Montgrain, argues that women often experience the intensity of sexual stimulation as "dangerous, fragmenting and destructive"; that for a woman, mastering sexual excitement "is more difficult [because] she cannot link it to an external organ that would localize it in space and would allow some control of its duration"; and that this lack of anatomical anchoring has "a correlative effect at the symbolic level. . . ."[77] The assumption here is that it is only possible to control anxiety (hold oneself) through a symbolic and physical focus of sensation. Woman's problem is that her desire is not "localized in space," that she lacks the phallic agency of control.

I am tempted to reverse the terms of Montgrain's conception of woman's problem—to see her sexual grounding in intersubjective space as her "solution." The relationship itself, or, more precisely, the exchange of gestures conveying attunement, and not the organ, serves to focus women's pleasure and contain their anxiety. Women make use of the space in-between that is created by shared feeling and discovery. The dance of mutual recognition, the meeting of separate selves, is the context for their desire. This facet of the erotic relationship is not articulated in the phallic symbolism of genital complementarity. Psychoanalytic valorization of genital sexuality has obscured the equal importance to erotic pleasure of the early attunement and mutual play of infancy. When the sexual self is represented by the sensual capacities of the whole body, when the totality of space between, outside, and within our bodies becomes the site of pleasure, then desire escapes the borders of the imperial phallus and resides on the shores of endless worlds.

At this point the reader might object that my argument ends up reestablishing the sexual polarity, at best altering the terms somewhat in favor of women. Given the pervasiveness of the sexual polarity, it is inevitable that any exploration of women's experience will pass through the language of the old dualisms. Indeed, it may not be possible to map previously neglected areas of experience without accepting a moment of reversal. But we need not remain there. I am arguing here for simultaneity and equality, not exclusion or privileging of either male or female experiences and capacities. I believe that individuals can integrate the gender division, the two sides of which have previously been considered mutually exclusive and the property of only one sex. I suggest that, ideally, an individual's relationship to desire should be formed through access to a range of experiences and identifications that are not restricted by rigid gender formulas. Thus girls should get what boys get from their father; and girls and boys should get it from their mothers as well—recognition of agency, curiosity, movement toward the outside. Consequently, I do not think that women should discount the world of phallic, symbolic functioning in order to celebrate their own sphere, nor do I think they should embrace the male world at the expense of denying the experiences that are part of the female world. By the same token, I believe that men should—and many do—have access to the intersubjective experience of space, for it is essential to the most various forms of recognition and creativity. The point, then, is not to invalidate the dominant mode of representation, but to challenge its privilege in expressing, and so circumscribing, desire. Having argued for the intersubjective self and its representations apart from the intrapsychic self, I must also stress their coexistence.

In this spirit we can value both traditional figures of infancy—the holding mother and the exciting father—as constituent elements of desire. As we have seen, holding and the space created by it allow the self to experience desire as truly inner; so it is not merely the recognizing response of the exuberant, exciting father that ignites the child's own sense of activity and desire. The mother's holding, or containment, is equally important.

As we have seen in the analysis of ideal love, women often seek their desire in another. The masochistic fantasy of *Story of O* is about being released into abandon by a powerful other who remains in control. Now we see how closely that search parallels and substitutes for the search for a desire of one's own. The ideal lover's power calls forth the freedom and abandon that are otherwise suppressed; he offers an alienated version—an "ever-ready look-alike," as Ghent calls it—of the safe space that permits self-discovery, aloneness in the presence of the other.[78]

Too often, woman's desire is expressed through such alienated forms of submission and envy, the products of idealization. This process of alienation works, in part, through the transformation of recognition from the concrete intersubjective mode to the symbolic phallic mode, in which recognition is not subject-to-subject but occurs through identification with the ideal; and the erotic relationship is organized into the complementarity of active and passive organs, subject and object of desire. Yet even then, the underlying wish for recognition of one's own desire remains.

Of course, this transformation from direct recognition into identification—a defensive process, the basis for self-alienation—is an unavoidable development. And it has its beneficial side when it occurs at the appropriate time in early childhood. Indeed, it is precisely because women have been deprived of early identificatory love, the erotic force behind separation, that they are so often unable to forge the crucial link between desire and freedom. The value of early identificatory love thus cannot be denied. But it reveals its negative side clearly when it takes the form of an opposition between mother and father, emphasizing freedom *from* a powerful mother, under the aegis of paternal power. Feminist theory aims to expand the idea of freedom *to,* offering a view of erotic union as a tension between separation from and attunement to an other. In the sustaining of this tension, I see an expansion of that space where subject meets subject. The phallus as emblem of desire has represented the meeting of subject and object in a complementarity that idealizes one side and devalues the other. The discovery of another dimension of desire can transform that opposition into the vital tension between subjects—into recognition between self and other self.

CHAPTER FOUR

The Oedipal Riddle

THE ROUTE TO individuality that leads through identificatory love of the father is a difficult one for women to follow. The difficulty lies in the fact that the power of the liberator-father is used to defend against the engulfing mother. Thus however helpful a specific change in the father's relationship to the daughter may be in the short run, it cannot solve the deeper problem: the split between a father of liberation and a mother of dependency. For children of both sexes, this split means that identification and closeness with the mother must be traded for independence; it means that being a subject of desire requires repudiation of the maternal role, of feminine identity itself.

Curiously enough, psychoanalysis has not found this split, with its devaluation of the maternal, to be a problem. As long as the father provided the boy with a way into the world and broke up the mother-son bond, no problem seemed to exist. After years of resistance, however, psychoanalysis seems finally ready to accept the idea that girls, too, need a pathway to the wider world, and that a girl's need to assert her subjectivity is not merely an envy-inspired rejection of her proper attitude. Nevertheless, man's occupation of this world remains a given; and few imagine that the mother may be capable of leading the way into it. By and large, the mainstream of psychoanalytic thought has been remarkably indifferent to feminist criticism of the split between a mother of attachment and a father of separation.

In questioning the terms of the sexual polarity, then, we cannot, as in the case of woman's desire, adapt a problem (penis envy) already identified by Freud. Rather, we have to illuminate a problem which psychoanalysis scarcely acknowledges. To do so, we will have to challenge the most fundamental postulates of psychoanalytic thinking as they appear in the centerpiece of Freud's theory, the Oedipus complex. For Freud, the Oedipus complex is the nodal point of development, the point at which the child comes to terms with both generational difference and sexual difference. It is the point when the child (the boy, more precisely)* accepts his ordained position in the fixed constellation of mother, father, and child.

This construction of difference, as we will see, harbors the crucial

---

*Much of my argument pertains to the model of the boy's development and requires the pronoun "he." At times, however, the oedipal model applies to both sexes, and I will then refer to "the child."

assumptions of domination. Analyzing the oedipal model in Freud's original formulations and in the work of later psychoanalysts, we find this common thread: the idea of the father as the protector, or even savior, from a mother who would pull us back to what Freud called the "limitless narcissism" of infancy. This privileging of the father's role (whether or not it is considered the inevitable result of his having the phallus) can be found in almost every version of the oedipal model. It also underlies the current popular diagnosis of our social malaise: a rampant narcissism that stems from the loss of authority or the absence of the father.

Paradoxically, the image of the liberating father undermines the acceptance of difference that the Oedipus complex is meant to embody. For the idea of the father as the protection against "limitless narcissism" at once authorizes his idealization and the mother's denigration. The father's ascendancy in the Oedipus complex spells the denial of the mother's subjectivity, and thus the breakdown of mutual recognition. At the heart of psychoanalytic theory lies an unacknowledged paradox: the creation of difference *distorts*, rather than fosters, the recognition of the other. Difference turns out to be governed by the code of domination.

The reader may well wonder that I have given so much credit to the father in preoedipal life only to diminish his importance in oedipal life. Having argued that little girls should have use of this very father, I now question his role as liberator. But this is not as contradictory as it seems. In the identification with the rapprochement father we saw both a defensive and a positive aspect. What I will argue is that in the Oedipus complex, this defensive aspect becomes much more pronounced. The boy does not merely disidentify with the mother, he repudiates her and all feminine attributes. The incipient split between mother as source of goodness and father as principle of individuation is hardened into a polarity in which her goodness is redefined as a seductive threat to autonomy. Thus a paternal ideal of separation is formed which, under the current gender arrangement, comes to embody the repudiation of femininity. It enforces the split between male subject and female object, and with it, the dual unity of domination and submission.

But we must not forget that every idealization defends against something: the idealization of the father masks the child's fear of his power. The myth of a good paternal authority that is rational and prevents regression purges the father of all terror and, as we will see, displaces it onto the mother, so that she bears the badness for both of them. The myth of the good father (and the dangerous mother) is not easily dispelled. That is why the critique of the oedipal model is so crucial. Perhaps the best way to understand domination is to analyze how it is legitimated in what is the most influential modern construction of psychic life.

UNDER FATHER'S PROTECTION

> The infant's helplessness and the longing for the father aroused by it seem to be incontrovertible. . . . I cannot think of any need in childhood as strong as the need for a father's protection. Thus the part played by the oceanic feeling, which might seek something like the restoration of limitless narcissism, is ousted from a place in the foreground.
>
> —Freud, *Civilization and Its Discontents* [1]

According to recent cultural criticism, Narcissus has replaced Oedipus as the myth of our time. Narcissism is now seen to be at the root of everything from the ill-fated romance with violent revolution to the enthralled mass consumption of state-of-the-art products and the "lifestyles of the rich and famous." The longing for self-aggrandizement and gratification, in this view, is no longer bound by authority and superego to the moral values of work and responsibility that once characterized the autonomous individual. Instead, people seek immedi-

ate experiences of power, glamor, and excitement, or, at least, identification with those who appear to possess them.

This social critique, best articulated by Christopher Lasch in *The
Culture of Narcissism,* argues that the unleashing of narcissism reflects
the decline of Oedipal Man.[2] The Oedipus complex, this critique
continues, was the fundament for the autonomous, rational individual,
and today's unstable families with their less authoritarian fathers no
longer foster the Oedipus complex as Freud described it. The individual who could internalize the father's authority into his own conscience and power is an endangered species. Whereas Oedipus
represented responsibility and guilt, Narcissus represents self-involve-
ment and denial of reality. At times, the popular versions of this
critique presented a view of narcissism amounting to little more than
a caricature of self-indulgence, whether in the counterculture of youth
revolt or in the solipsism of therapy addicts.

The invocation of myths, of course, oversimplifies a more complex
matter of psychic and cultural change. But it is nevertheless true that
Narcissus rivals Oedipus as the dominant metaphor of contemporary
psychoanalysis. Analysts no longer focus exclusively on the instinctual
conflicts that develop through the triangular relationship of child and
parents, the Oedipus complex. Now pathologies of the self, or narcissistic disorders, are at least of equal importance in psychoanalytic
practice and discussion.[3] But what does this change in the diagnosis of
psychological distress mean?

Many psychoanalysts agree that the change reflects the greater visi-
bility of preoedipal issues of early individuation and self formation.
Some think it reflects broader changes in family, childrearing, character formation, and the nature of civilization itself.[4] For example, Heinz
Kohut, the founder of the psychoanalytic school called self psychology, argues that the new focus on narcissistic disorders corresponds to
a spiritual transition from Guilty Man to Tragic Man, from the
problem of thwarted gratification to the desperation about self-ful-
fillment.[5] The great cause of discontent in civilization has reversed

since Freud's time: we suffer not from too much guilt but from too little.

The cultural critique of narcissism is based on this idea of too little guilt. It interprets the Oedipus complex primarily as the source of the superego, favoring a rather old-fashioned reading of Freud's theory. In Freud's conception, the Oedipus complex crystallizes the male child's triangular relationship with the parents. The boy loves his mother and wishes to possess her, hates his father and wishes to replace or murder him. Given the father's superior power (the threat of castration), the boy renounces the incestuous wish toward the mother and internalizes the prohibition and the paternal authority itself. Those wishes that the little boy once proclaimed openly ("When I grow up I'll marry you and be the daddy and we'll have a baby") now undergo repression; that is, their sexual and aggressive components are repressed, and what remains is civilized filial affection or competition.

Now the boy's superego will perform the paternal function within his own psyche: internal guilt has replaced fear of the father. Structurally, this means a differentiation within the psyche, a new arrangement of the agencies of superego, ego, and id.[6] The resolution of the complex includes the transition from fear of external authority to self-regulation, the replacement of authority and the desire for approval by conscience and self-control. The cultural critique emphasizes the importance of this process of internalization for the creation of the autonomous individual; and it interprets the current social malaise as the direct result of the weakening of authority and superego, the eclipse of the father. But in its lament for the lost prestige and normative power of Oedipal Man, it oversimplifies the psychoanalytic position. Thus Lasch presents a simple scheme in which the preoedipal fantasy of authority is archaic, primitive, "charged with sadistic rage," while the oedipal one is realistic and "formed by later experience with love and respected models of social conduct."[7] Implicit in this scheme is the assumption that the narcissistic or infantile components of the psyche are the more destructive ones, that psychological development is a progress away from badness. The comparison between Oedipal Man and the New Narcissist is permeated with nostalgia for old forms of authority and morality. The old authority may have engendered Guilty Man's conflicts but it spared him Tragic Man's disorganization of the self.

Lasch's analysis is a variation on the older theme of the fatherless society, a theory which explained many phenomena, including the popularity of fascism in Germany, as responses to the absence of paternal authority.[8] In Lasch's version, the "emotional absence of the father" who can provide a "model of self-restraint" is so devastating because it results in a superego that remains fixated at an early phase, "harsh and punitive" but without moral values. Other contemporary critics have echoed his analysis, claiming that changes in psychological complaints are the result of shifts in family politics.[9] Contemporary disorders result from the excessive distance of parents rather than overstimulation by them. Children no longer take their parents, especially their fathers, as their ideal, but distribute their identificatory love promiscuously in the peer group and among the superstars of commodity culture. Many explanations are offered for the weakening of parental authority in childrearing. Lasch particularly singles out the interference of the "experts": the vast proliferation of psychoanalytically informed literature, mental health agencies, and social welfare intervention directed at the family.[10]

Sociologically speaking, this viewpoint is one-sided. It simply dismisses all the opposing tendencies that enrich and intensify, as well as complicate, contemporary family life: fewer children per family, shorter working hours for parents, less labor in the home, a culture of family leisure, increased paternal involvement in the early phases of childrearing, and the trend toward understanding rather than merely disciplining children.[11]

As a reading of psychoanalytic discourse, this viewpoint is equally limited. We should start by noting that psychoanalysts do not commonly express the sort of crass nostalgia for authority that we find in the critique of the New Narcissist, even if they are in sympathy with it. It is true that psychoanalysts generally assume that a patient with an oedipal conflict has reached a higher level of development than a patient with a narcissistic or preoedipal one; but what they find positive about Oedipus and the superego, about the father and masculinity, is not primarily framed in terms of the internalization of authority.

Rather, psychoanalysis currently sees the oedipal conflict as the culmination of the preoedipal struggle to separate from the parents. Separation includes giving up the narcissistic fantasy of omnipotence—either as perfect oneness or self-sufficiency. Contemporary psychoanalytic discussions emphasize how the Oedipus complex organizes the great task of coming to terms with difference: when the oedipal child grasps the *sexual* meaning of the difference between himself and his parents, and between mothers and fathers, he has accepted an external reality that is truly outside his control. It is a given, which no fantasy can change. The sexual difference—between genders and between generations—comes to absorb all the childhood experiences of powerlessness and exclusion as well as independence. This interpretation, which understands oedipal development as a step forward into reality and independence, by no means devalues the positive aspect of the child's narcissism in the early relationship with the mother.[12]

This emphasis on separation in the oedipal model becomes problematic, however, because it is linked to the paternal ideal. The idea that the father *intervenes* in the mother–child dyad to bring about a boy's masculine identity and separation is, as I have suggested, hardly innocuous. This idea is actually the manifest form of the deeper (and less scientific) assumption that the father is the only possible liberator and way into the world.[13] Repeatedly, this defense of the father's role as the principle of individuation creeps into the theory even when the element of authority is de-emphasized. Whether the Oedipus complex is interpreted as a theory of separation or of the superego, it still contains the equation of paternity with individuation and civilization.

When Freud, for example, asserts the child's great need for the father's protection, telling us that it ousts "the oceanic feeling," what could this feeling refer to but the bond to the mother?* Freud then admits his discomfort with the ecstasy of oneness, with primordial states—in short, with the irrational; his preference is for the Apollonian world of dry land, and he quotes Schiller's diver: "Let him rejoice who breathes up here in the roseate light."[15] Likewise, when Lasch links together the absence of the father, the dependence on the mother, and the "persistence of archaic fantasies," he implies that without paternal intervention the image of the "primitive mother" necessarily overwhelms the child.[16] In other theories, as we shall see, the contrast between a primitive/narcissistic mother and a civilized/ oedipal father is explicitly stated.

There are several problems with this point of view. For one thing, the association of the father with oedipal maturity masks his earlier role in rapprochement as an ideal imbued with the fantasy of omnipotence. When paternal authority is presented as an alternative to narcissism, its role in preserving that fantasy is ignored. Furthermore, the sanitized view of oedipal authority denies the fear and submission that paternal power has historically inspired.

The roots of this denial lie in Freud's curious interpretation of the story he chose to represent the great conflict of childhood. Oedipus, it will be remembered, fled his home in Corinth, hoping to evade the Delphic oracle that he will murder his father and commit incest with his mother. What Oedipus does not know is that his real father who had set him out to die as an infant in order to evade the same prophecy is the man he has slain in his flight. When Oedipus learns the truth, that he has murdered his father and married his mother, he puts out his eyes, and exiles himself from the human community. For Freud, the tragedy of Oedipus was the key to our unconscious desires and our inevitable sense of guilt.

---

*In *The Future of an Illusion,* which immediately preceded *Civilization and Its Discontents,* Freud actually states that the child first is protected by the mother, but that "the mother is soon replaced by the stronger father."[14]

But as has often been observed, Freud's reading of the Oedipus myth "overlooked" the father's transgression: Laius's attempt to murder Oedipus in infancy, which sets in motion the awful course of events.[17] If we put this transgression back into the story, a very different reading emerges. Laius now appears as a father seeking to avoid what is, in some sense, the fate of all fathers—to die and be superseded by their sons. The oedipal father is one who cannot give up omnipotence; the thought of his own mortality, surrendering his kingdom to his son, is too much for him to bear. Oedipus, too, now appears in a different light. In Freud's version, Oedipus appears possessed by the wish to kill his father, whereas in this reading we also note Oedipus's efforts to evade the prophecy. The oedipal son, then, is one who cannot bear his wish to unseat his father, because its fulfillment would deprive him of the authority who protects him, the ideal that gives him life.[18]

This view of the father, although it nowhere appears in Freud's discussion of the Oedipus story, can be discovered in the frequent portrayal of father and son in his other writings. In *The Interpretation of Dreams* Freud explicitly depicts the dangerous father in the figure of Kronos; "Kronos devoured his children just as the wild boar devours the sow's litter; while Zeus emasculated his father and made himself ruler in his place. The more unrestricted was the rule of the father in the ancient family, the more must the son, as his destined successor, have found himself in the position of the enemy."*[19]

---

*Later, in The *Psychopathology of Everyday Life,* Freud acknowledges that his version of the myth contains a crucial slip, that it was actually Uranus who devoured his children and who was castrated by Kronos. Freud says that he was "erroneously carrying this atrocity a generation forward" (NB: he is referring to the atrocity of emasculating one's father, not of devouring one's children). These errors proceeded, he says, from his efforts to suppress thoughts about his own father, specifically, "an unfriendly criticism." And he links this mistake to another slip—in his account of Hannibal—in which he refers to the brother as the father, and makes the father into the grandfather. Freud states that this slip occurred because he had recently met his half-brother in England, his father's son by a previous marriage. This brother, whose first son was the same age as Freud,

The image of the dangerous father appears again in Freud's myth of the primal horde. At the beginning of history Freud imagines a primal horde ruled by a dreaded patriarch, whom the sons rise up against and murder. Freud cites the sons' murder of the primal father as the beginning of the Oedipus complex. Out of remorse, the sons create an ideal of goodness, in the hope of preventing the recurrence of the father's "extreme aggressiveness" and the murderousness it inspired in them. The good father and his law are thus created by the sons in the mental act of internalization.[21] The terrible primal father is transformed into the superego, who upholds the law against patricide, and moderates the force of omnipotence or narcissism. So the good father—as a mental creation—is a protection against the danger of irrational authority and the hatred it inspires. The British psychoanalyst Ronald Fairbairn called this kind of mental creation the "moral defense." The individual takes badness upon himself in order to preserve the goodness of authority: "It is better to be a sinner in a world ruled by God than a saint in a world ruled by the devil."[22]

Paternal authority, then, is a far more complex emotional web than its defenders admit: it is not merely rooted in the rational law that forbids incest and patricide, but also in the erotics of ideal love, the guilty identification with power that undermines the son's desire for freedom. The need to sustain the bond with the father makes it impossible for the sons to acknowledge the murderous side of authority; instead they create the "paternal law" in his name.

But the transformation of the father from a figure who inspires murderous revolt to a personification of rational law is not complete. Behind Laius still lurks the figure of the murderous, dreaded primal father. Freud's delineation of the father is ambiguous: although his

---

suggested to Freud that he more properly belonged to the "third generation," as if he were his own father's grandchild. All of this implies that Freud identifies his father with Uranus, his brother with Kronos, and himself with Zeus, who, by putting an end to his father's archaic violence, becomes upholder of the law.[20]

defense of paternal authority is quite obvious—the father is the progressive force—it is complicated by an awareness of danger. Freud's
partisanship for the moral father does not entirely obscure the darker
signs of the primal father.

The double image of the father also surfaces in Freud's discussion
of ideal love. In *Group Psychology and the Analysis of the Ego,* Freud
shows how what I have called identificatory love can either be the basis
of ordinary identification with the father or of bondage. On the one
hand, Freud associates the hypnotic leader who inspires mass adoration
with the "dreaded primal father," the man who loves no one but
himself, a leader who demands "passive-masochistic" surrender, and
satisfies his "thirst for obedience." Mass submission could thus be
understood as the group uniting in its narcissistic strivings by taking
this leader as its ideal.[23] On the other hand, Freud suggests that the
emotional tie of identification is readily observable in the little boy's
ordinary love for his father:

> A little boy will exhibit a special interest in his father; he would
> like to grow like him and be like him, and take his place
> everywhere. We may simply say that he takes his father as his
> ideal. This behavior has nothing to do with a passive or feminine
> attitude towards his father (and toward males in general); it is
> on the contrary typically masculine. It fits in very well with the
> Oedipus complex, for which it helps to prepare the way.[24]

The dangers of identification arise in adult life, Freud suggests, when
we cannot live up to our ideal and so make the loved one the
"substitute for some unattained ego ideal of our own." This love of
the ideal can become so powerful, Freud points out, that it is stronger
even than desire for sexual satisfaction. The "devotion" of the ego to
the object becomes so compelling that the subject loses all conscience:
"In the blindness of love remorselessness is carried to the pitch of
crime. The whole situation can be completely summarized in a for-
mula: *The object has been put in the place of the ego ideal.*"[25]

The social critics who turned to Freud in their efforts to understand fascism had no difficulty recognizing this constellation in which the leader is put in the place of the ideal image of the self. Deployed by a hypnotic leader, the narcissistic currents of identification can sweep people into dangerous social movements. But what did this have to do with the father? Since the hypnotic leader was conspicuously lacking in the qualities of the classic "father figure,"—the solid monarch, the wise and just ruler—he could not be a simple expression of paternal authority. T. W. Adorno solved the problem by proposing that the primal father whom Freud describes as the hypnotic leader should be understood as the preoedipal father. The classic father figure whose authority appeals not to dread but to reason is the oedipal father. Now the analysis of mass participation in fascism reads this way: In the absence of the oedipal father, the narcissistic tie to a figure of dreaded power can prevail in the psyche. This analysis of "fatherless" individuals seeking a powerful figure of identification could then, with slight modifications, be adduced to explain the fascination with the "superstars" of a "narcissistic" culture.[26]

The fatherless-society critics, then, see the oedipal authority as the rational figure who saves us from the dangerous preoedipal strivings associated with the archaic figure. But this hard and fast distinction between oedipal and preoedipal figures—one which Freud himself did not make—actually suggests that splitting is at work. All badness is attributed to the residue of the early phase, all goodness to that of the later phase. In fact, in each phase the father figure plays a role in the child's inner conflict, and in each case the child may use the father defensively or constructively. Which aspect of the father predominates depends largely on the relationship the father offers the child. To explain what Freud called the "short step from love to hypnotism," from ordinary identificatory love to bondage, we must look not merely to the distinction between oedipal and preoedipal, but to the fate of the child's love for the father in each phase. The bias in the fatherless-society critique consists of the effort to find pathology in the child's early love, rather than in the father's response to it. As I have argued in chapter 3, the idealization of the preoedipal father is closely associated with submission when it is thwarted, unrecognized. Yet if that early ideal love is gratified it can form the basis for autonomy. As Freud proposed, the child's early identification is not opposed to but paves the way for the oedipal relationship to the father.

One could plausibly argue that the surrender to the fascist leader is not caused by the absence of paternal authority, but by the frustration of identificatory love: the unfulfilled longing for recognition from an early, idealized, *but less authoritarian* father. As we have seen, if the child does not receive this recognition, the father becomes a distant, unattainable ideal. This failure of identificatory love does not imply the absence of authority; it often comes about precisely when the father is authoritarian and punitive. It is the combination of narcissistic disappointment and fear of authority that produces the kind of admiration mingled with dread noted by observers of fascism in the mass love of the leader.[27] The fascist leader satisfies the desire for ideal love, but this version of ideal love includes the oedipal components of hostility and authority. Again, it is not absence of a paternal authority—"fatherlessness"—but absence of paternal nurturance that engenders submission.

Thus both narcissistic and oedipal currents contribute to the fearful love of authority. The image of the "good father," free of irrationality, is but one side of the father, an image that can only be produced by splitting. Indeed, in the most common version of the oedipal model, the existence of the archaic, dangerous father is completely obscured, and the split between good and bad father is instead reformulated as the opposition between a progressive, oedipal father and a regressive, archaic mother. This opposition is, for us, the most serious problem in psychoanalytic theory; yet by analyzing this problem, we may begin to unravel the "great riddle of sex."

. . .

THE PRIMAL MOTHER

The notion that rational paternal authority constitutes the barrier to
irrational maternal powers hearkens back to long-standing oppositions
within the Western tradition—between rationalism and romanticism,
Apollo and Dionysus. It is significant that Chasseguet-Smirgel introduces her book on "the role of the mother and the father in the
psyche," *Sexuality and Mind,* with Thomas Mann's classic statement of
this opposition:

> In the garden of the world, oriental myths recognize two trees,
> to which they give a universal significance, which is both funda-
> mental and opposed. The first is the olive tree. . . . It is the tree
> of life, sacred to the sun. The solar principle, virile, intellectual,
> lucid, is linked to its essence. . . . The other is the fig tree. Its
> fruit is full of sweet, red seeds, and whosoever eats of them
> dies. . . .
>   The world of the day, of the sun, is the world of the mind.
> . . . It is a world of knowledge, liberty, will, principles and moral
> purpose, of the fierce opposition of reason to human fatality.
> . . . At least half of the human heart does not belong to this world,
> but to the other, to that of the night and lunar gods . . . not a
> world of the mind but of the soul, not a virile generative world,
> but a cherishing, maternal one, not a world of being and lucidity,
> but one in which the warmth of the womb nurtures the Uncon-
> scious.[28]

This opposition between the rational and the irrational is also intertwined with the sexual politics of psychoanalytic theory. The oedipal
model takes for granted the necessity of the boy's break with his early
maternal identification. It ratifies that repudiation on the grounds that
the maternal object is inextricably associated with the initial state of
oneness, of primary narcissism. In this view, femininity and narcissism
are twin sirens calling us back to undifferentiated infantile bliss. Com-

munion with others is understood as dangerous and seductive—as regression. The elevation of the paternal ideal of separation is a kind of Trojan horse within which is hidden the belief that we actually long to return to oceanic oneness with mother, that we would all sink back into "limitless narcissism" were it not for the paternal imposition of difference. The equation *oneness* = *mother* = *narcissism* is implicit in the oedipal model.

The contrast between paternal rescue and maternal danger emerges clearly in contemporary writing about the Oedipus complex.[29] Chasseguet-Smirgel's theory of the Oedipus complex offers a particularly striking version of the idea that the paternal law of separation is what protects us from regression.* Her theory, which is highly regarded among psychoanalysts here and in France, is worth a detailed discussion because it clearly spells out assumptions about the role of the mother in the Oedipus complex that remain *sub rosa* in previous formulations.

The distinction between ego ideal and superego is essential to Chasseguet-Smirgel's argument. In the evolution of psychoanalytic theory, the concept of the ego ideal preceded that of the superego. Freud originally developed the concept in his writing on narcissism. The ego ideal referred to an agency which was the locus of the child's desire for omnipotence and aspirations to perfection. Originally Freud gave the ego ideal such functions as self-observation and conscience. But when he later elaborated the theory of the Oedipus complex, he gave those functions to the superego, and henceforth used the terms ego ideal and superego interchangeably. Later writers tried to disentangle the two agencies, recalling that Freud called the ego ideal "heir to our narcissism" and the superego "heir to the Oedipus complex."[31] Accordingly, the superego could be defined as the agent that modifies our narcissism and keeps the ego ideal from getting out of hand. In

---

*This may be surprising in light of Chasseguet-Smirgel's well-known critique of Freud's views on female sexuality—but then again, her critique is based on the idea that Freud underestimates the unconscious power and dread of the mother.[30]

Chasseguet-Smirgel's interpretation, for example, the ego ideal represents the narcissistic love of the perfect being, whose nearness produces heights of fear and exhilaration, annihilation and self-affirmation. The superego represents a later, more rational authority, which admonishes us only to be good—to obey the prohibition against incest and patricide—but not to be powerful and perfect.[32]

Chasseguet-Smirgel reviews the Oedipus complex in light of this contrast between ego ideal and superego. For her, as for most contemporary theory, the oedipal conflict is a reformulation of the earlier preoedipal conflict between separation from and reunion with the mother. In her view, the oedipal wish to make the mother an exclusive loved one can be seen as a later expression of the early narcissistic longings, "the nostalgia for primary fusion, when the infant enjoyed fullness and perfection."[33] Thus, fulfillment of the incest wish would mean return to narcissistic oneness, loss of the independent self—psychic death.

In this reading, the superego upholds difference; it denies the wish for omnipotence and reunion that remains alive in the ego ideal. The superego, which says, "You may not *yet* . . ." offers only a long march, an evolutionary route to final satisfaction. By contrast, the ego ideal is the "inheritor of narcissism" and "tends to restore illusion"; it is devoted still to shortcuts, to the magical achievement of power through identification with the ideal. It is therefore opposed by the superego, which as "the inheritor of the Oedipus complex discourages this identification."[34]

The consequence of this definition is that these agencies are now aligned schematically with mother and father: the superego represents the paternal demand for separation, and the ego ideal represents the goal of maternal oneness. As Chasseguet-Smirgel puts it, "The superego cuts the child off from his mother; the ego pushes the child toward fusion with her."[35] This alignment defines narcissism *exclusively* in terms of maternal oneness, as if the identification with the ideal father of rapprochement played no part in the development of early narcissism. Likewise, it defines the longing for the mother as *only* narcissistic, denying the erotic, oedipal content of the child's desire for her.[36]

The oedipal superego in Chasseguet-Smirgel's reading does more, however, than represent the paternal law of separation; it also leads the child into reality—the reality of gender and generational difference. It is true that the oedipal injunction, "You must be like me," seems to be simply a continuation of that grandiose identification with the rapprochement father that already "saved" the child from immersion in the mother. As Chasseguet-Smirgel points out, it is incorrect to say that the oedipal father liberates the child from the dyad, for the preoedipal father has already done so.[37] But what the oedipal prohibition adds is that the parents cannot be split apart, that something powerful unites them from which the child is excluded. When the oedipal father says, "You *may not* be like me," thus denying the boy identification with him, he represents a reality principle, a limit. Of course, this limit is actually the result of the child's own recognition that he is too small to be what the father is to the mother. But the child prefers to hear this as prohibition ("You *may not* be like me") rather than as impotence ("You *cannot* be like me"). This denial of identification takes on a familiar, symbolic form. The phallus, once the token of sameness, now also becomes the sign of difference.[38]

The father and his phallus come to symbolize the child's whole sense of difference between himself and adults, as well as between men and women.* In order to inherit that phallus, to sustain identification with his father, the child must accept his separation from his mother. According to the oedipal model, it is precisely this recognition of difference and separateness that makes a person able to enjoy the possibilities of erotic union later in life. As Otto Kernberg points out, once the

---

*In my view, this should be understood to mean that it is the process of differentiation that stimulates the creation of a symbolic representation, not the symbol that creates difference. Any mother, or any combination of parenting figures (with or without an actual father) who are basically committed to their child's development as a separate person, can foster differentiation. That is why children without fathers still exhibit the symbolic representation.

oedipal separation is consolidated in the psyche, passion can be ignited by crossing the boundaries of the separate selves, and the narcissistic element can be safely enjoyed.[39]

I agree with the interpretation of the Oedipus complex as a confrontation with difference and limits. What is essential is the child's realization that he or she cannot be the mother's lover. In my view, the pressure points of development, like rapprochement or the Oedipus complex, reveal the child's striving to separate, to destroy, to let go of earlier connections and replace them with new ones. The child, as much as he desires the mother, fears incest as a kind of re-engulfment. The child fears being overwhelmed, overstimulated by the more potent parental object with adult desires. The limit set by the incest taboo is experienced as a protection, because the child wants to be his own person even as he resents having to be it. The idea of paternal intervention, in the most profound sense, is a projection of the *child's own desire.* He attributes this power to the father because he wants him to have it. Moreover, by accepting that the parents have gone off together without him, the child may go off without the parents. If father and mother fulfill one another's desire, the child is relieved of that overwhelming responsibility. By allowing their full sexuality, the child can fully identify with them as sexual subjects.

What I object to in Chasseguet-Smirgel's interpretation of the Oedipus complex is that this confrontation with reality is made contingent on the father's embodiment of difference and the reality principle. The mother here seems to play no active role in bringing the child to reality. In this polarized scheme, the mother exercises the magnetic pull of regression and the father guards against it; he alone is associated with the progression toward adulthood, separation, and self-control. The problems start, I suggest, when we take the symbolic figures of father and mother and confuse them with actual forces of growth or regression. There is no denying that unconscious fantasy is permeated with such symbolic equations. But even if the father does symbolize growth and separation—as he does in our culture—this does not mean that in actual fact the father is the one who impels the child to develop.

Chasseguet-Smirgel's idea that the paternal superego presides over growth and development collapses the distinction between symbolic representation and concrete reality.[40] The idea that the ego ideal derives from the experience of maternal union is likewise a mixing up of metaphor and reality. Real mothers in our culture, for better and worse, devote most of their energy to fostering independence. It is usually they who inculcate the social and moral values that make up the content of the young child's superego. And it is usually they who set a limit to the erotic bond with the child, and thus to the child's aspiration for omnipotent control and dread of engulfment.

Rather than opposing paternal superego to maternal ego ideal, we can distinguish between a maternal and a paternal ideal, and a paternal and a maternal superego. As recent feminist critiques have demonstrated, the dominant identification of little girls with their mothers impairs neither their social maturity nor their superego. Certainly the ideal that the female superego strives for is often different; thus Gilligan argues that it is defined more as concern for others than as separateness. The sense of responsibility promoted by the female superego (not the sense of separateness) curbs aggression and desire.[41] This suggests quite a different relationship between separation and morality than superego theory has maintained. It shows that the paternal principle of separation is not necessarily the royal road to selfhood and morality. The capacity for concern and responsibility allows the girl a sense of initiative and competence in personal relationships—though it may contain an inclination toward self-sacrifice. Girls learn to appreciate difference within the context of caring for others, identifying with the mother's ability to perceive the different and distinct needs of others.

Curiously, Chasseguet-Smirgel's own account of the concrete reality of mothering contradicts her neat division between a regressive, maternal ego ideal and a progressive, paternal superego. She, in fact, acknowledges that the mother helps her child project the ego ideal forward concretely through encouragement and recognition. Each time the child has to give up some illusion of perfection a new sense of mastery must replace it and be recognized. When the parent provides this "narcissistic confirmation," the child's agency (for example, being able to dress oneself) is invested with value.[42] Under these circumstances, the child's narcissism is a vehicle for development, not a pull toward regression. In the end, Chasseguet-Smirgel allows that the ego ideal itself develops, each phase assimilating new images into the idea of perfection. Thus our narcissism pushes us forward; it is not merely a siren luring us toward regression.[43]

But if narcissism impels us forward as well as backward, and if such development actually depends on the concrete activity of the mother *and* father, then why does the theory make the oedipal father represent *all* the progress and *all* the sense of reality that both parents foster? Why does the mother appear only as a feared, archaic figure whom the oedipal father must defeat?*

According to Chasseguet-Smirgel this is how the mother appears in the unconscious. But as we have seen, that is not all there is in the unconscious. There is also the oedipal mother, and, for that matter, the archaic father. Indeed, we are left wondering why the child's fantasy would pit a highly developed, mature, oedipal father against an earlier, preoedipal mother.

In Chasseguet-Smirgel's theory, the two phases of development are collapsed, and the Oedipus complex is reduced to a confrontation with

---

*It must be that idealization plays a role here. The oedipal father is in part a screen for the narcissistic ideal of rapprochement. And to this idealization is added his oedipal power to reunite with mother without being engulfed by her. The father and his phallus thus become the magnet for the (preoedipal and oedipal) strivings of narcissism: reunion and omnipotence. But it is also the father's very lack of concreteness, compared to the mother, which makes him this magnet. The symbolic dominance of father and phallus is intensified when he is outside the family. The father's inaccessibility, as we have seen in the case of the daughter, transforms identificatory love of the ideal father into penis envy. The missing father, who was not there to confirm his daughter's identificatory love, became the missing phallus. The father's distance and the mother's closeness conspire to produce the disproportionate idealization of the symbolic father.[44]

narcissism. Chasseguet-Smirgel fails to distinguish the differentiated eroticism the oedipal child feels toward the mother from the narcissism of oneness. And she fails to find the archaic father as well. For if the incest wish can shatter this more differentiated image of the oedipal mother and evoke the archaic one, would it not also shatter the oedipal father and evoke his archaic, punitive, primal aspect? As we have seen, this primal father is curiously missing from most versions of oedipal theory. How do we account for this constellation in which the father is progressive and developed while the mother is primitive and archaic? We might see it as the result of a defense: fear and dread are split off from paternal power and welded onto maternal power. Insofar as the child perceives the father as powerful and threatening, he dares not know him, and has to displace the danger—onto the mother.

This same displacement can be observed in Chasseguet-Smirgel's remarks on the dangers of striving after a maternal ideal. She argues that this striving is the inspiration for destructive group formations, such as Nazism,

> which was directed more toward the Mother Goddess *(Blut und Boden)* than God the Father. In such groups one witnesses the complete erasure of the father and the paternal universe, as well as all of the elements pertaining to the Oedipus complex. In Nazism, the return to nature, to the old German mythology, is an expression of this wish for fusion with the omnipotent mother.[45]

The notion that return to the omnipotent mother was the predominant motive in Nazism is an exemplary demonstration of the theoretical attempt to attribute all irrationalism to the maternal side and deny the destructive potential of the phallic ideal. Chasseguet-Smirgel's alignment of the ego ideal with the mother in general, and her example of Nazism in particular, are whitewashes of the vital part played by narcissistic identification with the father in the mass psychology of fascism—a part anticipated full well by Freud. This view justifies the father's domination of the mother on the grounds that, in the unconscious, she still reigns omnipotent.*

In Chasseguet-Smirgel's view, the roles played by mother and father are part of an inevitable unconscious structure, a condition that we must make the best of. She advocates a more equitable outcome to the "struggle between maternal and paternal law" in which we remember that "we are all children of Men and Women." She also envisions a balance of superego and ego ideal, salvaging our narcissism as a source of creativity and the aspiration to perfection.[47] The idea of psychic balance in which both ego ideal and superego have their say, where narcissistic and oedipal currents each play their role, seems to offer an ideal outcome of the Oedipus complex.

On closer examination, however, this vision of separate but equal roles is not equal at all. Citing the *Eumenides* of Aeschylus, Chasseguet-Smirgel compares the psychological evolution of the individual to the overthrow of matriarchy by patriarchy, the "subordination of the chthonic, subterranean forces by celestial Olympian law."[48] The most we can do to redress the balance, she says, is to remember the preoedipal mother, to acknowledge that beneath the appearance of male domination lies the reality of early maternal omnipotence—an

---

*A case in point is Chasseguet-Smirgel's illustration of her thesis that the absence of the father intensifies the destructive urges toward the archaic mother, that the child who "omits the identification with the father" and his phallus has no impediment to the destructive reentry into the maternal body. Her example is a perverse male patient whose fantasies of invading women's bellies reflect the "absence of a stable introjection of [the father's] penis" which would bar the way. This patient has a dream in which he puts a stone through a fish's smooth belly, which turns into a vagina, which is next to a museum exhibit about the Jews. She later mentions that shortly before entering analysis, the patient discovered that his father had been a fascist, in the Rumanian equivalent of the SS. This fact suggests to me that the patient does not live in a "fatherless universe," but that he lives rather with a dangerous father with whom he *has* identified. This father image, as the dream connection to Jews shows, is the source of the fantasy of attacking the mother's body. Here Chasseguet-Smirgel is describing not the *absence* of a father, but the presence of a *bad* father.[46]

idea prefigured by Freud's remark that the early attachment to the mother is like discovering "the Minoan-Mycenaean civilization behind the civilization of Greece."[49]

But why must one civilization bury the other? Why must the struggle between maternal law and paternal law end in unilateral defeat rather than a tie? Why must a patriarchal father supersede and depose the mother? If the struggle between paternal and maternal power ends in paternal victory, the outcome belies the victor's claim that the loser, the mother, is too dangerous and powerful to coexist with. Rather, it would seem that the evocation of woman's danger is an age-old myth which legitimates her subordination.

As our discussion of the rational father and irrational mother shows, the debate over Oedipus and Narcissus has an implicit sexual politics. This aspect of the debate has been more explicit outside the confines of psychoanalysis. When Lasch published *The Culture of Narcissism* a number of feminists criticized its nostalgia for paternal authority and the old gender hierarchical family. One feminist critic, Stephanie Engel, proposed that the denunciation of narcissism reflected a fear of "femininization."[50] She argued that narcissistic ties of identification were denigrated by virtue of their association with femininity, that is, with the early maternal experience. She supported her argument by reference to Chasseguet-Smirgel's work, and suggested a solution to the tension between superego and ego ideal in which neither agency would be devalued.

Engel made an eloquent case for a less one-sided view of narcissism, arguing that "the call back to the memory of original narcissistic bliss pushes us toward a dream of the future." She proposed that ideally one can find a balance between narcissistic aspirations and limitations:

Neither agency of morality should overpower the other—this challenge to the moral hegemony of the superego would not destroy its power but would instead usher in a dual reign. We

can remain aware of the danger of a politics founded on a fantasy
of infantile omnipotence or grandiosity, while remembering that
the total extinction of the ego ideal by the superego, which
would curtail creative fantasy, is neither possible nor desirable.[51]

A dual reign would acknowledge the ego ideal, with its fantasies and
longings, as an indispensable avant-garde, and accord it the same
respect as solid citizenry. It would be a rehabilitation of narcissism.

It appears that Lasch was profoundly influenced by Engel's critique.
In his next book, *The Minimal Self,* he dropped his panegyric to the
superego and adopted Chasseguet-Smirgel's theory, including her understanding of the early conflict between separation and dependency.[52]
Lasch also accepted Engel's case for a more balanced view of narcissism, but he balked at the gender implications of her argument. He
rejected her charge that the psychoanalytic model of a "radically
autonomous and individuated man" devalues both femininity and
primary narcissistic connectedness to the world. Having cited approv-
ingly Engel's vision of the dual reign of superego and ego ideal, Lasch
wants to know why feminists must ruin a good argument by bringing
up the matter of male domination:

> The case for narcissism has never been stated more persuasively.
> The case collapses, however, as soon as the qualities associated
> respectively with the ego ideal and the superego are assigned a
> gender so that feminine "mutuality" and "relatedness" can be
> played off against the "radically autonomous" masculine sense of
> self. That kind of argument dissolves the contradiction held in
> tension by the psychoanalytic theory of narcissism, namely, that
> all of us, men and women alike, experience the pain of separation
> and simultaneously long for a restoration of that union. Narcis-
> sism . . . expresses itself in later life both in the desire for ecstatic
> union with others, as in romantic love, and in the desire for
> absolute independence from others, by means of which we seek
> to revive the original illusion of omnipotence and to deny our

dependence on external sources of nourishment and gratification. The technological project of achieving independence from nature embodies the solipsistic side of narcissism, just as the desire for a mystical union with nature embodies its symbiotic and self-obliterating side. *Since both spring from the same source—the need to deny the fact of dependence—it can only cause confusion to call the dream of technological omnipotence a masculine obsession, while extolling the hope of a more loving relation with nature as a characteristically feminine preoccupation.* [53] (emphasis added)

Here it might appear that Lasch raises the same question I have raised. Why, indeed, should the ego ideal or the superego be assigned a gender? Yet Lasch himself makes such distinctions between mother and father, in spite of all his protests. First, like Chasseguet-Smirgel, he makes use of a gender scheme in which the father's phallus and prohibition play a decisive role in establishing the rule of difference. This leads him to the assertion that "the emotional absence of the father" is so devastating because it means "the removal of an important obstacle to the child's illusion of omnipotence."[54] And second, he adopts her theory, which privileges absolute independence over ecstatic union, by making the superego of separation a protection from the ideal of oneness.[55]

As we have seen in our discussion of early differentiation, separation from the mother is based on paternal identification. By the same logic, the attempt to master dependency through feelings of oneness preserves the identification with the mother. Each aspect of narcissism is thus associated with gender: independence with masculinity, oneness with femininity. Neither state of mind represents real relationships or the truth about gender—each is merely an ideal. But whether one idealizes the mother or the father, separation or connection, *does* make a great difference.

Either extreme, pure symbiosis or pure self-sufficiency, represents a loss of balance. Both are defensive denials of dependency and difference. But they are not equally powerful ideals. Lasch would like to downplay the inequality of power between the maternal and paternal ideals by arguing that both ideals serve the same psychic function. He would like to think that one can only criticize technological domination as a masculine strategy by turning the tables and celebrating an idealized oneness with mother nature.[56] He is wrong to think that his feminist critics fall into that trap; it *is* possible to criticize the consequences of the masculine strategy without embracing its opposite and believing in fantasies of maternal utopia (although such reversal is undeniably present in some feminist thought). Certainly, Engel's argument for a balance between separation and relatedness in the conception of the individual avoids that pitfall.

The controversy about Oedipus and Narcissus, superego and ego ideal, is really a debate about sexual difference and domination. In the oedipal model, the father, in whatever form—whether as the limiting superego, the phallic barrier, or the paternal prohibition—always represents difference and enjoys a privileged position above the mother. Her power is identified with early, primitive gratifications that must be renounced, while the father's power is associated with development and growth. His authority is supposed to protect us from irrationality and submission; she lures us into transgression. But the devaluation of femininity in this model undermines precisely what the Oedipus complex is purported to achieve: difference, erotic tension, and the balance of intrapsychic forces. The oedipal model illustrates how a one-sided version of individuation undoes the very difference that it purports to consolidate.

THE REPUDIATION OF FEMININITY

We often have the impression that with the wish for a penis and the masculine protest we have penetrated through all the psychological strata and have reached bedrock, and that thus our activities are at an end. This is probably true, since, for the psychical field, the biological field does in fact play the part of the underlying bedrock. *The repudiation of femininity can be nothing else than a biological fact, a part of the great riddle of sex.* [57] (emphasis added)

In this passage from "Analysis Terminable and Interminable," Freud sums up the deepest issues in psychoanalysis for men and women. It is interesting to observe how differently male and female "bedrock" have fared. When it came to penis envy, women offered no dearth of opposition, even if it took many years for psychoanalytic orthodoxy to reconsider the issue. But when it came to the other side of the great riddle, the repudiation of femininity, there was hardly an objection raised. Men did not dispute their fear of castration, or attribute their repudiation of femininity to social conditions. Nor did the two sides of the riddle share an equal place in the taxonomy of neurosis. While women's wish to be like men was deemed illness, men's fear of being like women was deemed universal, a simple, immutable fact. We might hope that the boy's "triumphant contempt"[58] for women would dissipate as he grew up—but such contempt was hardly considered pathological.

The repudiation of femininity does not offer us the same convenient avenue for theoretical revision as did the concept of penis envy. While current theories of gender identity dispute Freud's view that the penis wish is the core of femininity, they seem to confirm that the rejection of femininity is central to masculinity. Not a biological fact, perhaps, but an equally unavoidable psychological one. The boy's disidentification with his mother is considered a necessary step in the formation of masculine identity. With luck, the boy's disavowal of his own femininity would occur in a way that does not overly disparage his mother and exalt his father. Yet, in the oedipal model this polarity of a regressive mother and a liberating father seems inescapable.

Accepting the repudiation of femininity as "bedrock," psychoanalysis has normalized it, glossing over its grave consequences not only for theory, but also for the fate of relationship between men and women. But the damage this repudiation inflicts on the male psyche is indeed comparable to woman's "lack"—even though this damage is disguised as mastery and invulnerability.

In the psychoanalytic picture of development, gender polarity and the privileging of the father become far more intense in the oedipal phase. In the preoedipal period, as we saw in the discussion of rapprochement, gender difference is still somewhat vague. The boy's ego ideal may still include identification with the mother; he still dresses up in her clothes and, like Freud's famous patient "Little Hans," still "believes" he might have a baby even though he knows he can't. But the oedipal resolution banishes this ambiguity in favor of an exclusively masculine ideal of being the powerful father capable of leaving mother as well as of desiring and uniting with her. In oedipal reality sexual difference becomes a line that can no longer be breached.

After Oedipus, both routes back to mother—identification and object love—are blocked. The boy must renounce not only incestuous love, but also identificatory love of the mother. In this respect the contrary commands of the oedipal father—"You must be like me" and "You may not be like me"—unite in a common cause, to repudiate identity with the mother.[59] The oedipal injunctions say, in effect: "You may not *be like* the mother, and you must *wait* to love her as I do." Both agencies, paternal ego ideal and superego, push the boy away from dependence, vulnerability, and intimacy with mother. And the mother, the original source of goodness, is now located outside the self, externalized as love object. She may still have ideal properties, but she is not part of the boy's own ego ideal. The good mother is no longer inside; she is something lost—Eden, innocence, gratification, the bounteous breast—that must be regained through love on the outside.

What really changes, then, in the oedipal phase is the nature of the boy's tie to the mother. I have already made the point that the oedipal identification with the father is actually an extension of a powerful erotic connection, identificatory love. In this sense, the term narcissism does not mean self-love or a lack of erotic connection to the other, but a love of someone *like* oneself, a homoerotic love.[60] In the oedipal phase a new kind of love emerges, which Freud, perhaps unfortunately, called object love. But it is not an entirely unhappy phrase, for it does connote that the other is perceived as existing objectively, outside, rather than as part of the self. In the Oedipus complex the important change is the transformation of the original preoedipal object of identification into an oedipal object of "outside love." This outside love, according to the theory, would threaten to dissolve back into "inside love" if the incest barrier did not prohibit it. A major function of the incest barrier thus seems to be making sure the love object and the "like" object are not the same. It is not just a literal forbidding of sexual union, but also a prohibition on identification with the mother.[61]

In my view—and, in a way, in Freud's view too—the boy's repudiation of femininity is the central thread of the Oedipus complex, no less important than the renunciation of the mother as love object. To be feminine like her would be a throwback to the preoedipal dyad, a dangerous regression. The whole experience of the mother-infant dyad is retrospectively identified with femininity, and vice versa. Having learned that he cannot have babies like mother, nor play her part, the boy can only return as an infant, with the dependency and vulnerability of an infant. Now her nurturance threatens to re-engulf him with its reminder of helplessness and dependency; it must be countered by his assertion of difference and superiority. To the extent that identification is blocked, the boy has no choice but to overcome his infancy by repudiation of dependency. This is why the oedipal ideal of individuality excludes all dependency from the definition of autonomy.

Generally the road back to the mother is closed off through devaluation and denigration; as observed before, the oedipal phase is marked by the boy's contempt for women. Indeed, the boy's scorn, like penis envy, is a readily observable phenomenon, and it often becomes more pronounced once the oedipal stance is consolidated. Consider the great distance between boys and girls during the period of latency: the pejorative charge of "sissy"; the oedipal boy's insistence that all babies are "she."

With the exception of dissidents like Karen Horney, most psychoanalytic writers have denied the extent to which envy and feelings of loss underlie the denigration or idealization of women.[62] Male envy of women's fecundity and ability to produce food is certainly not unknown, but little is made of it. Similarly, the anxiety about the penis being cut off is rarely recognized as a metaphor for the annihilation that comes from being "cut off" from the source of goodness. As Dinnerstein has noted, once the mother is no longer identified with, once she is projected outside the self, then, to a large extent, the boy loses the sense of having this vital source of goodness inside.[63] He feels excluded from the feminine world of nurturance. At times he feels the exclusion more, as when he idealizes the lost paradise of infancy; at other times he feels contempt for that world, because it evokes helplessness and dependency. But even when mother is envied, idealized, sentimentalized, and longed for, she is forever outside the masculine self. The repudiation of the mother, to whom the boy is denied access by the father—and by the outside world, the larger culture that demands that he behave like a little man—engenders a fear of loss, whether the mother is idealized or held in contempt.

As the discussion of intersubjective space in chapter 3 suggested, the identification with the holding mother supplies something vital to the self: in the case of the boy, losing the continuity between himself and mother will subvert his confidence in his "inside." The loss of that in-between space cuts him off from the space within. The boy thinks: "Mother has the good things inside, and now that she is forever separate from me and I may not incorporate her, I can only engage in heroic acts to regain and conquer her in her incarnations in the outside world." The boy who has lost access to inner space becomes enthralled with conquering outer space.

But in losing the intersubjective space and turning to conquest of the external object, the boy will pay a price in his sense of sexual subjectivity. His adult encounter with woman as an acutely desirable object may rob him of his own desire—he is thrown back into feeling that desire is the property of the object. A common convention in comedy is the man helpless before the power of the desirable object *(The Blue Angel);* he is overpowered by her attractiveness, knocked off his feet. In this constellation, the male's sexual subjectivity becomes a defensive strategy, an attempt to counter the acute attractive power radiating from the object. His experience parallels woman's loss of sexual agency. The intense stimulation from outside robs him of the inner space to feel desire emerging from within—a kind of reverse violation. In this sense, intersubjective space and the sense of an inside is no less important for men's sexual subjectivity than for women's. In the oedipal experience of losing the inner continuity with women and encountering instead the idealized, acutely desirable object outside, the image of woman as the dangerous, regressive siren is born. The counterpart of this image is the wholly idealized, masterful subject who can withstand or conquer her.

The upshot of the repudiation of femininity, then, is a stance toward women—of fear, of mastery, of distance—which by no means recognizes her as a different but like subject. Once the unbridgeable sexual difference is established, its dissolution is threatening to male identity, to the precious identification with the father. Holding on to the internalized father, especially by holding on to the ideal phallus, is now the means of protection against being overwhelmed by the mother. But this exclusive identification with the father, achieved at the expense of disavowing all femininity, works against the differentiation that is supposed to be the main oedipal achievement.

We can see this in the fact that the oedipal model equates sexual renunciation of mother with recognition of her independent subjectivity. In giving up the hope of possessing her, in realizing that she belongs to the father, the child presumably comes to terms with the limits of his relationship with her. But true recognition of another person means more than simply not possessing her. In the parents' heterosexual love, the mother belongs to and acknowledges the father, but the father does not necessarily acknowledge her in return. The psychoanalytic literature consistently complains of the mother who denies the child the necessary confrontation with the father's role by pretending that he is unimportant to her, that she loves only the child. Yet seldom do psychoanalysts raise a comparable complaint about the father who denigrates the mother. Realizing that mother belongs to father, or responds to his desire, is not the same as recognizing her as a subject of desire, as a person with a will of her own.

This is the major internal contradiction in the oedipal model. The oedipal resolution is supposed to consolidate the differentiation between self and other—but without recognizing the mother. What the Oedipus complex brings to the boy's erotic life is the quality of outside love for the mother, with all the intensity that separation produces. This erotic potential is further heightened by the incest prohibition, the barrier to transgression, stimulated by the awareness of difference, boundaries, and separation. Yet all of this does not add up to recognition of her as an independently existing subject, outside one's control. It could mean, after all, that she is in the control of someone else whom one takes as one's ideal. The point of the oedipal triangle should be the acknowledgment that "I must share mother, she is outside my control, she is involved in another relationship besides the one with me." Yet—and here we come to the unhappy side of the phrase "object love"—at the same time that the boy acknowledges this outside relationship, he may devalue her and bond with father in feeling superior to her. She is at best a desired object one may not possess.

The problem with the oedipal model should come as no surprise when we consider that men have generally not recognized women as equal independent subjects, but rather perceived them as sexual objects (or maternal helpmeets). If the disavowal of identity with the mother is linked to the denial of her equal subjectivity, how can the mother survive as a viable other with whom mutual recognition is possible? Psychoanalysis has been careful to evade this contradiction by defining differentiation not as a tension or balance, not in terms of mutual recognition, but solely as the achievement of separation: as long as the boy gets away from the mother, he has successfully become an individual.

Perhaps the starkest denial by psychoanalysis of the mother's subjectivity is Freud's insistence that children do not know about the existence of the female sexual organs. According to Chasseguet-Smirgel, the real flaw in Freud's thinking was this idea of "sexual phallic monism," the assertion that there is only one genital organ of significance to both boys and girls, the penis.[64] No matter what competing evidence he stumbled over, Freud insisted that children do not know about the existence of the vagina until puberty, and that, until then, they perceive women as castrated men.[65]

The theory of the castrated woman is itself an example of this denial. What is denied, Chasseguet-Smirgel says, is the image of woman and mother as she is known to the unconscious: the frightening and powerful figure created out of the child's helpless dependency. "The theory of sexual phallic monism (and its derivatives) seems to me to eradicate the narcissistic wound which is common to all humanity, and springs from the child's helplessness, a helplessness which makes him completely dependent upon his mother."[66] When the oedipal child denies the existence of a vagina in favor of the phallic mother it is because "the idea of being penetrated by a penis is less invasive than that of a deep and greedy womb."[67]

The idea of phallic monism is clearly at odds with the acceptance of difference that the Oedipus complex is supposed to embody. It denies the difference between the sexes, or rather it reduces difference to absence, to lack. Difference then means plus-or-minus the penis. There is no range of qualitative divergence; only presence or absence, rich or poor, the haves and the have-nots. There is no such thing as woman: woman is merely that which is not man.* Like the oedipal

---

*In her remarks on Luce Irigaray's critique of Freud, "The Blind Spot in an Old Dream of Symmetry," Jane Gallop emphasizes this point. The blind spot, the denial of women's

symbolization of the mother as either a lost paradise or a dangerous siren, the denial of her sexual organs makes her always either more or less than human.

Thus within the oedipal model, difference is constructed as polarity; it maintains the overvaluation of one side, the denigration of the other. Although Chasseguet-Smirgel recognizes that the real issue is that mother's vagina is too big, she accepts as inevitable the outcome that denies women's sexuality. She argues that children of both sexes, in the wish to escape the primal mother, "project her power on to the father and his penis, and so more or less decathect specifically maternal qualities and organs." Consequently the boy's "passing devaluation of the mother and women is 'normal.' "[69]

Implicit in this account is that devaluation of the other is a normal aspect of heterosexuality that can be modified in later life. Similarly, the transfer of erotic idealization to the father's penis by both sexes is presented as a normal feature of heterosexuality. Accepting the penis is psychoanalytic shorthand for separating from and recognizing the mother. In these terms, only heterosexual relationships acknowledge the father's penis and therefore show respect for difference. Accepting the vagina is *not* psychoanalytic shorthand for the father's recognition of the mother's equal subjectivity, or for the boy's learning to accept difference.[70]

Chasseguet-Smirgel glosses over the contradictory finale of the Oedipus complex, its false resolution. She remains hopeful that the boy whose relationship with the mother has been "sufficiently good" (once again, it is up to the individual mother) will not reactively denigrate femininity, or at any rate will not "prolong" this reaction into adulthood. At best, then, we can say that the resolution of Oedipus awaits adolescence or adulthood.[71] Once the possibility of real, concrete

---

genitals, prohibits "any different sexuality." The other, woman, is circumscribed "as man's complementary other, his appropriate opposite sex." Instead of real difference there is only a mirror image.[68]

sexual interaction emerges, once the boy has renewed access to women, the symbolic level on which they are depreciated can be counteracted. But the symbolic depreciation of women and their sexuality permeates adult culture, just as it did Freud's own theory, which retained the oedipal boy's phallocentric perception of women. All the evidence of woman's objectification testifies that the oedipal riddle—the repudiation of femininity—continues to bar the way between men and women.

Thus the Oedipus complex does not finally resolve the problem of difference, of recognizing an other. The mother is devalued, her power and desire are transferred to the idealized father, and her nurturance is inaccessible. The same phallus that stands for difference and reality also stands for power over and repudiation of women. By assuming the power to represent her sexuality as well as his, it denies women's independent sexuality. Thus, masculinity is defined in opposition to woman, and gender is organized as polarity with one side idealized, the other devalued.

Although the oedipal construction of difference seems to be dominant in our cultural representation of gender, it is not the only possible one. The oedipal phase is, after all, only one point at which gender difference is integrated in the psyche. Once we recognize the consequences of the repudiation of femininity, we may speculate that the boy's stance toward femininity has something in common with the girl's toward masculinity, that it, too, is a reaction to blocked identification. As we have seen in the case of the girl, a successful identificatory love of the father may "solve" the problem of penis envy. Perhaps repudiation is not all that different from envy, in which it is partially rooted.

Irene Fast's distinction between repudiation and renunciation of femininity suggests another route to the integration of difference. Repudiation, Fast suggests, is an unsuccessful mode of differentiation; "ideally" boys ought to renounce, not repudiate, femininity, after a period of identification with it.[72] She points out that girls, too, must overcome the primary identification with the mother and replace it with more generalized gender identifications that do not equate all femininity with the mother. If the girl tries to differentiate exclusively by repudiating the mother in favor of the father rather than by also developing generalized gender identifications, she never really separates from the mother: "Repudiation leaves the primitive identifications and the fusion with the mother intact."[73] We could then speculate that for boys, repudiation also forecloses the development of a more mature maternal identification; it perpetuates the power of the merging, omnipotent mother in the unconscious. Without this mature identification, the boy does not develop a differentiated mother image. Thus a longer period of "bisexuality," of allowing both feminine and masculine identifications to coexist, would aid boys in becoming *more* differentiated from mother and obviate the need for such defenses as repudiation, distance, and control.

Perhaps, then, the way out of the oedipal repudiation of femininity must be sought in the period that comes before it. Between the boy's early disidentification with the mother and his oedipal separation from her is a neglected phase of playful, secondary identification with femininity. Insofar as the culture forecloses this possibility by demanding a premature entry into the oedipal world, gender identity is formed by repudiation rather than by recognition of the other. But the changing social relations of gender have given us a glimpse of another world, of a space in which each sex can play the other and so accept difference by making it familiar. As we give greater value to the preoedipal world, to a more flexible acceptance of difference, we can see that difference is only truly established when it exists in tension with likeness, when we are able to recognize the other in ourselves.

THE POLARITY PRINCIPLE

In the oedipal model, the distinction between the two parents—the holding, nurturing mother and the liberating, exciting father—is expressed as an irreconcilable difference. Even though the rapprochement conflict already opposed the father to the mother, it did not wholly abrogate the maternal identification. But in the oedipal construction of difference, this coexistence is no longer possible. Separation takes precedence over connection, and constructing boundaries becomes more important than insuring attachment. The two central elements of recognition—being like and being distinct—are split apart. Instead of recognizing the other who is different, the boy either identifies or disidentifies. Recognition is thus reduced to a one-dimensional identification with likeness; and as distinct from early childhood, where any likeness will do, this likeness is sexually defined.

The denial of identification with the mother also tends to cut the boy off from the intersubjective communication that was part of the primary bond between mother and infant. Emotional attunement, sharing states of mind, empathically assuming the other's position, and imaginatively perceiving the other's needs and feelings—these are now associated with cast-off femininity. Emotional attunement is now experienced as dangerously close to losing oneself in the other; affective imitation is now used negatively to tease and provoke. Thus the intersubjective dimension is increasingly reduced, and the need for mutual recognition must be satisfied with mere identification of likeness (which the industry of mass culture is only too happy to promote in the gender stereotyping of children's playthings). Recognition works more through ideal identifications and less through concrete interaction. What comes to fruition in this psychic phase, then, is a one-sided form of differentiation in which each sex can play only one part. Concrete identifications with the other parent are not lost, but they are excluded from the symbolically organized gender identity.[74]

Although I have dealt with the oedipal model exclusively in its masculine form, it is easy to see how the model constructs femininity as a simple mirror image of masculinity. The ideal type of femininity (which, as we observed earlier, is constituted as whatever is opposite to masculinity) absorbs all that is cast off by the boy as he flees from mother. The main difference is simply that for girls, masculine traits are not a threat to identity, as feminine traits are for boys, but an unattainable ideal. But for both sexes the important oedipal limit is the same: identify only with the same-sex parent. Even if the mirror relationship does not fit seamlessly in real life, the oedipal model defines gender as just such a complementarity. Each gender is able to represent only one aspect of the polarized self-other relationship.

To the extent that this scheme actually does prevail, no one can truly appreciate difference, for identification with the other parent is blocked. Identification no longer functions as a bridge to the experience of an other; now it can only confirm likeness. Real recognition of the other entails being able to perceive commonality through difference; and true differentiation sustains the balance between separateness and connection in a dynamic tension. But once identification with the other is denied, love becomes only the love of an object, of The Other. Since the mother is deprived of subjectivity, identification with her involves a loss of self. When the oedipal standpoint takes over completely, men no longer confront women as other subjects who can recognize them. Only in other men can they meet their match. Women can gain this power of recognition only by remaining desirable yet unattainable, untouched and unconquered, and ultimately dangerous. Loss of mutual recognition is the most common consequence of gender polarity.

The other important consequence of this polarity is the one-sided ideal of autonomous individuality, the masculine ideal. The identification with the father functions as a denial of dependency. The father's phallus stands for the wholeness and separateness that the child's real helplessness and dependency belie. Denying dependency on the mother by identifying with the phallic ideal amounts to sustaining the rapprochement fantasy of omnipotence, only modified by projecting it into the future ("You must *wait* to be like me"). The devaluation of the need for the other becomes a touchstone of adult masculinity.

Thus, I believe, the deep source of discontent in our culture is not repression or, in the new fashion, narcissism, but gender polarity. Many of the persistent symptoms of this discontent—contempt for the needy and dependent, emphasis on individual self-reliance, rejection of social forms of providing nurturance—are not visibly connected to gender. Yet in spite of the fact that these attitudes are almost as common among women as they are among men, they are nevertheless the result of gender polarity. They underlie the mentality of opposition which pits freedom against nurturance: either we differentiate or remain dependent; either we stand alone or are weak; either we relinquish autonomy or renounce the need for love. No doubt many individuals are flexible enough to forge less extreme solutions, but the polarities tug mightily whenever dependency is an issue.

In spite of the many arguments that individuality is waning, the ideal of a self-sufficient individual continues to dominate our discourse. The power of this ideal is the chief manifestation of male hegemony, far more pervasive than overtly authoritarian forms of male domination. Indeed, this one-sided ideal of individuality has not been diminished by the undermining of paternal authority and superego. It may even have been strengthened: the lack of manifest authority intensifies the pressure to perform independently, to live up to the ideal without leaning on a concrete person who embodies it. The idealization of masculine values and the disparagement of feminine values persist unabated even though individual men and women are freer to cross over than before. The very idea that this form of individuality is not universal and neutral, but masculine, is highly controversial, as we saw in Lasch's outraged denial of the relevance of gender to narcissism. It challenges the repudiation of femininity, and the equation of masculinity with humanity—and so it challenges men's right to make the world in their own image.

Despite the appearance of gender neutrality and the freedom to be whatever we like, gender polarity persists. And it creates a painful division within the self and between self and other; it constantly frustrates our efforts to recognize ourselves in the world and in each other. My analysis of the oedipal model points beyond the obvious way that sexual difference has been linked to domination—the old authority of the father over children and wife—to its updated, subtler form. It points to a version of male dominion that works through the cultural ideal, the ideal of individuality and rationality that survives even the waning of paternal authority and the rise of more equitable family structures.

What sustains this ideal is the confusion between total loss of self and dependency. As we have seen, in recent versions of the oedipal model the revolt against maternal power is actually portrayed as a reaction against the experience of helplessness. According to the theory, we begin in an original state of primal oneness in which helplessness is not yet realized. The journey of differentiation takes us away from this perfect oneness with the beloved source of goodness, into revulsion and fear of fusion with her. But what if the idea of such a state is a symbolic condensation, a retroactive fantasy that "oversimplifies" a rather complicated intersubjective relationship? As I have shown, that relationship was neither oneness nor perfect—it was always marked by alterations between helplessness and comfort, by the contrast between attunement and disjunction, by an emerging awareness of separation and individual differences.

The vision of perfect oneness, whether of union or of self-sufficiency, is an *ideal*—a symbolic expression of our longing—that we project onto the past. This ideal becomes enlarged in reaction to the experience of helplessness—in the face of circumstance, powerlessness, death—but also by the distance from mother's help that repudiation of her enforces. What makes helplessness more difficult to bear is the feeling that one does not have the source of goodness inside, that one can neither soothe oneself nor find a way to communicate one's needs to someone who can help. It seems to me that the confidence that this other will help, like the confidence created by early attunement, is what mitigates feelings of helplessness. Such confidence is enhanced by a cultural life in which nurturance, responsiveness, and physical closeness are valued and generalized, so that the child can find them everywhere and adopt them himself. It is vitiated when those values are associated exclusively with infancy and must be given up in exchange for autonomy.

When individuals lose access to internal and external forms of maternal identification, independence backfires: it stimulates a new kind of helplessness, one which has to be countered by a still greater idealization of control and self-sufficiency. A usable maternal identification promises the possibility of regaining the satisfactions of dependency, the faith that we can rely on our environment to fulfill us; it is also associated with the confirmation that we contain within ourselves the source of satisfaction. But so long as this identification threatens male identity, men only have access to the mother outside. They react against this dependency by doing without her or by dominating her.

The inaccessibility of the mother who has been projected outside lends to the image of reunion—whether utopian return to nature or irrational regression—the qualities of an absolute, a journey away from civilization with no return ticket. To the flexible ego (which neither fears its desire nor is inebriated by the ideal) the experience of union is simply an excursion. The feeling of losing oneself in erotic union, like the experience of attunement in infancy, does not obliterate the self that possesses a sense of distinctness: one does not really *lose* oneself. But when the desire for unattainable reunion is construed as an absolute, it appears to be our deepest longing, while differentiation appears to be imposed from outside. And autonomy, although in conflict with our deepest desire, is, alas, the necessary goal of maturation.

For those, like Chasseguet-Smirgel, who conceive of infancy essentially as helplessness, the yearning for a "return" to the undifferentiated oneness of the womb seems to be the most profound psychological force. Only an equally omnipotent father appears strong enough to counteract this regressive urge and bring the child to the reality principle. But if, as my discussion of infancy in chapter 1 argued, we believe that infants take pleasure in interpersonal connection and are motivated by curiosity and responsiveness to the outside world, we need not agree to the idea that human beings must be pulled by their fathers away from maternal bliss into a reality they resent. I am not disputing the readily observable wishes—of infants and adults—to withdraw from the world into a state of rest or to experience the sensuous gratification and attunement of erotic union. But we do not have to see them as dangerous forces of regression that threaten to cancel all strivings toward differentiation.

When we *do* see them that way, the mother inevitably appears as a figure who would permit endless merging, blurring all differences and keeping the child in a swamp of narcissistic bliss. This image of the archaic mother from whom the father protects us appears to psychoanalysis as a basic construction of the human psyche. As Stoller has argued, the dreaded image of the mother arises as a male response to the need to separate from the primary identification with her. The threat which the original sense of bodily continuity poses to male identity remains as the unassailable explanation for male fear and dread of woman.[75] But this explanation does not account for the persistence of this threat once masculine identity is consolidated. How else may we explain the persistence of this dreadful apparition of maternal power?

Here we may recall our discussion of the difference between renunciation and repudiation. The persistence of the maternal threat can be explained, at least in part, by the prohibition on maternal identification which deprives the boy of the opportunity to develop a more differentiated image of the mother. The repudiation of the mother gives her the aura of lost perfection, but it also makes her the object of destructive envy: "Mother does not need me, so I don't need her; she is the source of perfect oneness, but this oneness can turn against me; Mother can retaliate for my envy by 'smothering' me with love." The blocking of identification reduces the mother to the complementary other who easily turns into the enemy, the opposite in the retaliatory power struggle between the sexes. This view of the mother meshes with the defensive stance assumed in reaction to the paradox of recognition, when the power of the one we have depended on may begin to appear threatening to the vulnerable self. When this defensive stance is institutionalized in a coherent symbolic system of gender—as in the

Oedipus complex—it cancels access to direct experience of the other. The symbolic system locks into place the sense of the mother's dangerous but alluring power and the need for paternal defense against it. The more violent the repudiation of the source of nurturance, the more dangerous and tempting it begins to appear. The demonic view of maternal love is analogous to the revulsion that repression confers upon a forbidden wish.

Quite possibly, the dangerous apparition of women only takes final form in the symbolic unconscious once domination is institutionalized. I suggested in chapter 2 that the dilemma of omnipotence may be a consequence of the loss of tension that results from reducing the other to object. Similarly, the lack of opportunity to encounter woman's subjectivity makes it impossible to break the magic spell of the omnipotent mother. The effort to destroy or reduce the other is an inevitable part of the childhood struggle for recognition, as well as a way of protecting independence. But it is another matter when—as in the domination of women by men—the other's independent subjectivity really is destroyed, and with it the possibility of mutual recognition. It may be impossible to say where this cycle of real domination and the fantasy of maternal omnipotence begins, but this does not mean that we can never break that cycle and restore the balance of destruction and recognition. The answer awaits the social abolition of gender domination. And this means not just equality for women, but also a dissolution of gender polarity, a reconstruction of the vital tension between recognition and assertion, dependency and freedom.

THE NEW OEDIPUS

Freud's opposition between rational paternal authority and the maternal underworld still resonates today. And I believe that the father's authority will persist as long as we accept the ideal of rationality as the antithesis of "limitless narcissism." The persistence of this dualism alerts us to an unchanging image of the father in the deep strata of the psyche where sexual difference takes hold. This dualism operates just as powerfully, it should be noted, for social critics like Brown and Marcuse, who defend the desire for union with the bounteous mother against the rational reality principle of the father. Their positions accept the characterization of the maternal world as found in the discourse of gender domination: they affirm the "limitless narcissism" of the babe at the breast who does not recognize the mother's, or anyone else's, equal subjectivity.[76] A deeper critique is necessary, one which rejects the terms of sexual polarity, of subject and object, and so rejects any revolt that merely reverses these terms. The point is to get out of the antithesis between mother and father, this revolving door between the regressive maternal warmth and the icy paternal outside.

One step in the dissolution of this dualism is to reinterpret the Oedipus complex in such a way that it is no longer the summation of development. Rather than emphasizing the overcoming of preoedipal identifications, a new perspective on the Oedipus complex might see it as only a step in mental life, one that leaves room for earlier and later levels of integration. Significantly, Hans Loewald, a prominent exponent of the object relations tendency in American psychoanalysis, proposed in "The Waning of the Oedipus Complex" that psychoanalysis should question the exclusion of "the whole realm of identification and empathy from normality." The focus on preoedipal life has created "a growing awareness of the force and validity of another striving, that for unity, symbiosis, fusion, merging, identification. . . ."[77]

The validation of this striving helps to redress the repudiation of the maternal that informed the earlier rationalism of psychoanalysis. It opens a place in the reality principle for bodily continuity with an other; it includes the intersubjective experience of recognition and all the emotional elements that go into appreciating, caring for, touching, and responding to an other, many of which are developed in infancy. I suspect that this change in psychoanalysis is an indirect result of women's increased status and freedom, which have proven that the maternal bond is not founded on a denial of reality. It may also reflect an incipient critique of pure autonomy, based on the observation that the denial of the need for nurturance takes a tremendous toll on those who live by it, as well as on those who cannot or will not live up to it.

While Loewald's interpretation of the Oedipus complex is an attempt to soften the antithesis between rationality and affectivity, it is also a new approach to paternal authority. He no longer sees patricide as forbidden, but as figuratively necessary. "The assumption of responsibility for one's own life and its conduct is in psychic reality tantamount to the murder of the parents. . . . Not only parental authority is destroyed by wresting authority from the parents and taking it over, but the parents . . . are being destroyed as libidinal objects as well."[78] This, of course, presumes that the parents survive the destruction without retaliating, something only the "generous father" can do.[79] But Oedipus, and countless sons before and after him, did not have a generous father. Theirs was the father of Kafka's story "The Judgment," who leaps from his sickbed to condemn his son to death for the crime of taking over the family business and planning to marry. Along with the social decline in paternal authority, the plot has gradually changed: from murdering the father to leaving home. Rebelling against the father now appears to our conscious minds as a stage in life rather than a transgression punishable by death.* Likewise, women's emancipation has contributed to the transformation of reunion: from an image of death or primordial oneness to a moment of connection. As women

---

*In his discussion on dreams of the death of parents Freud himself observed how the rule of the father created a link between independence and patricide: "Even in our middle-class families fathers are as a rule inclined to refuse their sons independence and the means necessary to secure it and thus to foster the growth of the germ of hostility which is inherent in their relation. A physician will often be in a position to notice how a son's grief at the loss of his father cannot suppress his satisfaction at having at length won his freedom."[80]

achieve greater equality and mothers become equally important re-
presentatives of the outside, the desire for mother no longer evokes
complete loss of self. The mother's ability to balance separation and
connection can also become a model for the child, and the child can
leave this mother without fear of destroying her. Thus both separation
and connection become disentangled from the archaic fears.

In this sense, we can conceptualize a *post* oedipal phase of separation
in which the metaphoric death of the parents as loved ones who are
responsible for us is accompanied by the joy of successful survival and
the grief of loss. This joy and grief could be, at least partially, disentangled from the polarized, archaic images of reunion and separation,
murder and guilt (the lasting imprint of the oedipal phase on the
symbolic unconscious) and be felt as conscious ambivalence. This
would make it possible for sons and daughters, as Loewald says, to take
responsibility for their own desires—by responding to them, not
relinquishing them.[81]

This formulation revises the old oedipal notion of responsibility in
which the sons assumed the guilt for the father's transgression and
made his oppressive power into law. This act of internalization substituted identification with the aggressor for separation from authority,
and so perpetuated the guilt-ridden desire to become the authority
oneself. Identification with the aggressor, embodying the wish to
merge with and be like the all-powerful other, is an effort to escape
the necessity of destroying the father, and insures the same refusal to
be superseded by one's own offspring. The desire to be one with such
an authority is equally dangerous, whether it is expressed through
overt submission, conformity, or domination.

Internalization of authority proceeds by turning the frustrated wish
for power inward: we may not be able to affect the world, but we
can at least control ourselves; we may not be able to truly achieve
independence from all other creatures, but we can distance ourselves
from them so that we *appear* completely autonomous. That this acceptance of powerlessness in the guise of autonomy may deny our respon-

sibility to care for others is rationalized by the notion that we can, after all, do nothing to help them. This compact with the reality principle was expressed most eloquently by Descartes:

> My third maxim was to try to conquer myself rather than fortune, and to change my desires rather than the order of the world, and generally to accustom myself to believing that there is nothing entirely in our power except our thoughts. . . . And this alone seemed to me to be sufficient to prevent me from desiring anything in the future that I could not obtain.[82]

Freud brought about a dramatic break in the Cartesian worldview by showing that controlling our thoughts is not sufficient to change our desires. He revealed that even in withdrawing from the world the ego remains subject to the pressures of the unconscious which confront it as "external" reality. But Freud's great discovery was still only another stage of the journey inward, away from the impact of the outside world. Freud's reading of Oedipus exclusively as a story of unconscious desire and not of real transgression shows how difficult it is to know—and face—external reality, how difficult it is to confront not only one's own aggression and desire, but that of the father as well. The New Oedipus, the rereading of the story as a confrontation with knowledge of self and other, holds out the prospect of understanding not only the hidden inner world, but also the mystifying outer world of power and powerlessness. It presumes the possibility of a postoedipal separation in which individuals are able to turn back and look at their parents, and to assess critically their legacy rather than simply identifying with their authority.

The breakdown of paternal authority and the resulting search for a different route to individuation are the context for the controversy over Oedipus and Narcissus with which we began this chapter. But this does not mean that the decline of authority has "caused" the demise of a once successful form of individuality; rather, it has revealed the contradiction once hidden within that individuality: the inability to confront the independent reality of the other. Men's loss of absolute control over women and children has exposed the vulnerable core of male individuality, the failure of recognition which previously wore the cloak of power, responsibility, and family honor. It is this inability to recognize the other which the psychoanalytic focus on narcissism has finally brought to the surface.

The oedipal model rationalized and concealed this failure by assuming that differentiation cannot occur within the mother–child dyad, that the father must intervene to impose independence. The three pillars of oedipal theory—the primacy of the wish for oneness, the mother's embodiment of this regressive force, and the necessity of paternal intervention—all combine to create the paradox that the only liberation is paternal domination. Oedipal theory thus denies the necessity of mutual recognition between man and woman. Construing the struggle for recognition in terms of the father-son rivalry, the theory reduces woman to a contested point on the triangle, never an other whose different and equal subjectivity need be confronted. By going beyond Oedipus we can envisage a direct struggle for recognition between man and woman, free of the shadow of the father that falls between them. By rejecting the false premise of paternal authority as the only road to freedom, we may recover the promise on which oedipal theory has defaulted: coming to terms with difference.

CHAPTER FIVE

Gender and Domination

OUR DISCUSSION OF the oedipal model has already revealed the difficulty with the idea that the infant begins with a primal oneness from which he must gradually break free. It follows from this that the mother becomes the force of irrationality and undifferentiation, a threat and a promise calling from the infant past. The return to this mother, invoked by oedipal desire, must be warded off by the father, who accordingly stands for rationality and separateness. This polarized structure of gender difference leaves only the alternatives of irrational oneness and rational autonomy. In the wake of this splitting, the image of feminine connection appears the more dangerous, the goal of masculine separation the more rational.

Oedipal gender polarity, so compelling in its logic and so formidable in its unconscious roots, is not restricted to the individual psyche, where it is expressed in terms of mother and father. This polarity, as I have already said, has its analogue in other long-standing dualisms of Western culture: rationality and irrationality, subject and object, autonomy and dependency. In this chapter, I will offer some observations on how the split that constitutes gender polarity is replicated in intellectual and social life, and how it eliminates the possibilities of mutual recognition in society as a whole.

The opposition between paternal subject and maternal object clearly reveals the gender structure that analogous dualisms conceal. Significantly, in the cultural representation of dualism the gender aspect is generally unacknowledged. Whereas psychoanalysis unselfconsciously took the oedipal boy as its standard—the male as the model of the individual—much of modern thought claims to speak for the neuter subject, gender-free and universal. Yet the idea of the individual in modern liberal thought is tacitly defined as masculine even when women are included. Identifying the gender content of what is considered to be gender-neutral can be as difficult as undoing the assumption of essential gender differences. We must look for male hegemony where social and cultural theories have seen the workings of neither sex nor psyche.

Feminist criticism in many disciplines has demonstrated that the concept of the individual is really a concept of the male subject.[1] Likewise I will argue that the principle of rationality which social theorists since Weber have seen as the hallmark of modernity—the rationality that reduces the social world to objects of exchange, calculation, and control—is in fact a male rationality. Rationalization, at the societal level, sets the stage for a form of domination that appears to be gender-neutral, indeed, to have no subject at all. Yet its logic dovetails with the oedipal denial of woman's subjectivity, which reduces the other to object. The psychic repudiation of femininity, which includes the negation of dependency and mutual recognition, is homologous with the social banishment of nurturance and intersubjective relatedness to the private domestic world of women and children. The social separation of private and public spheres—long noted by feminists as the crucial form of the sexual division of labor and thus the social vehicle of gender domination—is patently linked to the split between the father of autonomy and the mother of dependency.[2]

The separation of spheres intensifies as society is increasingly rationalized. As in erotic domination, the process replicates the breakdown in tension: the subject fears becoming like the object he controls, which no longer has the capacity to recognize him. As the principle of pure self-assertion comes to govern the public world of men, human agency is enslaved by the objects it produces, deprived of the personal authorship and recognizing reponse that are essential to subjectivity. On the other hand, private life, which preserves authorship and recognition, is isolated, deprived of social effectiveness. Thus societal rationalization negates what is truly "social" in social life.

The subordination of all aspects of life to the instrumental principles of the public world also subverts the very values of private life, and thus threatens the maternal aspects of recognition: nurturance (the recognition of need), and attunement (the recognition of feeling). Some social critics blame the erosion of such maternal qualities on women's efforts to enter the public world. But this diagnosis misconstrues the symptoms and ignores their cause. The destruction of maternal values is not the result of women's liberation; it is the consequence of the ascendance of male rationality.

MALE INDIVIDUALITY, MALE RATIONALITY

Rationalization, as Weber conceived it, defines the process in which abstract, calculable, and depersonalized modes of interaction replace those founded on personal relationships and traditional authority and beliefs. Instrumental rationality elevates means to the status of ends. Formal procedures (like law) and abstract goals (like profit) replace the traditional values and customs that form a common cultural life and serve to legitimate authority. Political domination is no longer embodied in personal authority (monarchs), but in the system of bureaucratic rationality ("the administration").[3] For Weber, instrumental rationality leads to a culture of disenchantment in which substantive values are no longer collectively shared, universal, or social; they become private, particular, and personal. Thus the gain in individual authority that emerges in liberal, enlightened society is simultaneously vitiated by the loss of moral reason that gives this authorship its social meaning and impact.[4]

For the Frankfurt theorists, individual authority and agency are only an appearance contradicted by the reality of economic powerlessness and dependency. Following Georg Lukacs, they joined Weber's concept of rationalization to Marx's idea that domination is located in the principle of commodity exchange.[5] A worker sells his labor power in exchange for a wage; but his labor produces more value (surplus value) than that wage; and this surplus is appropriated by capital and wielded as power. Likewise, the worker loses control of the object he produces, in which he might recognize his own labor. Thus the formal principle of "equal" exchange subordinates all other principles of social recognition and masks the domination of one class by another. As domination is rationalized and depersonalized, it becomes invisible, and seems to be natural and necessary.[6]

The idea of rationalization forms a bridge between intellectual history and the history of social and economic relationships. It describes the essence of modern social practice and thought. It is, in Foucault's sense, a discourse.[7] My argument is that it is a *gendered* discourse, that the instrumental orientation and the impersonality that govern modern social organization and thought should be understood as masculine. This means that male domination, like class domination, is no longer a function of personal power relationships (though these do exist), but something inherent in the social and cultural structures, independent of what individual men and women will.

Thus regardless of woman's increasing participation in the public, productive sphere of society, it remains, in its practices and principles, "a man's world." The presence of women has no effect on its rules and processes. The public institutions and the relations of production display an apparent genderlessness, so impersonal do they seem. Yet it is precisely this objective character, with its indifference to personal need, that is recognized as the hallmark of masculine power. It is precisely the pervasive depersonalization, the banishment of nurturance to the private sphere, that reveal the logic of male dominance, of female denigration and exclusion. Invisible, the structure of gender domination is nevertheless materialized in the rationality that pervades our economic and social relations. The apparent gender neutrality is a kind of mystification, like the mystification that Marx identified as commodity fetishism—an illusion created by the social relations themselves.

Feminist theory has already exposed the mystification inherent in the ideal of the autonomous individual. As our discussion of Oedipus showed, this individual is based on the paternal ideal of separation and denial of dependency. The feminist critique of the autonomous individual closely parallels the Marxian critique of the bourgeois individual, elaborated by the Frankfurt theorists.[8] As Marcuse points out, the denial of dependency is central to the bourgeois ideal of individual freedom:

> Self-sufficiency and independence of all that is other and alien is the sole guarantee of the subject's freedom. What is not dependent on any other person or thing, what possesses itself, is free. . . . A relationship to the other in which one really reaches and is united with him counts as loss and dependence.[9]

The ideal of the bourgeois individual, Marcuse shows, is created by an act of abstraction, which denies his real dependency and social subordination. Consequently, his freedom consists of protection from the control or intrusion of others. It is a *negative* ideal of freedom: freedom as release from bondage, individuality stripped bare of its relationship with and need for others.

From a feminist point of view, the missing piece in the analysis of Western rationality and individualism is the structure of gender domination. The psychosocial core of this unfettered individuality is the subjugation of woman by man, through which it appears that she is his possession, and therefore, that he is not dependent upon or attached to an other outside himself. As a psychological principle, autonomous individuality derives from the male posture in differentiation; that is, from the repudiation of the primary experience of nurturance and identity with the mother. The individual's abstractness lies in the denial not merely of the nourishing and constraining bonds that engage him in society, as Marcuse argues, but also of the primary emotional bonds, conscious and unconscious, that foster and limit his freedom.

Submerged beneath the universal claims of this individual, then, is not only his historic and cultural specificity, but also his gender. While most modern theory has considered this masculine identity too self-evident to be mentioned (the particularity of gender would compromise his universality), it is, nevertheless, retained as an "option": when necessary, it can always be mobilized to exclude or devalue women. It has uncovered the masculine identity of the seemingly neutral universal individual of modern thought and society; indeed, it has shown that neutrality itself is the sign of masculinity, its alliance with rationality and objectivity. The feminist critique has rejected the assumption in modern thought that individuality and rationality are universals while gender is particular, secondary, not essential to their constitution.

Let us be clear about the stakes of this critique: it is not a matter merely of exposing bias, or of the exclusion of women from a world they wish to enter. If the rational, autonomous individual's claim to neutrality is compromised, then so is his claim to universality. If his way of being in the world is not simply human, but specifically masculine, then it is not universal. And this means that his way is not the only or inevitable way of doing things. Furthermore, if this subject establishes his identity by splitting off certain human capabilities, called feminine, and by refusing to recognize the subjectivity of this feminine other, then his claim to stand for equality, liberty, free thought, and recognition of the other is also invalidated. And this means that his way cannot be the best way of doing things.

OBJECTIVITY AND AUTONOMY

In her book *Reflections on Gender and Science* Evelyn Keller makes a convincing case for the masculine character of modern scientific objectivity. Her work adds the missing piece—gender—to the well-known critique of modern science as fundamentally inspired by the project of control and domination of nature. She argues that the relationship between the subject of knowledge and his object may be represented in terms of the relationship between the subject and his love object. Contrasting Plato's metaphor of knowledge as homoerotic union *(knowledge = eros)* with Bacon's metaphor of heterosexual conquest *(knowledge = power),* she shows how gender frames the relationship between mind and nature. She contends that as the character of male dominion over woman has changed, so has the metaphor of scientific knowledge. Beginning with Bacon, modern science adopted the metaphor of subduing nature and wresting her secrets from her.[10] "Instead of banishing the Furies underground, out of sight, as did the Greeks, modern science has sought to expose female interiority, to bring it into the light, and thus to dissolve its threat entirely."[11]

Yet while denying invisibility to nature, the contemporary scientist maintains the invisibility of his personal authorship, protecting his autonomy behind a screen of objectivity. This impersonality of modern science, Keller argues, is actually the signature of its masculine identity.[12] We may note that this image of the scientist as impersonal knower who "tears the veil" from nature's body is reminiscent of the master in the fantasy of erotic domination, and his quest for knowledge parallels the rational violation in which the subject is always in control.

Indeed, Keller proposes that modern scientific detachment from the object derives from the relation to the mother that I have called one-sided differentiation. Because men originally define themselves through separation from and opposition to the mother, Keller argues, they reject experiences of merging and identification that blur the boundary between subject and object. Thus the masculine stance toward difference accords with the cultural dominance of a "science that has been premised on a radical dichotomy between subject and object."[13] The world outside, the other, is always object. As the first other, the mother, becomes an object, Keller explains, her object status infuses the world and the natural environment.[14]

In the radical separation of subject and object we perceive again the inability to grasp the aliveness of the other; we hear the echo of the unmovable, unmoving character of the master. And yet again the denial of recognition leaves the omnipotent self imprisoned in his mind, reflecting on the world from behind a wall of glass.

This is the impasse of rationalism, analogous to the impasse of omnipotence, in which the subject completely assimilates the outside. It is not a problem exclusive to modern science; it runs throughout Western thought. Lukacs and the Frankfurt theorists identified this tendency in the history of philosophy: as the rational subject of thought became increasingly separated from the object, he internalized the qualities of that lost object, and attributed to himself all that was once part of the objective world. In Kant, for example, space and time, the basic categories of sensuous knowledge, do not exist objectively in reality, which we can never know, but are rather part of the mind of the knower. The transcendental subject "eats up" the reality of the world, claiming that everything perceived is in the eye of the beholder.[15] Thus for the Frankfurt theorists the thinking subject has sucked the life out of the social and natural world, and now, like a swollen tick, is stuck, embedded, in this lifeless world. Of course its lifelessness does not prevent the host-world from suffocating the subject with its dead weight.

Despite this critique of how the radically separate mind dominates and so destroys objective reality, the Frankfurt theorists could find no other antidote than an even greater self-awareness. In order to break with the rationalist tradition of the individual as "windowless monad," to release the mind from its narcissistic bubble, they looked for some other principle that would limit the absolute self by restoring its connection to the world. In Freud, they found a perspective that challenged the mind's disconnection from the body, and saw omnipotence for the danger it is; but Freud did not address the gap between the self and other selves.[16] The Frankfurt theorists lacked a model of the psyche in which the self truly seeks to know the outside world and longs for contact with the other. Their difficulty was precisely their lack of an intersubjective theory. They could only envision connection as a return to oneness, as dedifferentiation and irrationality—a romantic, and ultimately dangerous reunion with nature.* The only "solution" to the impasse of the rational mind, then, was constant reflection on its tendency toward domination.

---

*Marcuse, less resigned than Adorno and Horkheimer, did propose the idea of a dialogic interaction with nature, although his adherence to drive theory made him unable to ground it psychoanalytically. Marcuse's vision of a different science and technology has been criticized by Habermas. Though he agreed that the motive of domination and control was embedded in modern rationality itself, especially in science and technology, Habermas disputed the possibility of a different relation to nature in which it was not objectified and instrumentalized but known as an independent, subjective other. He argued that the search for an arena of intersubjectivity (a project which he first formulated and to which he is committed) to counter the goal rationality of science must look elsewhere, in symbolic interaction. But Marcuse's utopianism is, in its intention, closer to the feminist critique of rationality than Habermas's. The latter's argument merely displaces the problem of rationalism—the inability to recognize the other—to the area of symbolic interaction and moral discourse. And there, the same issue arises as in science: only formal procedures and abstraction allow a universal form of recognition, but these negate the recognition of the other's particular subjectivity.[17]

The feminist critique of rationality is able to take the intersubjective route out of this impasse. It is not necessary, as Keller shows, to abandon the scientific project of knowing the world, only to redefine it. While the separation that recognizes the world's outside existence is a condition of vitality, the complete rupture of our connection to the world makes our perception of it static and rigid. Thus Keller proposes a new concept of dynamic objectivity that "actively draws on the commonality between mind and nature," and suggests the reconstitution of the subject–object relationship as one that permits attunement and similarity between knower and known.[18]

This intersubjective perspective envisions a more complex world than the realm of lifeless objects created by the radical separation of subject and object, self and other. By investing one's full attention in the object, one allows it to emerge as real and whole, so that the self is not lost but heightened through pleasure in the object.[19] Here we see how the intersubjective experiences of infancy—the awareness that different minds can share the same perceptions, the experience of a transitional space that is not sharply defined as inside or outside—may become the basis for knowledge and recognition of the other. Keller reminds us that an esoteric tradition of knowledge that respects its object exists as an alternative in Western science. This alternative, "intersubjective" tradition is exemplified in recent years by the work of the biologist Barbara McClintock, whose original work in genetics lay outside the dominant paradigm of "breaking the code." Of her experience studying chromosomes, she observed: "When I was really working with them I wasn't outside, I was down there. I was part of the system. I was right down there with them, and everything got big. I even was able to see the internal parts of the chromosomes. It surprised me, because I actually felt as if I was right down there and these were my friends. . . . As you look at these things, they become part of you. And you forget yourself."[20] McClintock's moving image reminds us that the act of knowing can be felt as communion, not conquest.

The feminist critique of rationality thus leads us to redraft our map of the mind to include the territory of self and other, that space in which we know, discover, and create the world through our connection to it. It identifies the element within the project of knowledge that leads to domination and destructiveness as well as the excluded element that might redeem it. In exposing the structure of rationality and individuality as masculine and one-sided, the feminist critique points out both the origins of domination and the potential for a more balanced differentiation of self and world. To assert that rationality is contaminated by control is not a proposal to scrap it in favor of romantic anti-rationality; it is meant to redefine rationality and expand its boundaries. The point is not to undo all of modern science but to acknowledge the value of what has been banished as irrational and infantile.

Modern science's definition of knowledge in terms of a controlling subject and an objectified world is one instance of the hegemony of male rationality. Let us now consider a related critique: Carol Gilligan's analysis of the masculinist orientation of moral psychology.

While other fields have grown accustomed to feminist theorizing about the subject's gender, psychology was taken unawares when the issue of gender was finally brought to its door. Gilligan's challenge to the exclusion of women's experience from psychology, In a Different Voice, drove home the moral and political implications of theories of individual development. Gilligan exposes the gender assumptions in moral development and life-cycle theories, some of which have been widely influential outside the bounds of the discipline of psychology. Thus she criticizes Erik Erikson's model of identity development, in which the stages of life are seen as a progress in separation, and the definition of maturity subordinates relational responsibilities to autonomy and achievement.[21]

Gilligan's research is primarily designed to challenge Lawrence Kohlberg's model of moral development, a theory that originated in studies of male subjects only. When Kohlberg applied his model to women, he found they were less likely than men to reach the "highest stage" of moral reasoning, the ability to reason in formal terms about universal goals, independent of concrete considerations, conventions, and self-interest. In Kohlberg's theory, this stage is characterized by the ability to recognize and apply universal norms such as justice and equality.[22] Gilligan argues that this conception of morality is one-sided, and specifically, that it reflects the masculine experience. Her own research shows that women do progress toward higher levels of universal judgment, but that their values—such as psychological truth, caring, nonviolence—are not identical with those of men. Although women and men are able to take either position, women are more likely to espouse an ethics of care and responsibility, men an ethics of rights and justice. Women who have demonstrated the ability to reason formally and abstractly nonetheless prefer a style of moral thinking that is contextual and concrete, that sees the self in relation to others.

Gilligan revalues woman's moral position and, more generally, redeems previously denied aspects of feminine experience. Her intention is to correct an individuation that has been centered on the goal of separation.* She shows how Kohlberg's conception of moral reasoning is grounded in a notion of abstract, formal recognition independent of specific needs or ties ("I recognize you as having the same rights as I have myself"). The moral subject can take the role of the other and can accept the principle of reciprocity in the abstract, but only by constituting a general point of view, not by taking the other's subjective point of view. The particular other is subsumed by the universal "generalized other."[24] We may say that reciprocity of rights is based on the most abstract common denominator—what makes one person like the other—and denies all that is "individual." This symme-

---

*There is an element of reversal in Gilligan's argument but I believe that those critics who see only this element and thus claim that she espouses a "feminine ethos" have overlooked her critique of feminine self-sacrifice and her repeated statements in favor of psychological tension and ambiguity. This misinterpretation has arisen, as Seyla Benhabib suggests, because Gilligan's book contained no explicit discussion of the historical "*constitution* of these gender differences . . . in light of woman's oppression."[23]

try of rights presumes the competition of all against all—the limit and the affirmation of pure assertion. Thus the individual is not "interested" in the other's needs, indeed, does not recognize them because they may oppose his own. Paradoxically, then, this abstraction from personal needs and the other's subjective viewpoint militates against recognition of difference. Only the other (my complementary opposite) who does *not* have the same rights as I do, and against whom I do *not* compete, may claim respect for needs—in this category we find the helpless wife, the child, the deprived. Thus the formal acceptance of difference opposes the intersubjective appreciation of it, which includes recognition of the particular, individual needs of the other.

This kind of moral knowledge, Gilligan argues, "in the end is always self-referenced"; despite his encounter with the other, "the self oddly seems to stay constant."[25] The impact of the other's difference is never really felt; the collision with reality never shatters the bubble of the self; the "news of difference," as Gregory Bateson calls it, never gets through. In intersubjective terms, the other is, we might say, not recognized as someone who can be different and yet share the same subjective state. Without concrete knowledge, empathy, and identification with the other subject—with the other's needs, feelings, circumstances, and history—the self continues to move in the realm of subject and object, untransformed by the other. The self says, "You cannot affect or negate my identity, you can only be the object of my assertion." What is absent is the tension of recognizing the outside other as both different *and* alike. While the idea of reciprocal rights appears to define recognition, it actually defines only one condition of it. When this condition—equal rights—is confused with recognition itself, it actually makes the recognition of individual needs and differences more difficult. Thus Gilligan's challenge to the ideal of the autonomous individual also alerts us to the insufficiency of the political ethos of rights.

Kohlberg, and other adherents of his moral philosophy, have rejected Gilligan's critique on the grounds that women's concerns with care and emotional truth belong to values of "the good life," that is, to private choice rather than public ethics. Furthermore, Kohlberg argues that, unlike justice and rights, women's moral concerns are not sufficiently abstract and universal to be considered proper categories of moral reasoning—they are merely aspects of ego development.[26] It is as if these values were fit only for the nursery, not for the public world. In the public world, only values abstracted from individual, particular needs can claim universal validity—to generalize any individual's needs would compromise the right of every individual to choose his values and pursue the fulfillment of his needs.*

But as political philosopher Seyla Benhabib points out, this very insistence on the division between questions of public and private expresses an unavowed sexual politics.

> This traditional distinction in moral and political theory between justice and the good life does not only reflect a cognitive concern, but has also been a means of legitimizing the split between the public and the private spheres, as these reflect the sexual division of labor current in our societies. The public sphere, the sphere of justice . . . is regarded as the domain where independent, male heads of household transact with one another, while the private-intimate sphere is put beyond the pale of justice and restricted to the reproductive and affective needs of the bourgeois pater

---

*The inability to reconcile individual needs with universal goals is a serious problem for feminist politics as well. Thus feminists opposed the use of universals as a feature of male discourse, but wanted to retain universalism for themselves—as in the claim for a universal woman's essence, or in the idea that women are the new revolutionary subject whose liberation will free everyone. The same groups that once embraced the idea of the unity of women based on their common essence then leapt to a "new" awareness that differences of race and class were the real truth and that all universal categories only serve to deny such difference. In this turnabout there was no stopping point, no consideration of how to sustain the tension between universal commonality and specific differences.

familias. . . . An entire domain of human activity, namely, nurture, reproduction, love and care, which became women's lot in the course of modern bourgeois society, was thereby excluded from moral and political consideration, and relegated to the realm of nature.[27]

The ideal of the autonomous individual could only be created by abstracting from the relationship of dependency between men and women. The relationships which people require to nurture them are considered private, and not truly relationships with outside *others*. Thus the other is reduced to an appendage of the subject—the mere condition of his being—not a being in her own right. The individual who cannot recognize the other or his own dependency without suffering a threat to his identity requires the formal, impersonal principles of rationalized interaction, and is required by them.

The unbreachable line between public and private values rests on the tacit assumption that women will continue to preserve and protect personal life, the task to which they have been assigned. In this way the political morality can sustain the fiction of the wholly independent individual, whose main concern is a system of rights that protects him from other individuals like himself. The public world is conceived as a place in which direct recognition and care for others' needs is impossible—and this is tolerable as long as the private world "cooperates." The public sphere, an arrangement of atomized selves, cannot serve as the space between self and other, as an intersubjective space; in order to protect the autonomy of the individual, social life forfeits the recognition between self and other.

This public rationality necessitates that woman's different voice be split off and institutionalized in the private sphere. This voice is, I suspect, part of the "pianissimo" Weber had in mind when he wrote:

It is the fate of our times, with its characteristic rationalization and intellectualization, and above all disenchantment, that precisely the ultimate, most sublime values have withdrawn from public life either into the transcendental realm of mysticism or the brotherliness of direct personal relationships. It is not accidental that our greatest art is intimate and not monumental, nor is it accidental that today only within the smallest, intimate circles, from person to person, in *pianissimo,* this Something pulsates that corresponds to the prophetic *pneuma,* which in former times swept through the great communities like a firebrand, welding them together.[28]

DEFENDERS OF THE PRIVATE SPHERE

Weber observes that sublime values have become the preserve of private life, with regret rather than satisfaction. This is not the case for many who have come after him. A strain of social criticism has arisen (right *and* left, feminist *and* antifeminist) that celebrates the private sphere of female nurturance and criticizes social rationality while accepting this division, and indeed all gender polarity, as natural and inevitable. This fantasy of separate but equal spheres denies that rationalization is a form of male hegemony; that the modern sexual division, like its more authoritarian predecessors, is still a relationship of domination.

The several versions of this position, which I shall refer to as gender conservatism, display a common contradiction. Although they criticize the effects of rationalization (for example, the invasion of family life by state institutions and mental health professionals) they accept its premise: that the split between nurturance and rationality in social life is unavoidable. Gender conservatives offer a well-worn alternative to the repudiation of maternal nurturance by male enterprise: the restoration of gender polarity in a best-of-all-possible separation of spheres. They want to restore the traditional sexual division of labor in the family precisely because they see it as the matrix for the growth of the autonomous individual.* Conversely, they attribute the break-down of this family form not to the dissolution of larger kin and neighborhood ties, but to the demise of the independent male wage earner. Thus they would recreate the conditions in which the whole family depends on the male wage earner in order to promote the purported stability of the old sexual division. For gender conservatives, the feminist project of bringing women into the public world is the main obstacle to restoring familial and societal stability.

The defense of "the family" has been formulated not only by avowed conservatives like Brigitte and Peter Berger, sociologists who see themselves as Weberian critics of rationalization, but also by historian Christopher Lasch, who calls himself a radical, and political theorist Jean Bethke Elshtain, who calls herself a feminist.[30] Although each of these authors has a somewhat different position, all are gender conservatives who criticize rationalization in the name of protecting the family, its sexual division of labor, and, above all, women's mothering. All see the idea of reforming public life to provide more nurturance as a dangerous invitation to state expansion and further rationalization of private life. As they see it, to put more areas of life under the jurisdiction of public policy and organization would only disrupt the domestic arrangements that offer a last refuge of warmth and safety. But here arises the dilemma that gender conservatives cannot solve. Although their ideal is the structure of gender polarity, which upholds masculine rationality and autonomy in the public world and honors feminine

---

*The idea that changes in family life have undermined individualism and the work ethic is a shibboleth of social criticism closely allied with the criticism of the "New Narcissism." But, as the sociologist Robert Bellah and his colleagues have recently documented, the old work ethic of competitive individualism is still flourishing and is quite compatible with the narcissistic focus on the self.[29] What has changed is that the struggle for individual achievement or survival is no longer endowed with meaning by the broader society; individual performance is now divorced from participation in community life.

nurturance in the home, the masculine principle cannot in fact be contained in public life. It inevitably threatens to exceed these limits and devalue the cherished haven of home.

For the defenders of the family, the damage done by the rationalized public world of men can be repaired by women, if only they will play by the rules of gender polarity and devote their lives to the endangered maternal role. In *The War over the Family,* for example, the Bergers make no bones about defending the bourgeois family in its classic nineteenth-century form, in which "the woman is paramount in the home" and has a "civilizing mission" outside of it. They state categorically that "the bourgeois family is the necessary social context for the emergence of the autonomous individuals who are the empirical foundation of political democracy." This family, they claim, was based on an ethos of *balance* which "made it possible to socialize individuals with singularly stable personalities, . . . a balance between individualism and social responsibility, between 'liberation' and strong communal ties, between acquisition and altruism."[31] The balance the Bergers celebrate is, of course, the one between public and private, based on the separate spheres of mother and father.

The Bergers concede that the extension of individualism and rationalization into every area of life has rent the old fabric of society.[32] Individualism has brought about its own demise; it has undermined the very family that gave birth to the stable individual. But since the Bergers consider the family woman's domain, we are not surprised to discover, as we read on, that what they lament is not so much the general expansion of male rationality but the particular extension of individualism to women. The Bergers suggest that the family is undermined by feminist "hyperindividualism"; women are no longer willing to devote themselves to fostering the individuality of others.[33] In a similar vein, Lasch and Elshtain, who know better, equate feminism with the ethos of corporate liberalism and individualist competition— as if it all came down to more places for women financial executives.[34]

The Bergers appear entirely ignorant of the feminist critique of individualism and rationality, and attribute to feminists an ideal of the individual which is really their own. In feminism, they claim, "the individual woman is now emphasized over against every communal context in which she may find herself—a redefinition of her situation that breaks not only the community between the spouses but (more fundamentally) the mother-child dyad, . . . the most basic human community of all."[35] The Bergers believe that women's independence virtually threatens life itself, the most vital human bond.

The problem with this defense of the family as matrix for the autonomous individual is, again, the one that arises from the language of gender-neutral universality: the moment women take advantage of the logic of universality and rebel against their confinement to the domestic sphere, the advocates of autonomy trot out the hidden gender clause. The unspoken assumption is that women, by upholding the private sphere and creating a nurturing environment, create the framework for the autonomous individuality of men. The Bergers finally hope that women "will come to understand that life is more than a career and that this 'more' is above all to be found in the family. But, however individual women decide, *they should not expect public policy to underwrite and subsidize their life plans.*"[36] (emphasis added) Thus, while men can have a career and "more," subsidized by the care and labor of the wife-mother, women should realize that this offer is not open to them. Their role is to *produce* autonomous individuals (boys) who can balance their public and private lives, not to *be* such individuals. Berger and Berger present their proposal for women with no thought of the contradiction between the democratic ethos of formal equality and substantive inequality—let alone domination—nor with any thought of the inherent instability of such a contradiction.

The Bergers' plea also exemplifies the other contradiction that arises from gender polarity: defending the traditional female ethos of nurturance while affirming its exclusion from the public social world.[37] While they object to women sharing in the pursuit of individualism, they continue to defend the individualist ethos. They are convinced that any limitation placed on free enterprise, and any state program for social support, is a step away from democracy, a step toward the death of individualism. This is why no woman should expect public policy to support her "life plans"—even if these plans include no more than single-handedly feeding, clothing, and sheltering her children through minimum-wage employment.

Although they acknowledge that the family is the victim of the very forces of rationalization to which it gave birth, the Bergers never pause to question the principle of rationality, especially the principle of capitalist economy (production for profit, all services organized through economic exchange, unchecked competition). Nor do they see how these principles threaten the ideal of mutual responsibility which their bourgeois family stands for. The lack of support and responsibility in public life creates unremitting anxiety about being at the mercy of a heartless rationality. This is why the *idea* that women are needed in the home—increasingly impossible in actuality except for the well-to-do—has once again become so popular, an enchanted vision of a maternal haven.[38]

I believe that this insistence on the division between public and private is sustained by the fear that anything public or "outside" would merely intensify individual helplessness, that only the person we have not yet recognized as outside (mother and wife) can be trusted to provide us with care, that the only safe dependence is on someone who is not part of the struggle of all against all, and indeed, who is herself not independent. Thus we can only protect our autonomy and mask our vulnerability by keeping nurturance confined to its own sphere.

Perhaps, also, the social provision of nurturance is too threatening a reminder of early dependency in the very outside sphere which was supposed to be our escape from it. The kind of social support that might spark our identification with the helplessness of the needy is bitterly resisted. This attitude generates a vicious cycle in which the unconscious revulsion against early states of dependency or helplessness is reinforced by the spectacle of those who are left in the lurch. The visible consequences of our failure to provide socially organized nurturance—a safe holding environment—intensify our distance and disidentification from those who require support. Witness the refusal to recognize the increasing number of women and children below the poverty line.

While the values of competition, success, and hard work seem to thrive as ever, the values of collective nurturance and responsibility for others have suffered. Of course, these are not intrinsically female values, but in our society they are almost exclusively familial and private, and thus associated with women. It would be more accurate to say they are *parental* values, part of the private lives of women and the growing number of men who are consciously emphasizing father-hood. But in the logic of gender polarity, *nurturance = private = mother.* This equation insists on the division of labor between the parents, and so acts against the creation of conditions that would allow fathers *and* mothers to nurture their children.

While conservatives like the Bergers blame feminists for the condi-tions of marital instability and mothers' unwillingness to stay home with their children, they are silent about the lack of social support for families. Nor have they anything to say about the relationship between fathers and children. Here we might note a peculiarity common to all of the authors cited. Their response to the feminist proposal of dual parenting and to the critique of instrumental rationality as masculine is to change the subject and talk loudly of the dangers of collective childrearing. In *The Minimal Self* Lasch reports, accurately enough, that psychoanalytic feminists believe that the problem of instrumental rationality will persist "as long as society assigns children exclusively to the care of women and subordinates the work of nurture to the masculine projects of conquest and domination." Rather than directly confront this idea, Lasch simply asserts that Freudian feminists want more than "an expanded role for men in childcare"—yes, they want an *equal* role. "They call for the collectivization of childrearing."[39] Without any comment on male responsibility for children, Lasch changes the subject to public childcare.

This sudden change of subject struck me as significant when I found identical elisions in other defenses of the traditional family. Thus in her book *Public Man, Private Woman* Elshtain dismisses Chodorow's idea that male parenting would change the male stance toward women as "counterfactual," and goes on to denounce collective childrearing and, specifically, the destruction of individualism in the kibbutz. To back up her argument, she calls on the evidence that without specific attachments children are damaged, and the correlate assumption that daycare means the substitution of temporary attachments for permanent ones.[40] The feminist proposal that fathers nurturing children would simultaneously repair the repudiation of the mother and reconcile men to nurturance is transformed into a nightmare vision of raising children like Perdue chickens.

I think this displacement reveals something about the fear of being left in the father's care—the preconscious assumption that men would either neglect children or raise them with the same instrumental rationality (impersonality, lack of care and attunement) that they display in public enterprise. It reveals that the state, that purveyor of instrumental rationality, really is symbolically equated with the detached father. We can speculate that the insistence on maintaining the separation between public and private simply repeats the splitting of father and mother. As we have seen, this split grows out of the conflict between autonomy and attachment. The child, fearing that dependency will contaminate his autonomy, develops a one-sided version of independence. But splitting backfires: for now masculine separation and repudiation of femininity have destroyed maternal love; and having left mother, there is no turning back.

Gender conservatism accepts the instrumentalism of society as long as society permits the existence of a private refuge. Indeed, it fears any extension of public nurturance and support as an encroachment on autonomy, a violation of the territory of pure individuality. Restricted to the private enclave, the mother is equated with the infantile ideal: she is the constant source of goodness, the one who can make everything right with the world. This scheme preserves the split between outside and inside, so that the individual appears self-sufficient in public but can relax and regress in the safe enclave of the wife-mother. Yet it is precisely this split on the psychic and social level that provokes the deep anxiety about losing access to home, mother, dependency, and nurturance—about being exposed to the cold, ruthless outside.

This anxiety is, in turn, plowed back into the urgent wish to restore the boundaries between personal and public that "ideally" protect the inner, private core of the self. The idea of home functions metaphorically to protect the needy, dependent, and vulnerable self from exposure and violation. The inner core of need (still seen as infantile since the autonomous adult should not need anyone) can never be revealed "outside," in public, except as weakness. The ideal mother-wife protects the autonomous individual from having to admit his needs by meeting them in advance; she protects him from the shame of exposure, allowing him to appear independent and in control. Therefore losing control over her, the object, is a threat to the individual's self-control, to his sense of an intact self.

As long as the father (and men in general) cannot be depended upon in the same reliable way for tenderness and holding, as long as he represents selfish autonomy, mother (and women in general) will remain the only source of goodness. The problem is that using the wife-mother as a prop for autonomy threatens to reduce her to a mere extension of the self; it risks using her up. The ideal of autonomous individuality with its stress on rationality, self-sufficiency, performance, and competition threatens to negate the mother so completely that there may be no one to come home to. This is a version of the contradiction we saw in erotic domination, the fear that we have destroyed or wholly objectified the other whom we need. It is also another version of the oedipal model: wanting to devalue and control the other while still drawing sustenance from her, wanting to keep mother in captivity and yet alive and strong, protected by a separate and yet responsible father. The panic about women leaving home does express a psychic reality: the fear of paying the price for individual autonomy and social rationalization, the fear that being grown up means feeling "like a motherless child." But it is not women's abandonment of the home that stimulates this fear. Rather, the social division of gender—with its idealization of autonomous individuality—is at fault, bringing about the loss of the very maternal nurturance it is meant to protect.

THE LOST IDEAL OF MOTHERHOOD

> If there is no true recognition of the mother's part, then there must remain a vague fear of dependence. This fear will sometimes take the form of a fear of women in general or fear of a particular woman, and at other times will take on less easily recognised forms, always including the fear of domination.
>
> Unfortunately, the fear of domination does not lead groups of people to avoid being dominated; on the contrary, it draws them towards a specific or chosen domination. . . .
>
> —D. W. Winnicott, *The Child, the Family, and the Outside World*[41]

In acknowledging the erosion of maternal nurturance by societal rationalization, I do not intend to idealize private motherhood as the advocates of gender polarity have done. The sentimental ideal of motherhood is the product of the historic separation of public and private spheres that gave gender polarity its present form as an institutionalized opposition between male rationality and maternal nurturance. To idealize maternal nurturance, a position some feminists share with gender conservatives, only confirms the dualism and denies historical reality. To accept the old ideal of motherhood—even as an ideal—is to remain inside the revolving door of gender polarity.

The contemporary celebrations of motherhood are a classic example of reenchantment, which is the attempt to replace a lost relationship with an ideal. Disenchantment (the impersonality and neutrality bred by rationalization) inevitably stimulates the search for reenchantment, in this case, for a regendered version of society. Such regressive reenchantment can rely on the structure of gender polarity that is preserved, albeit beneath the surface, by rationalization. Thus as the concrete forms of maternal care and recognition diminish, their loss is repaired by the symbolic evocation of motherhood.

The symbolism of ideal motherhood actually obscures the waning of the sociable domestic world that originally supported it. The isolation of the nuclear family household in the post-war era and the reduction of its social ties with the outside world (which are now largely ties of consumption) deprived the mother of her own holding environment—the web of kin and neighborhood relationships that supported, advised, and nurtured her. The loss of this support was compensated for by a more equal sharing of tasks and a more intimate personal cooperation between man and wife: the separate spheres were replaced by a new image of marital solidarity, the so-called "partnership marriage," which became the model of the post-war era. But the ideal of marital solidarity was simply grafted on to the old sexual division of labor, leaving mothers of this era at home, more isolated and dependent than ever.[42]

The contradiction between the ideal of marital solidarity and the framework of gender polarity, especially the public-private split, has largely worked to women's detriment. While men's greater participation in domestic life offers some women greater intimacy and support, it hardly offsets the greater isolation, disenfranchisement, and dependency that characterize privatized motherhood. The inequality between men and women at work and at home constantly undermines the intimacy and solidarity which are the theoretical goal of modern marriage. This disparity between ideal and reality is obviously a major cause of marital disharmony and divorce—still a very different experience for women than for men. Women's dependence on men continues to be reinforced by the wage structure; this is especially the case when women interrupt work to care for children. Yet women are likely to have sole responsibility for raising and supporting children after divorce.[43] As a result, mothers are almost as helpless as they were in the days of total economic dependency—and in some ways more so.

The nostalgia for gender polarity, as many feminist observers have pointed out, is a reaction against the present desolate condition of motherhood. It reflects the misguided hope that by returning women to dependency, by blaming women (and not men) for the destructive effects of autonomy, men can be lured back to familial responsibility.[44] It also reflects the assumption that it is women's job to restore and repair the private sphere. As Elshtain declares in her challenge to feminism, if women are relocated in the public world, no one will tend the private "little world" with its "joys and tragedies."[45] In other words, nurturance is particular and feminine; private life is a delicate plant whose growth requires the exclusive devotion of the gentler sex.

But ironically, the new conditions of mothering, even as they have generated a longing for the maternal ideal, have made it even more unrealistic.[46] The all-giving woman who finds fulfillment in her home and children is no longer well respected. Yet she is *still* considered the best possible, indeed the only good, mother; she is *still* a reproach to the many who work. The moral authority of motherhood has been damaged, yet motherhood remains the backbone of socialization and care. Though maternal care is still regarded as vital for small children, its values are nearly irrelevant for life outside the nursery.

The restriction of mothering tenderness to the early years creates a sense of scarcity; giving an infant or small child into someone else's care is tantamount to depriving them of their only shot at intimacy, protection, and warmth. The early years are not only formative; they seem to be the *only* time when any sort of protection is available from the hardness and profligacy of the culture. The thought of losing this protection stimulates intense fears of helplessness and abandonment. It is hardly surprising that the idea of daycare arouses so much passion. As we have already seen, daycare is the lightning rod that attracts all the fears and fantasies about the mother's role. In her book *Every Child's Birthright; In Defense of Mothering,* child psychoanalyst Selma Fraiberg (well known to parents for her guide, *The Magic Years*) offers a good illustration of the use and abuse of psychoanalysis in the daycare-versus-exclusive-mothering debate. Fraiberg's argument, and others like it, have persuaded countless people that we need not try to provide good daycare for children since it is impossible in any case.

It is worth considering briefly Fraiberg's argument: she begins with the well-known work on the infant's need for attachment, but quickly distorts it with her own observation that a baby cannot "switch partners and bestow his love upon a stranger."[47] But the issue is not *switching,* it is *adding* partners (a limited number, of course). Most babies who are firmly attached to mother (and, let us add, father) *can,* as Bowlby acknowledges, acquire other attachment figures—the people they see on a daily or regular basis. Such babies greet their regular sitters with pleasure, and, since they are used to forming new relationships, can (perhaps with difficulty but not damage) switch to a new sitter if necessary.* Furthermore, by eighteen months most infants can form strong attachments to other children, whom they greet with a special joy.

Fraiberg abandons empirical evidence altogether when she turns to what she defines as the preschool group: ages three to six (not a meaningful category, since six-year-olds are twice as autonomous as three-year-olds, and are considered schoolchildren). At this age, she claims, children still do not become attached to groups or teachers; they require an individual mother substitute, and can stand "the strain of prolonged separation from mother" in nursery school for only a few hours. Citing directors of "daycare centers known to me," Fraiberg contends that children who spend the day in nursery care show "by afternoon, after nap time, restlessness, tearfulness, whininess, or lassitude."[48] My own (equally subjective) evidence indicates otherwise: the symptoms Fraiberg describes are the ones I have seen in late afternoon

---

*In my own research I have found that when one-year-old babies were left alone with the stranger in the Ainsworth experiment ("strange situation"), the babies of working mothers who had had regular sitters related to and "used" the stranger to remain calm. Of the babies in exclusive-mother care, most showed stranger anxiety and became upset when left by mother with the stranger. All babies were upset when left completely alone, as expected.

tours of households in which babies and toddlers were in the sole care of their (good enough) mothers; and they are much worse in winter when mother has been tending to a small infant since 6 A.M. In daycare centers known to *me,* at the end of the day children still concentrate when listening to stories or coloring, play actively outdoors, and get a new burst of enthusiasm when the parent appears. What happens at that moment of reunion—and here I absolutely agree about the importance of primary attachment—makes all the difference.

Although Fraiberg does not flatly equate daycare with abandonment, the Bergers are not so careful. They actually go so far as to quote Bowlby's research findings (that infants left alone in hospitals become apathetic and dejected) as proof of the damage done by daycare. "The setting was a hospital but the same results would apply to any facility," claim the Bergers.[49] This is an equation Bowlby explicitly rejected. Bowlby has stated unequivocally that daycare does not interfere with attachment to the parents; and the literature on attachment has long since disconfirmed his original theory that attachment devolves on only one person in favor of the idea of multiple attachment figures, as the Bergers must surely know.[50]

The pleas for exclusive mothering function as insulation against the frightening facts about what is in actuality happening to the increasing numbers of infants and young children whose parents must choose between poor daycare and poverty. There is no question that much childcare outside the home in this country is grossly inadequate. This is hardly surprising, since virtually no public resources go into providing it.[51] Neither is there any question that, ideally, working parents should be more available to their young children, and less burdened by conflicting demands. But it is not obvious why critics of daycare do not advocate the alterations in work organization that would accommodate parenting. Nor is it clear why those who concede that high-quality daycare does not damage and may even help children accept the fact that such care is available only to the privileged few. How would it look if a study of the school system, finding it wanting except for the private schools attended by the rich, suggested that the public schools be abandoned and all their students be educated at home? And what about the parents who would have to stay home and tutor them?

Although actual mothering and fathering would be more effective if our organization of work and childcare were improved, the *ideal* of the mother—the all-giving, self-contained haven—would be damaged by it. When the ideal of the self-contained mother clashes with external reality, the defenders of gender polarity will inevitably rush to protect the ideal. As the conditions of mothering become more difficult and the sense of living in a dangerous world increases, the need for the ideal of motherhood becomes more acute. As is so often the case, the symbolic invocation of an ideal and what threatens it mobilizes more political energy than the appeal for concrete social reform. Here we see the truly dangerous consequences of regressive reenchantment. When antiabortionists invoke the image of the fetus being torn from the womb and left to die, or the image of the maternal body being violated, this mobilizes mass passion.[52] The practical demand for a system of prenatal care that would lower the high infant-mortality rate in the United States has not, because it is not "enchanted," is not linked to a powerful chain of symbolic images. The real problems that endanger mothers and children—inadequate daycare, unavailable medical care, lack of maternity leave and flexible work time—hide behind the ideal of motherhood, the vision of a self-sufficient family guarded by an omnicompetent angel of the house.

What can our psychoanalytic perspective tell us about the power of this ideal, a power that overcomes concrete needs and empirical facts? How can we understand the extreme passion that is aroused by the specter of mothers leaving their helpless infants in the care of others (a practice once typical in most families that could afford servants)? What fantasy about separation is at work?

One element of this fantasy is the notion that the infant is infinitely fragile in his dependency and insatiable in his need. Thus Lasch: "It is because the biological need for nourishment is suffused with desire that the infant's greed is insatiable; even the temporary absence of the mother gives rise to frustration and to feelings of rage."[53] Now there is no evidence that the infant is insatiable—although his needs may exceed what one person who has been awake half the night feels happy providing in a given day. Nor does his "desire" (which, as we have seen in chapter 3, develops later, along with symbolic representation and the sense of subjectivity) devolve on only one person. Furthermore, the image of maternal absence Lasch evokes is abstract and fantastic: does he mean an infant left alone in the crib to cry or an infant left in the care of a familiar adult who is holding and entertaining him?

Ordinary experiences of separation and reunion, anger and resolution, go with the territory of infancy and childhood; working these experiences through is vastly more productive than never experiencing them at all. Obviously these experiences are quite different from being neglected, abandoned, or treated with consistent indifference. Yet many people at quite different points along the sexual-political spectrum—including many a guilty mother—are stirred by the conviction that separation is destructive, infantile wrath swift and dangerous. But there is a distortion in perception here. This is the stuff that the idealized image of motherhood, "the fantasy of the perfect mother,"[54] is made of.

Let us consider once again the relationship between real separation (the experience of someone leaving) and mental separation (the internal conviction that someone is outside the self). When someone who is not felt to be outside the self leaves, one may feel hopelessly alone and yet enmeshed with an undependable, abandoning object who keeps everyone else away. If the child feels unable to contain or express the anger at being left, anger threatens to destroy the object. This is so frightening to the child that the object must be protected at all costs ("Mother is wonderful, I would never be angry at *her*"). If the child cannot get angry about his mother's leaving, or about any other frustration, he never enjoys the positive experience of destruction that Winnicott describes: "that he has destroyed everyone and everything, and yet the people around him remain calm and unhurt." As a result, he continues to experience the object as inside; he does not learn that "what he feels to be true is not necessarily real, that fantasy and fact, both important, are nevertheless different from each other."[55]

This distinction between inner and outer reality—the result of successful destruction—is crucial to perceiving the other as a separate person who does not need to be perfect or ideal to satisfy you. It is also crucial to reducing the fear of a retaliatory object who embodies one's own omnipotent aggression. A successful experience with the real vitiates the need for the ideal—the ideal may still have allure, but it is no longer such a vital protection against loss or attack.[56]

Separation—whether really leaving or simply asserting one's own will—is often interpreted as a hostile act, by both parties. Both must manage not only separation, but the associated aggression. As we have seen, the inability to survive separation and aggression keeps mother and child locked in the field of omnipotence. The child misses not only the encounter with mother's independent subjectivity (she goes away), but also the opportunity to work through the pain of that encounter, turn it into an *internal* emotional reality ("I am sad and angry; I've destroyed her; I've lost her") that can be distinguished with relief from the *external* reality ("She has returned; she accepts my grief and loves me still; she is not destroyed"). Similarly, when the mother fears that her act of leaving will destroy her child, she does not see him as separate. Consciously, her child is perfect (as her own mother was) and no sacrifice is too great; unconsciously, he is powerful and destructive (as she was, when she wanted to separate or when she denied her mother's independence). Neither she nor her child could tolerate the disillusionment of knowing that she exists independently of him. Mother and child must cooperate in the fantasy that he is the center of her life.*

At the source of the ideal of motherhood is the belief in maternal omnipotence which, as we have seen in the oedipal model, legitimates

---

*Freud himself was not free of this idealization, expressing repeatedly the certainty that a woman's greatest love is for her first-born son, that the son gets the love the husband hoped for, and so forth.[57]

male domination. The idea that mother is or should be all-giving and perfect (just a kiss away from all-controlling) expresses the mentality of omnipotence, the inability to experience the mother as an independently existing subject. This idealization testifies to the failure of destruction; hate has not been able to come forth and make the experience of love less idealized and more authentic. It is a maxim of psychoanalysis that idealization is a defense against aggression and so emerges when hate cannot be integrated with love; this failure of integration is the essential element in splitting. What determines whether hatred becomes the destruction that dispels idealization or, instead, goes inside where it requires idealization as a defense is, finally, *what happens in real life.* The child can only perceive the mother as a subject in her own right if the mother *is* one. And here we must be clear that the mother's subjectivity (in contrast to the maternal ideal) must include imperfection to be real, to her and her child; real subjectivity does not require her to be self-sufficient, perfect, and omni-competent. Yet this ideal of self-sufficiency commonly goes unquestioned, as it did for the mother who, when asked what care and support *mothers* need, could not understand the question and finally replied, "Someone taking care of *me? . . . I'm* the mother, *I'm* the one, I take care of *him!"*

The fantasy of the omnipotent mother is the result of psychic splitting, replicated at many levels of cultural and social experience. We can imagine a cycle something like this: The negation of the mother's independent subjectivity in social and cultural life makes it harder for her to survive her child's psychic destruction and become real to him. Since the child has not been able to engage in successful destruction, he is less able to distinguish the real person from the fantasy. The larger cultural reality then reinforces his fantasy that women's subjectivity is nonexistent or dangerous. And so on.

The symbolic structure of gender polarity produces the fantastic ideal of motherhood even as it stimulates the fear of destroying all maternal goodness. On the social level, male rationality sabotages maternal recognition, while on the psychic level, the oedipal repudiation of the mother splits her into the debased and the idealized objects. The reparation for debasing her takes the form of sentimentalizing and idealizing the mother, a strategy that locks both men and women into an inner fantasy world and evades the real issue: recognition of each other.

The dynamic which first undermines the mother concretely and then attempts to repair her through symbolic reenchantment gives rise to two ideal figures: the perfect mother and the autonomous individual, bound in a relationship of of domination. The more the individual repudiates the mother, the more he is threatened by his own destructiveness and her all-powerful weakness or retaliation. The more the subject splits off his dependency, the more his unconscious dependency increases and internally threatens his sense of independence. The self's aspiration to be absolute destroys the self, as well as the other, for as long as the other cannot face the self as an equal in the struggle, the battle results in loss, and not mutual recognition. The ideal mother is the after-image of the true lost other, who can return only when she ceases to be split off from the autonomous individual.

We have seen how the universal structures of individuality and rationality in our culture are gendered and represent a basic split between subject and object. We have seen how this rationality expresses masculinity and suppresses femininity, and how the increasing hegemony of rationality leads to a paradoxical reaction: the attempt to reenchant the world by appealing to the same gender splitting that gives disenchantment its character.

This strategy is not only appealing to gender conservatives, but also to feminists, who, in the effort to unveil the neutral discourse and reveal its gender often forget that this neutrality is precisely where male domination is located. They are mystified by the fact that the underlying structure of male domination is so depersonalized and has so little, apparently, to do with individual men. Thus many feminists have turned to the movement against pornography which repersonalizes domination by focusing on men's sexual violence. Presenting woman as pure victim and man as pure destroyer, the anti-pornography movement sees male violence as the basis of male power—and the essence of heterosexuality. As Andrea Dworkin insists, "The process of killing . . . is the prime sexual act for men in reality and/or imagination."[58] Similarly, women's subordination, heterosexuality, and gender identity, are all defined by sexual violation. In the words of the movement's main theorist, Catherine MacKinnon, "To be about to be raped is to be gender female in the process of going about life as usual."[59] It is probably no accident that MacKinnon's main project as a lawyer is to expose the violence and domination that are protected by formal legal principles of equality and justice. But her analysis of these principles misses the point that impersonal legal structures are not merely a cover for male violence, that they themselves express the primary course of gender domination.

It is difficult to grasp the fact that the center of male domination lies not in direct expressions of personal violence (rampant though they are) but in the societal rationality which may or may not be defended by men. Male domination, as Weber said of rationalization, works through the hegemony of impersonal organization: of formal rules that refer to the hypothetical interaction of autonomous individuals; of instrumental knowledge founded in the subject's control of the object world; of the accumulation of profit, which bows neither to need nor tradition. It is this protean impersonality that makes it so elusive.

Societal rationalization has a paradoxical tendency to neutralize gender difference and yet to intensify the dichotomies that are rooted in it. The terms of the dichotomy are often neutral, abstracted from gender; yet they can be regendered at any moment. The polarity of subject and object is the enduring skeletal frame of domination, ready to be fleshed out with manifest gender content when the situation demands. This is especially true of the distinction between public and private: at one moment it is ostensibly about "work" and "family," at another, clearly about men and women. Thus we are often confused by the way that gender difference "floats" in social reality, inconstant but never truly eliminated. As we have seen, this inconstancy is exacerbated by the fact that the dichotomous structure informs both individual psychic representations and collective cultural representations.

The pervasive effects of gender polarity demand a radical extension of the feminist critique—beyond the critiques of the family, the images of mother and father, or patriarchy. The proposal for dual parenting exemplifies both the virtues and the limitations of the psychoanalytic feminist approach. Chodorow and Dinnerstein conclude from their analysis of female mothering that if both men and women raised children, both would become associated with primary oneness. Presumably, then, the child could not resolve the ambivalence toward the earliest parent by splitting the two parents. This would mean that males would no longer have to break that bond in order to identify with their own sex, and thus they would not have to repudiate and denigrate the maternal. They would retain the value of nurturance and empathy, and this might begin to dissolve the rationality that supports the masculine side and determines all the major binary oppositions: public and private, universal and particular, rational and empathic, subject and object.

But the reorganization of parenting in individual families cannot wholly eliminate the effects of binary opposition—though it can mute the splitting that underlies it, weaken the conviction that it is a function of gender, and sequester it in fantasy. The core feature of the gender system—promoting masculinity as separation from and femininity as continuity with the primary bond—is maintained even when mother and father participate equally in that bond. For example, the father's primary care of the infant does not detract from the boy's readiness to identify with the standard cultural representations of masculinity and to locate his fantasy play "outside" the parent-infant relationship, not with dolls but with space ships. This may occur because parents are not only objects of identification; they actively, albeit unconsciously, shape the child's identity in accordance with the culture—continuity in girls, discontinuity in boys. At times it even seems that regardless of what real parents do, the cultural dualisms sustain the splitting of gender and recreate parental images as polar opposites. Chodorow grants that the reorganization of parenting alone would not break up the gender polarity; and she points out that this reorganization could not occur without vaster changes that would challenge other aspects of rationalization—above all, the relation between public and private. But this still casts the problem in terms of the relationship between family and social organization. In my view it is equally important to grasp the deep structure of gender as a binary opposition which is common to psychic and cultural representations.[60]

This opposition, which at the psychic level is called splitting, has its analogue in many other levels of experience, and is the pattern for every form of domination. As we have repeatedly seen, domination ultimately deprives both subjugator and subjugated of recognition. Gender polarity deprives women of their subjectivity and men of an other to recognize them. But the loss of recognition between men and women as equal subjects is only one consequence of gender domination. The ascendancy of male rationality results finally in the loss and distortion of recognition in society as a whole. It not only eliminates the maternal aspects of recognition (nurturance and empathy) from our collective values, actions, and institutions. It also restricts the exercise of assertion, making social authorship and agency a matter of performance, control, and impersonality—and thus vitiates subjectivity itself. In creating an increasingly objectified world, it deprives us of the intersubjective context in which assertion receives a recognizing response. We must face the enormity of this loss if we are ever to find our way back through the maze of domination to the heart of recognition.

CHAPTER SIX

Conclusion

DOMINATION, I HAVE argued, is a twisting of the bonds of love. Domination does not repress the desire for recognition; rather, it enlists and transforms it. Beginning in the breakdown of the tension between self and other, domination proceeds through the alternate paths of identifying with or submitting to powerful others who personify the fantasy of omnipotence. For the person who takes this route to establishing his own power, there is an absence where the other should be.

This void is filled with fantasy material in which the other appears so dangerous or so weak—or both—that he threatens the self and must be controlled. A vicious cycle begins: the more the other is subjugated, the less he is experienced as a human subject and the more distance or violence the self must deploy against him. The ensuing absence of recognition, indeed of an outside world, breeds more of the same. What has always been assumed but not explicated is this psychological destruction of the other which is the condition of any particular fantasy of domination.

The role of "the other," which for so many is their only moral refuge and political hope, is no less complicated. The subjugated, whose acts and integrity are granted no recognition, may, even in the very act of emancipation, remain in love with the ideal of power that has been denied to them. Though they may reject the master's right to dominion over them, they nevertheless do not reject his personification of power. They simply reverse the terms and claim his rights as theirs.

This cycle of reproducing the idealized authority even in the act of liberation is the cycle Freud described in the father-son struggle. Conceived in terms of two selves who both wish to be absolute, the father-son struggle does not allow for the recognition of someone outside the self, since the son is constantly taking the father inside himself, trying to become him. The father-son relationship, like the master-slave relationship, is a model in which the opposition between self and other can only reverse—one is always up and the other down, one is doer and the other done-to.

This reversible complementarity is the basic pattern of domination, and it is set in motion by the denial of recognition to the original other, the mother who is reduced to object. The resulting structure of subject and object (gender polarity) thoroughly permeates our social relations, our ways of knowing, our efforts to transform and control the world; and it is this gendered logic which ultimately forecloses on the intersubjective realm—that space in which the mutual recognition of subjects can compete with the reversible relationship of domination.

The denial of subjectivity to women means that the privilege and power of agency fall to the father, who enters the stage as the first outsider, and so represents the principle of freedom as denial of dependency. Ironically, then, the ideal of freedom carries within it the seeds of domination—freedom *means* fleeing or subjugating the other; autonomy means an escape from dependency. The ideal of individual power and freedom is all the more seductive once the breakdown of mutual recognition has locked the self in the vacuum of zero tension.

To halt this cycle of domination, I have argued, the other must make a difference. This means that women must claim their subjectivity and so be able to survive destruction. They may thus offer men a new possibility of colliding with the outside and becoming alive in the presence of an equal other. The conception of equal subjects has begun to seem intellectually plausible only because women's demand for equality has achieved real social force. This material change makes the intersubjective vision appear as more than a utopian abstraction; it makes it seem a legitimate opponent of the traditional logic of subject and object. The vision of recognition between equal subjects gives rise to a new logic—the logic of paradox, of sustaining the tension between contradictory forces. Perhaps the most fateful paradox is the one posed by our simultaneous need for recognition and independence: that the other subject is outside our control and yet we need him. To embrace this paradox is the first step toward unraveling the bonds of love. This means not to undo our ties to others but rather to disentangle them; to make of them not shackles but circuits of recognition.

Even in theory, of course, this is not a simple proposition. The basic tension between self and other which intersubjective theory illuminates is only one side of the story. The intersubjective model of self and other is abstracted from the web of intrapsychic life, which has stamped the history of the individual and the culture with its symbols and fantasies, its drama of subject and object. I have condensed the intrapsychic side of the story as the splitting of tension into complementary forms: subject and object, idealization and repudiation, good and bad, doer and done-to. But my point is that it is crucial to respect the different realities that intersubjective and intrapsychic theory describe, and not to see one as epiphenomenal and the other as essential. To assert the possibility of mutual recognition is not to suggest that in an ideal world recognition would never falter, and the tension between and within individuals would never break down. Such ideal constructions do not help us to understand the subtle way by which what we most desire may alternatively enthrall or liberate us.

The close kinship of thralldom and liberation, their common roots, requires us to recognize the doubleness of psychological reality. Thus beginning with the first relationship—of parent and child—we note the uneasy coexistence of contradictory tendencies: mutual recognition and unequal complementarity. We observe how complementarity subsumes mutuality in erotic domination, where the idea of a powerful person acting on a powerless one inspires the thrill of transgression. Again, beginning with the infant's struggle to individuate, we see how readily the reaction against dependency can turn into ideal love of paternal power. This process of defensive idealization marks the entry into a gendered reality. To be sure, the idealization of the early figures who raise us is to some extent inevitable. It is one pathway of the desire for recognition, a welcome escape at just the moment when the child's awareness of opposition between self and other brings the fall from grace: the confrontation with difference.

What is not inevitable is that this confrontation will be resolved only by splitting, and that this splitting will be conventionalized as gender opposition. It is not inevitable that the knowledge of difference be reduced to the complementarity of male and female—a parallel to the split between subject and object, good and bad, doer and done-to. It is this complementarity which, even as it appears to idealize sexual difference, recasts the knowledge of difference as invidious comparison. As we have seen, the spurious embrace of difference only defines the other in mirror opposition to the self. It thus precludes the necessity of dealing with the contradictory tendencies within the self. This escape from the knowledge of self is what constitutes temptation in the struggle to deal with the complexity of life outside the garden.

It is possible to resist this temptation; it is possible to analyze the psychic processes that foster splitting and underlie domination without casting them as unambiguously good or evil, or equating them with masculine and feminine attributes. Feminism has by no means transcended this temptation. But because feminist theory necessarily addresses the psychological bond between the powerful and the powerless, it has begun to question the logic of splitting—with its dualism, polarization, and simple reversal of roles. My purpose in putting forth an intersubjective theory is not to engage in such a reversal: I do not posit an original pure culture of intersubjectivity, a feminine realm corrupted by the culture of phallic symbolization and paternal idealization. Such a scheme of feminine innocence and phallic evil would only restore the old gender opposition; it would simply repeat the strategy of the opponents of instinct theory, which reversed the model of original evil controlled by culture in favor of a model of original goodness distorted by culture. It is important to be cautious of falling into such a reactive position—this caveat applies even in proposing that certain psychic processes underlie the breakdown of tension into domination. After all, breakdown of tension is as much a part of life as recreating it once more. The logic of paradox includes the acknowledgment that breakdown occurs. A sufficient ground for optimism is the contention that if breakdown is "built into" the psychic system, so is the possibility of renewing tension. If the denial of recognition does not become frozen into unmovable relationships, the play of power need not be hardened into domination. As the practice of psychoanalysis reveals, breakdown and renewal are constant possibilities: the crucial issue is finding the point at which breakdown occurs and the point at which it is possible to recreate tension and restore the condition of recognition.

My conclusion is both modest and utopian. The renewal of mutual recognition in the wake of its breakdown is not a final, redemptive "end of prehistory"; rather, it is a necessary part of the continuing process of individual and social change. To aspire to this renewal is to accept the inevitable inconstancy and imperfection of our efforts, without relinquishing the project. Feminism, though many think the contrary, has opened up a new possibility of mutual recognition between men and women. It has allowed men and women to begin confronting the difficulties of recognizing an other, and to expose the painful longing for what lies on the other side of these difficulties. To attempt to recover recognition in personal life does not mean to politicize personal life relentlessly or to evade politics and give up the hope of transformation—though all these failures do happen in real life. It means to see that the personal and social are interconnected, and to understand that if we suffocate our personal longings for recognition, we will suffocate our hope for social transformation as well.

BIBLIOGRAPHY

ABELIN, ERNEST. "Triangulation, the Role of the Father, and the Origins of Core Gender Identity During the Rapprochement Subphase." In R. F. Lax, S. Bach, and J. A. Burland, eds., *Rapprochement: The Critical Subphase of Separation-Individuation.* New York: Jason Aronson, 1980.

ADORNO, T. W. "Sociology and Psychology." *New Left Review,* 46, 47 (1967, 1968): 67–80, 79–91.

———. "Freudian Theory and the Pattern of Fascist Propaganda." In *Gesammelte Werke* vol. 8. Frankfurt: Suhrkamp, 1972.

ADORNO, T. W., ELSE FRENKEL-BRUNSWIK, DANIEL J. LEVINSON, and R. NEVITT SANFORD. *The Authoritarian Personality*. New York: Harper and Row, 1950.

AINSWORTH, M. D. S. "Object Relations, Dependency, and Attachment: A Theoretical Overview of the Infant-Mother Relationship." *Child Development* 40 (1969): 969–1025.

AINSWORTH, M. D. S., and S. BELL. "Attachment, Exploration, and Separation Illustrated by the Behavior of One-Year-Olds in a Strange Situation." *Child Development* 41 (1970): 49–67.

————. "Mother-Infant Interaction and the Development of Competence." In K. J. Connolly and J. Bruner, eds., *The Growth of Competence*. London and New York: Academic Press, 1974.

ALPERT, JUDITH, and JODY BOGHOSSIAN SPENCER. "Morality, Gender, and Analysis." In J. Alpert, ed., *Psychoanalysis and Women: Contemporary Reappraisals*. Hillsdale, N.J.: The Analytic Press, 1986.

BACH, SHELDON. "Self-Love and Object-Love: Some Problems of Self- and Object-Constancy, Differentiation and Integration." In R. F. Lax, S. Bach, and J. A. Burland, eds., *Rapprochement: The Critical Subphase of Separation-Individuation*. New York: Jason Aronson, 1980.

BAHRICK, LORRAINE, and JOHN WATSON. "Detection of Intermodal and Proprioceptive Visual Contingency as a Basis of Self-Perception in Infancy." *Developmental Psychology* 21 (1985): 963–73.

BALINT, MICHAEL. *The Basic Fault*. London: Tavistock Publications, 1968.

BALMARY, MARIE. *Psychoanalyzing Psychoanalysis: Freud and the Hidden Fault of the Father*. Baltimore: Johns Hopkins University Press, 1982.

BARRET, MICHELE, and MARY MCINTOSH. *The Anti-Social Family*. London: Verso/New Left Books, 1982.

BASSIN, DONNA. "Women's Images of Inner Space: Data Toward Expanded Interpretive Categories." *International Review of Psycho-analysis* 9 (1982): 200.

BATAILLE, GEORGES. *Death and Sensuality*. New York: Walker and Company, 1962.

————. "Hemingway in the Light of Hegel." *Semiotext[e]* 2, No. 2 (1976): 12–22.

BEAUVOIR, SIMONE DE. *The Second Sex*. New York: Knopf, 1952.

BEEBE, BEATRICE. "Mother-Infant Mutual Influence and Precursors of Self and Object Representations." In J. Masling, ed., *Empirical Studies of Psychoanalytic Theories,* vol. 2. Hillsdale, N.J.: Lawrence Erlbaum, 1985.

BEEBE, BEATRICE, and DANIEL STERN. "Engagement-Disengagement and Early

Object Experiences." In N. Freedman and S. Frand, eds., *Communicative Structures and Psychic Structures.* New York: Plenum Press, 1977.

BEEBE, BEATRICE, DANIEL STERN, and JOSEPH JAFFE. "The Kinesic Rhythm of Mother-Infant Interactions." In A. W. Siegman and S. Felstein, eds., *Of Speech and Time: Temporal Patterns in Interpersonal Contexts.* Hillsdale, N.J.: Lawrence Erlbaum, 1979.

BELL, R. Q. "The Contribution of Human Infants to Caregiving and Social Interaction." In Lewis and Rosenblum, eds., *The Effect of the Infant on Its Caregiver.* New York: John Wiley, 1974.

BELLAH, ROBERT, RICHARD MADSEN, WILLIAM SULLIVAN, ANN SWIDLER, and STEVEN TIPTON. *Habits of the Heart.* Berkeley: University of California Press, 1985.

BENHABIB, SEYLA, and DRUSILLA CORNELL, eds. *Feminism as Critique.* Minneapolis: University of Minnesota Press, 1987.

BENJAMIN, JESSICA. "The End of Internalization: Adorno's Social Psychology." *Telos* 32 (1977): 42–64.

————. "Authority and the Family Revisited; or, A World Without Fathers?" *New German Critique* 13 (1978): 35–58.

————. "The Alienation of Desire: Women's Masochism and Ideal Love." In Judith Alpert, ed., *Psychoanalysis and Women: Contemporary Reappraisals.* Hillsdale, N.J.: The Analytic Press, 1986.

BERGER, BRIGITTE and PETER. *The War over the Family: Capturing the Middle Ground.* Garden City, N.Y.: Anchor Books, 1983.

BERNARD, JESSIE. *The Future of Motherhood.* New York: Penguin Books, 1974.

BERNHEIMER, CHARLES, and CLAIRE KAHANE, eds. *In Dora's Case: Freud-Hysteria-Feminism.* New York: Columbia University Press, 1985.

BERNSTEIN, DORIS. "The Female Superego: A Different Perspective." *International Journal of Psycho-analysis* 64 (1983): 187–202.

BERSANI, LEO. *Baudelaire and Freud.* Berkeley: University of California Press, 1977.

BLOS, PETER. "The Genealogy of the Ego Ideal." *Psychoanalytic Study of the Child* 29 (1974): 43–88.

BLUM, HAROLD. "Masochism, the Ego Ideal, and the Psychology of Women." In Harold Blum, ed., *Female Psychology.* New York: International Universities Press, 1977.

BONAPARTE, MARIE. *Female Sexuality.* New York: International Universities Press, 1953.

BOTT, ELIZABETH. *Families and Social Networks: Roles, Norms and External Relationships in Ordinary Urban Families.* New York: Free Press, 1957.

BOWLBY, JOHN. *Maternal Care and Mental Health.* (1951) New York: Schocken, 1966.

————. "The Nature of the Child's Tie to His Mother." *International Journal of Psycho-analysis* 39 (1958): 350–73.

————. *Attachment.* London: Penguin Books, 1971.

BRAZELTON, T. B. "Neonatal Assessment." In S. I. Greenspan and G. H. Pollock, eds., *The Course of Life: Psychoanalytic Contributions Toward Understanding Personality Development.* Vol. 1. *Infancy and Early Childhood.* Rockville, Md.: NIMH, 1980.

BRAZELTON, T. B., B. KOSLOWSKI, and M. MAIN. "The Origins of Reciprocity." In M. Lewis and L. Rosenblum, eds., *The Effect of the Infant on Its Caregiver.* New York: Wiley, 1974.

BROWN, N. O. *Life Against Death.* Middletown, Conn.: Wesleyan University Press, 1959.

CALIFIA, PAT. "Jessie." In *Coming to Power; Writings and Graphics on Lesbian S/M.* Boston: Samois, 1982.

CAPLAN, PAULA. "The Myth of Woman's Masochism." *The American Psychologist* 39 (1984): 130–39.

CARPENTER, G. "Mother's Face and the Newborn." *New Scientist* 61 (1974): 742–46.

CHASSEGUET-SMIRGEL, JANINE. "Feminine Guilt and the Oedipus Complex." In Janine Chasseguet-Smirgel, ed., *Female Sexuality.* Ann Arbor: University of Michigan Press, 1970.

————. "Freud and Female Sexuality." *International Journal of Psycho-analysis* 57 (1976): 275–87.

————. "Some Thoughts on the Ego Ideal." *Psychoanalytic Quarterly* 45 (1976): 349–60.

————. "Reflections on the Connections between Perversion and Sadism." *International Journal of Psycho-analysis* 59 (1978): 27–35.

————. "Perversion and the Universal Law." *International Review of Psycho-analysis* 10 (1983): 293–301.

————. *The Ego Ideal: A Psychoanalytic Essay on the Malady of the Ideal.* New York: Norton, 1985.

————. *Sexuality and Mind.* New York: New York University Press, 1986.

CHASSEGUET-SMIRGEL, JANINE, ed. *Female Sexuality*. Ann Arbor: University of Michigan Press, 1970.

CHILDREN'S DEFENSE FUND. "U.S. Work Force in the Year 2000: A National Catastrophe in the Making." Washington, D.C., 1987.

CHODOROW, NANCY. *The Reproduction of Mothering: Psychoanalysis and the Sociology of Gender*. Berkeley: University of California Press, 1978.

―――. "Gender, Relation, and Difference in Psychoanalytic Perspective." In Hester Eisenstein and Alice Jardine, eds., *The Future of Difference*. Boston: G. K. Hall, 1980.

―――. "Beyond Drive Theory: Object Relations and the Limits of Radical Individualism." *Theory and Society* 14 (1985): 271–319.

CHODOROW, NANCY, and SUSAN CONTRATTO. "The Fantasy of the Perfect Mother." In Barrie Thorne, ed., *Rethinking the Family: Some Feminist Questions*. New York: Longman, 1982.

CLARKE-STEWART, ALISON. *Daycare*. Cambridge, Mass.: Harvard University Press, 1982.

CLOWER, V. L. "Theoretical Implications in Current Views of Masturbation in Latency Girls." In Harold Blum, ed., *Female Psychology*. New York: International Universities Press, 1977.

COOLEY, C. H. *Human Nature and the Social Order*. (1902) New York: Schocken, 1970.

CORBETT, KEN. "Illness, Variation, Liberation: Psychoanalytic Interpretations of Male Homosexual Development." Unpublished paper.

COTT, NANCY. *The Bonds of Womanhood: "Woman's Sphere" in New England, 1780–1835*. New Haven, Conn.: Yale University Press, 1977.

DECASPER, A., and W. FIFER. "Of Human Bonding: Newborns Prefer Their Mother's Voices." *Science* 208 (1980): 1174–76.

DEFORGES, REGINE. *Confessions of O: Conversations with Pauline Réage*, trans. S. d'Estree. New York: Viking, 1979.

DERI, SUSAN. "Transitional Phenomena: Vicissitudes of Symbolization and Creativity." In Simon Grolnick and Leonard Barkin, eds., *Between Reality and Fantasy*. New York: Jason Aronson, 1978.

DESCARTES, RENÉ. *Discourse on Method*. (1637) Harmondsworth, U.K.: Penguin Books, 1968.

DEUTSCH, HELENE. *The Psychology of Women*, vols. 1 & 2. New York: Grune and Stratton, 1944, 1945.

DEVEREUX, GEORGE. "Why Oedipus Killed Laius: A Note on the Complementary Oedipus Complex in Greek Drama." *International Journal of Psychoanalysis* 34 (1953): 132–41.

DIMEN, MURIEL. *Surviving Sexual Contradictions.* New York: Macmillan, 1986.

DINNERSTEIN, DOROTHY. *The Mermaid and the Minotaur.* New York: Harper and Row, 1976.

DONZELOT, JACQUES. *The Policing of Families.* New York: Pantheon, 1979.

DUBOIS, ELLEN, and LINDA GORDON. "Seeking Ecstasy on the Battlefield: Danger and Pleasure in Nineteenth-Century Feminist Sexual Thought." In Carol Vance, ed., *Pleasure and Danger: Exploring Female Sexuality.* Boston: Routledge and Kegan Paul, 1984.

DWORKIN, ANDREA. "Woman as Victim: *Story of O.*" *Feminist Studies* 2, No. 1 (1974): 107–11.

———. "Pornography and Grief." In Laura Lederer, ed., *Take Back the Night.* New York: William Morrow, 1980.

ECHOLS, ALICE. "The New Feminism of Yin and Yang." In Ann Snitow, Christine Stansell, and Sharon Thompson, eds., *Powers of Desire.* New York: Monthly Review Press, 1983.

EHRENREICH, BARBARA. *The Hearts of Men: American Dreams and the Flight from Commitment.* Garden City, N.Y.: Anchor Books, 1984.

EIGEN, MICHAEL. "The Area of Faith in Winnicott, Lacan and Bion." *International Journal of Psycho-analysis* 62 (1981): 413–33.

ELSHTAIN, JEAN BETHKE. *Public Man, Private Woman.* Princeton, N.J.: Princeton University Press, 1981.

———. "Feminism, Family, and Community." *Dissent* 29 (1982): 442–49.

EMDE, R. N., and J. E. SORCE. "The Rewards of Infancy: Emotional Availability and Maternal Referencing." In J. D. Call, E. Galenson, and R. Tyson, eds., *Frontiers of Infant Psychiatry,* vol. 2. New York: Basic Books, 1983.

ENGEL, STEPHANIE. "Femininity as Tragedy: Re-examining the New Narcissism." *Socialist Review* 53 (1980): 77–104.

ERIKSON, ERIK H. *Childhood and Society.* New York: Norton, 1950.

———. "Womanhood and the Inner Space." In *Identity, Youth and Crisis.* New York: Norton, 1968.

FAIRBAIRN, RONALD. *Psychoanalytic Studies of the Personality.* London: Routledge and Kegan Paul, 1952.

———. "Steps in the Development of an Object-Relations Theory of the Personality." In *Psychoanalytic Studies of the Personality.*

FARR, SUSAN. "The Art of Discipline." In *Coming to Power; Writings and Graphics on Lesbian S/M.* Boston: Samois, 1982.

FAST, IRENE. *Gender Identity: A Differentiation Model.* Hillsdale, N.J.: The Analytic Press, 1984.

FIEDLER, LESLIE. "Come Back to the Raft, Huck Honey." In *Love and Death in the American Novel.* New York: Stein and Day, 1966.

FIELD, TIFFANY. "Infant Gaze Aversion and Heart Rate During Face-to-Face Interactions." *Infant Behavior and Development* 4 (1981): 307–15.

FIRST, ELSA. "The Leaving Game: I'll Play You and You Play Me: The Emergence of the Capacity for Dramatic Role Play in Two-Year-Olds." In Arieta Slade and Denny Wolfe, eds., *Modes of Meaning: Clinical and Developmental Approaches to Symbolic Play.* New York: Oxford University Press, 1988.

FLAX, JANE. "Mother-Daughter Relationships: Psychodynamics, Politics and Philosophy." In Hester Eisenstein and Alice Jardine, eds., *The Future of Difference.* Boston: G. K. Hall, 1980.

FLIEGEL, ZENIA ODES. "Feminine Psychosexual Development in Freudian Theory: A Historical Reconstruction." *Psychoanalytic Quarterly* 42 (1973): 385–409.

———. "Women's Development in Analytic Theory: Six Decades of Controversy." In Judith Alpert, ed., *Psychoanalysis and Women: Contemporary Reappraisals.* Hillsdale, N.J.: The Analytic Press, 1986.

FOUCAULT, MICHEL. *The Archaeology of Knowledge and The Discourse on Language.* New York: Pantheon, 1972.

———. *History of Sexuality. Vol. 1. An Introduction.* New York: Pantheon, 1978.

———. *Power/Knowledge: Selected Interviews & Other Writings.* Ed., Colin Gordon. New York: Pantheon, 1980.

FRAIBERG, SELMA. *Every Child's Birthright: In Defense of Mothering.* New York: Basic Books, 1977.

FRANKFURT INSTITUTE FOR SOCIAL RESEARCH. *Aspects of Sociology.* Boston: Beacon Press, 1972.

FREEDMAN, NORBERT. "On Splitting and Its Resolution." *Psychoanalysis and Contemporary Thought* 3 (1980): 237–66.

FREUD, ANNA. *The Ego and Its Mechanisms of Defense.* (1936) New York: International Universities Press, 1954.

FREUD, SIGMUND. *The Interpretation of Dreams.* (1900) *The Standard Edition of the Complete Psychological Works* (hereafter SE), 4 and 5. London: Hogarth Press, 1953–.

————. *The Psychopathology of Everyday Life.* (1901) SE 6.

————. *Three Essays on the Theory of Sexuality.* (1905) SE 7: 125–245.

————. "Formulations on the Two Principles in Mental Functioning." (1911) SE 12: 213–26

————. "On Narcissism: An Introduction." (1914) SE 14: 67–102.

————. "Instincts and Their Vicissitudes." (1915) SE 14: 11–140.

————. "Mourning and Melancholia." (1917) SE 14: 239–58.

————. "A Child Is Being Beaten: A Contribution to the Origin of the Study of Sexual Perversions." (1919) SE 17: 175–204.

————. "The 'Uncanny.' " (1919) SE 17: 217–52.

————. *Beyond the Pleasure Principle.* (1920) SE 18: 7–64.

————. *Group Psychology and the Analysis of the Ego.* (1921) SE 18: 65–144.

————. *The Ego and the Id.* (1923) SE 19: 1–66.

————. "The Dissolution of the Oedipus Complex." (1924) SE 19: 173–82.

————. "The Economic Problem of Masochism." (1924) SE 19: 155–72.

————. "Some Psychical Consequences of the Anatomical Distinction Between the Sexes." (1925) SE 19: 243–58.

————. *Inhibitions, Symptoms and Anxiety.* (1926) SE 20: 75–176.

————. *The Future of an Illusion.* (1927) SE 21: 77–174.

————. *Civilization and Its Discontents.* (1930) SE 21: 57–146.

————. "Female Sexuality." (1931) SE 21: 223–43.

————. "Femininity." In *New Introductory Lectures on Psycho-Analysis.* (1933) SE 22: 3–182.

————. "Analysis Terminable and Interminable." (1937) SE 23: 211–53.

————. *An Outline of Psychoanalysis.* (1940) SE 23: 139–208.

————. "The Splitting of the Ego in the Process of Defence." (1940) SE 23: 271–78.

FROMM, ERICH. *Escape from Freedom.* (1941) New York: Discus Books, 1971.

GALENSON ELEANOR, and HERMAN ROIPHE. "Some Suggested Revisions Concerning Early Female Development." In Harold Blum, ed., *Female Psychology.* New York: International Universities Press, 1977.

————. "The Preoedipal Relationship of a Mother, Father, and Daughter." In S. H. Cath, A. R. Gurwitt, and J. M. Ross, eds., *Father and Child.* Boston: Little, Brown, 1982.

————. *The Daughter's Seduction: Feminism and Psychoanalysis.* Ithaca, N.Y.: Cornell University Press, 1982.

————. *Reading Lacan.* Ithaca, N.Y.: Cornell University Press, 1985.

GARNER, SHIRLEY N., CLAIRE KAHANE, and MADELON SPRENGNETHER. *The (M)other Tongue*. Ithaca, N.Y.: Cornell University Press, 1985.

GHENT, EMMANUEL. "Masochism, Submission, and Surrender." Colloquium, New York University Postdoctoral Psychology Program, 1983.

———. "Credo: The Dialectics of One-Person and Two-Person Psychologies," Colloquium, New York University Postdoctoral Psychology Program, 1986.

GILLIGAN, CAROL. *In a Different Voice: Psychological Theory and Women's Development*. Cambridge, Mass.: Harvard University Press, 1982.

———. "On *In a Different Voice:* An Interdisciplinary Forum." *Signs* 11 (1986): 304–34.

———. "Remapping the Moral Domain: New Images of the Self in Relationship." In Thomas Heller, Morton Sosna, and David Wellbery, eds., *Reconstructing Individualism: Autonomy, Individuality, and the Self in Western Thought*. Stanford, Calif.: Stanford University Press, 1986.

GILLIGAN, CAROL, and EVE STERN. "The Riddle of Femininity and the Psychology of Love." Paper presented at the Seminar on the Psychology of Love, Douglass College, 1986.

GOLDBERG, S. "Social Competence in Infancy: A Model of Parent-Infant Interaction." *Merrill-Palmer Quarterly* 23 (1977): 163–77.

GORDON, LINDA. "Why Nineteenth-Century Feminists Did Not Support Birth Control and Twentieth-Century Feminists Do: Feminism, Reproduction, and the Family." In Barrie Thorne, ed., *Rethinking the Family: Some Feminist Questions*. New York: Longman, 1982.

GREEN, ANDRÉ. "The Analyst, Symbolization and Absence in the Analytic Setting." In *On Private Madness*. New York: International Universities Press, 1986.

———. "Potential Space in Psychoanalysis: The Object in the Setting." In *On Private Madness*. New York: International Universities Press, 1986.

GREENBERG, JAY, and STEPHEN MITCHELL. *Object Relations in Psychoanalytic Theory*. Cambridge, Mass.: Harvard University Press, 1983.

GREENSON, RALPH. "Dis-identifying from Mother: Its Special Importance for the Boy." *International Journal of Psycho-analysis* 49 (1968): 370–74.

GRIFFIN, SUSAN. *Woman and Nature*. New York: Harper and Row, 1978.

———. *Pornography and Silence: Culture's Revenge Against Nature*. New York: Harper and Row, 1981.

GRUNBERGER, BELA. *Narcissism*. New York: International Universities Press, 1979.

GUNSBERG, LINDA. "Selected Critical Review of Psychological Investigations of the Early Father-Infant Relationship." In S. H. Cath, A. R. Gurwitt, and J. M. Ross, eds., *Father and Child*. Boston: Little, Brown, 1982.

GUNTRIP, HARRY. *Personality Structure and Human Interaction*. New York: International Universities Press, 1961.

HABERMAS, JÜRGEN. "A Theory of Communicative Competence." In H. P. Dreitzel, ed., *Recent Sociology* no. 2. New York: Macmillan, 1970.

————. *Knowledge and Human Interests*. Boston: Beacon Press, 1971.

————. "Technology and Science as Ideology." In *Toward a Rational Society*. Boston: Beacon Press, 1971.

————. "Moral Development and Ego Identity." In *Communication and the Evolution of Society*. Boston: Beacon Press, 1979.

HARDING, SANDRA, and MERYL HINTIKKA, eds. *Discovering Reality: Feminist Perspectives on Epistemology, Metaphysics, Methodology, and the Philosophy of Science*. Boston: Reidel, 1983.

HARRIS, ADRIENNE. "The Rationalization of Infancy." In John Broughton, ed., *Critical Theories of Psychological Development*. New York: Plenum Press, 1987.

HARRIS, ELIZABETH. "Sadomasochism: A Personal Experience." In R. Linden, D. Pagano, D. Russell, and S. Star, eds., *Against Sadomasochism*. Palo Alto, Calif.: Frog in the Well, 1982.

HARTMANN, HEINZ. *Ego Psychology and the Problem of Adaptation*. (1939) New York: International Universities Press, 1958.

HEGEL, G. W. F. *Phänomenologie des Geistes*. Hamburg: Felix Meiner Verlag, edition of 1952.

HINES, PAULETTE MOORE, and NANCY BOYD-FRANKLIN. "Black Families." In M. McGoldrick, J. Pearce, and J. Giardano, eds., *Ethnicity and Family Therapy*. New York: Guilford, 1982.

HONEY, MARGARET, and BROUGHTON, JOHN. "Feminine Sexuality: An Interview with Janine Chasseguet-Smirgel." *Psychoanalytic Review* 72 (1985): 527–48.

HORKHEIMER, MAX. "Authority and the Family" (originally in *Studien über Autorität und Familie*, Paris: Felix Alcan, 1936). In *Critical Theory*. New York: Seabury Press, 1972.

————. "Authority and the Family Today." In Ruth Anshen, ed., *The Family: Its Function and Destiny*. New York: Harper and Row, 1949.

————. "Traditional and Critical Theory." In *Critical Theory*. New York: Seabury Press, 1972.

HORKHEIMER, MAX, and T. W. ADORNO. *Dialectic of Enlightenment.* (1947) New York: Seabury Press, 1972.

HORNEY, KAREN. "On the Genesis of the Castration Complex in Women." (1924) In *Feminine Psychology.* New York: Norton, 1967.

———. "The Flight from Womanhood." (1926) In *Feminine Psychology.*

———. "The Dread of Woman." (1932) In *Feminine Psychology.*

———. "The Denial of the Vagina." (1933) In *Feminine Psychology.*

———. "The Problem of Feminine Masochism." (1933) In *Feminine Psychology.*

IRIGARAY, LUCE. *Speculum of the Other Woman.* (1974) Ithaca, N.Y.: Cornell University Press, 1985.

———. "This Sex Which Is Not One." (1977) In *This Sex Which Is Not One.* Ithaca, N.Y.: Cornell University Press, 1985.

JACOBSON, EDITH. *The Self and the Object World.* New York: International Universities Press, 1964.

JACOBY, RUSSELL. *Social Amnesia.* Boston: Beacon Press, 1975.

JOHNSON, MIRIAM. "Fathers and 'Femininity' in Daughters: A Review of the Research." *Sociology and Social Research* 67 (1983): 1–17.

KAPLAN, LOUISE. "Symposium on *The Interpersonal World of the Infant.*" In *Contemporary Psychoanalysis* 23 (1987): 27–45.

KELLER, EVELYN. *A Feeling for the Organism: The Life and Work of Barbara McClintock.* San Francisco: W. H. Freeman, 1983.

———. *Reflections on Gender and Science.* New Haven, Conn.: Yale University Press, 1985.

———. "Making Gender Visible in the Pursuit of Nature's Secrets." In Teresa de Lauretis, ed., *Feminist Studies/ Critical Studies.* Bloomington: Indiana University Press, 1986.

KERNBERG, OTTO. *Borderline Conditions and Pathological Narcissism.* New York: Jason Aronson, 1975.

———. *Internal World and External Reality.* New York: Jason Aronson, 1980.

KESTENBERG, J., J. H. MARCUS, K. M. SOSSIN, and R. STEVENSON. "The Development of Paternal Attitudes." In S. H. Cath, A. R. Gurwitt, and J. M. Ross, eds., *Father and Child.* Boston: Little, Brown, 1982.

KHAN, MASUD. *Alienation in Perversions.* New York: International Universities Press, 1979.

KLEIN, MELANIE. *Envy and Gratitude.* New York: Basic Books, 1957.

KLINNERT, M. D., et al. "Emotions as Behavior Regulators: Social Referencing in Infancy." In R. Plutchik and H. Kellerman, eds., *Emotion: Theory, Research, and Experience,* no. 2. New York: Academic Press, 1983.

KOHLBERG, LAWRENCE. *The Philosophy of Moral Development.* San Francisco: Harper and Row, 1981.

———. "Reply to Owen Flanagan and Some Comments on the Puka-Goodpaster Exchange." *Ethics* 92 (1982): 513–28.

KOHLBERG, LAWRENCE, and R. KRAMER. "Continuities and Discontinuities in Childhood and Adult Moral Development." *Human Development* 12 (1969): 93–120.

KOHUT, HEINZ. *The Analysis of the Self.* New York: International Universities Press, 1971.

———. *The Restoration of the Self.* New York: International Universities Press, 1977.

KOVEL, JOEL, *The Age of Desire.* New York: Pantheon, 1982.

KRISTEVA, JULIA. "Women's Time." *Signs* 7 (1981): 13–35.

———. "About Chinese Women." In Toril Moi, ed., *The Kristeva Reader.* New York: Columbia University Press, 1986.

KUNDERA, MILAN. *The Unbearable Lightness of Being.* New York: Harper and Row, 1984.

LACAN, JACQUES. "The Mirror-Stage as Formative of the Function of the I." (1949) In *Ecrits, A Selection.* New York: Norton, 1977.

LAMB, MICHAEL. "The Development of Parental Preferences in the First Two Years of Life." *Sex Roles* 3 (1977): 495–97.

LAMPL–DE GROOT, JEANNE. "The Evolution of the Oedipus Complex in Women." (1927) In *The Development of the Mind.* London: Hogarth Press, 1966.

LAPLANCHE, J. *Life and Death in Psychoanalysis.* Baltimore: Johns Hopkins University Press, 1976.

LASCH, CHRISTOPHER. *Haven in a Heartless World: The Family Besieged.* New York: Basic Books, 1977.

———. *The Culture of Narcissism.* New York: Norton, 1979.

———. "The Freudian Left and the Cultural Revolution." *New Left Review* 129 (1981): 23–34.

———. *The Minimal Self: Psychic Survival in Troubled Times.* New York: Norton, 1984.

———. "Why the Left Has No Future." *Tikkun* 1 (1986): 92–94.

LAZARRE, JANE. *On Loving Men.* New York: Dial Press, 1980.

LEVENSON, RICKI. "Intimacy, Autonomy and Gender: Developmental Differences and their Reflection in Adult Relationships." *Journal of the American Academy of Psychoanalysis* 12 (1984): 529–44.

———. "Boundaries, Autonomy, and Aggression: An Exploration of Women's Difficulty with Logical and Abstract Thinking." In press.

LEWIS, M., and GOLDBERG, S. "Perceptual-Cognitive Development in Infancy: A Generalized Expectancy Model." *Merrill-Palmer Quarterly* 15 (1969): 81–100.

LEWIS, M., and ROSENBLUM, L., eds. *The Effect of the Infant on Its Caregiver.* New York: John Wiley, 1974.

LICHTENBERG, JOSEPH. *Psychoanalysis and Infant Research.* Hillsdale N.J.: The Analytic Press, 1983.

LOEWALD, HANS. "Ego and Reality." (1951) In *Papers on Psychoanalysis.* New Haven, Conn.: Yale University Press, 1980.

———. "The Therapeutic Action of Psychoanalysis." (1960) In *Papers on Psychoanalysis.*

———. "The Waning of the Oedipus Complex." (1979) In *Papers on Psychoanalysis.*

LUKACS, GEORG. *History and Class Consciousness.* (1918–30) Cambridge, Mass.: M.I.T. Press, 1971.

———. "The Antinomies of Bourgeois Thought." In *History and Class Consciousness.*

MACFARLANE, J. "Olfaction in the Development of Social Preferences in the Human Neonate." In M. Hofer, ed., *Parent-Infant Interaction.* Amsterdam: Elsevier, 1975.

MACKINNON, CATHERINE. *Feminism Unmodified: Discourses on Life and Law.* Cambridge, Mass.: Harvard University Press, 1987.

MAHLER, MARGARET, FRED PINE, and ANNI BERGMANN. *The Psychological Birth of the Human Infant.* New York: Basic Books, 1975.

MANNHEIM, KARL. *Man and Society in an Age of Reconstruction.* London: Routledge and Kegan Paul, 1940.

MARCUSE, HERBERT. "Philosophy and Critical Theory." (1934–38) In *Negations: Essays in Critical Theory.* Boston: Beacon Press, 1968.

———. *Eros and Civilization.* New York: Vintage Books, 1962.

———. "The Obsolescence of the Freudian Concept of Man." In *Five Lectures.* Boston: Beacon Press, 1970.

MARX, KARL. *Capital I.* New York: International Publishers, 1974.

MEADE, GEORGE HERBERT. *Mind, Self, and Society.* Chicago: University of Chicago Press, 1955.

MENAKER, ESTHER. *Masochism and the Emerging Ego.* New York: Human Sciences Press, 1973.

————. "Some Inner Conflicts of Women in a Changing Society." In A. Roland and B. Harris, eds., *Career and Motherhood.* New York: Human Sciences Press, 1979.

MILLER, JEAN BAKER. *Toward a New Psychology of Women.* Boston: Beacon Press, 1976.

————. "What Do We Mean by Relationships?" In *Works in Progress* of the Stone Center, Wellesley, Mass., 1987.

MILLER, NANCY. "Changing the Subject: Authorship, Writing and the Reader." In Teresa de Lauretis, ed., *Feminist Studies/Critical Studies.* Bloomington: Indiana University Press, 1986.

MILLET, KATE. *Sexual Politics.* New York: Avon Books, 1971.

MILNER, MARION. "D. W. Winnicott and the Two-Way Journey." In Simon Grolnick and Leonard Barkin, eds., *Between Reality and Fantasy.* New York: Jason Aronson, 1978.

MITCHELL, JULIET. *Psychoanalysis and Feminism.* New York: Pantheon, 1974.

————. "Introduction." In Juliet Mitchell and Jacqueline Rose, eds., *Feminine Sexuality: Jacques Lacan and L'École Freudienne.* New York: Norton, 1982.

MITSCHERLICH, ALEXANDER. *Society Without the Father.* New York: Harcourt, Brace, and World, 1970.

MODELL, ARNOLD. *Object Love and Reality.* New York: International Universities Press, 1968.

————. *Psychoanalysis in a New Context.* New York: International Universities Press, 1984.

MONEY, J. "Gender Role, Gender Identity, Core Gender Identity: Usage and Definition of Terms." *Journal of the American Academy of Psychoanalysis* 1 (1973): 397–402.

MONEY, J., and A. A. ERHARDT. *Man and Woman, Boy and Girl.* Baltimore: Johns Hopkins University Press, 1972.

MONTGRAIN, NOEL. "On the Vicissitudes of Female Sexuality: The Difficult Path from 'Anatomical Destiny' to Psychic Representation." *International Journal of Psycho-analysis* 64 (1983): 169–86.

MURPHY J. M., and C. GILLIGAN. "Moral Development in Late Adolescence and

Adulthood: A Critique and Reconstruction of Kohlberg's Theory." *Human Development* 23 (1980): 77–104.

OLESKER, WENDY. "Sex Differences in Two- and Three-Year-Olds." *Psychoanalytic Psychology* 1 (1982): 269–89.

OLINER, MARION. "The Anal Phase." In D. Mendell, ed., *Early Female Development*. New York: Spectrum, 1982.

PERSON, ETHEL. "Sexuality as the Mainstay of Identity." *Signs* 5 (1980): 605–30.

PERSON, ETHEL, and OVESEY, LIONEL. "Psychoanalytic Theories of Gender Identity." *Journal of the American Academy of Psychoanalysis* 11 (1983): 203–26.

PETCHESKY, ROSALIND. "Fetal Images: The Power of Visual Culture in the Politics of Reproduction." *Feminist Studies* 13 (1987): 263–93.

PETERFREUND, EMANUEL. "Some Critical Comments on Psychoanalytic Conceptualizations of Infancy." *International Journal of Psycho-analysis* 59 (1978): 427–41.

PIAGET, JEAN. *The Construction of Reality in the Child.* (1937) New York: Basic Books, 1954.

PIAGET, JEAN, and BARBEL INHELDER. *The Psychology of the Child.* New York: Basic Books, 1969.

PINE, FRED. "In the Beginning: Contributions to a Psychoanalytic Developmental Psychology." *International Review of Psycho-analysis* 8 (1981): 15–33.

PRUETT, KYLE. *The Nurturing Father.* New York: Warner Books, 1987.

RÉAGE, PAULINE. *Story of O.* New York: Grove Press, 1965.

REICH, ANNIE. "Pathological Forms of Self-Esteem Regulation." (1960) In *Psychoanalytic Contributions.* New York: International Universities Press, 1973.

REICH, WILHELM. *The Mass Psychology of Fascism.* (1933) New York: Simon and Schuster, 1970.

———. "The Imposition of Sexual Morality." In Lee Baxandall, ed., *Sex-Pol: Essays, 1929–1934.* New York: Vintage Books, 1972.

———. "What Is Class Consciousness?" In *Sex-Pol: Essays, 1929–1934.*

ROGOW, ARNOLD. *The Dying of the Light.* New York: Putnam, 1975.

ROIPHE, HERMAN, and ELEANOR GALENSON. *Infantile Origins of Sexual Identity.* New York: International Universities Press, 1981.

ROSALDO, MICHELE. "Women, Culture, and Society: A Theoretical Overview." In Michele Rosaldo and Louise Lamphere, eds., *Woman, Culture, and Society.* Stanford, Calif.: Stanford University Press, 1974.

ROSE, JACQUELINE. "Introduction." In Juliet Mitchell and Jacqueline Rose, eds., *Feminine Sexuality: Jacques Lacan and L'École Freudienne.* New York: Norton, 1982.

RUSTIN, MICHAEL. "A Socialist Consideration of Kleinian Psychoanalysis." *New Left Review* 131 (1982): 71–96.

RYAN, MARY. *Cradle of the Middle Class: The Family in Oneida County, New York, 1790–1865.* New York: Cambridge University Press, 1981.

SANDER, LOUIS. "Polarity, Paradox, and the Organizing Process in Development." In J. D. Call, E. Galenson, and R. L. Tyson, eds., *Frontiers of Infant Psychiatry,* no. 1. New York: Basic Books, 1983.

SCHACHTEL, ERNST. *Metamorphosis.* New York: Basic Books, 1959.

SCHAFER, ROY. *Aspects of Internalization.* New York: International Universities Press, 1968.

SCHAFFER, H. R. *The Growth of Sociability.* Harmondsworth, U.K.: Penguin Books, 1971.

————. *Mothering.* Cambridge, Mass.: Harvard University Press, 1977.

SCHAFFER, H. R., and P. E. EMERSON. "The Development of Social Attachments in Infancy." *Monograph of the Society for Research in Child Development* 29 (1964).

SENNETT, RICHARD. *The Fall of Public Man.* New York: Knopf, 1977.

————. *Authority.* New York: Knopf, 1980.

SHREVE, ANITA. "The Working Mother as Role Model." *The New York Times Magazine,* September 9, 1984.

SLATER, PHILIP. "Toward a Dualistic Theory of Identification." *Merrill-Palmer Quarterly* 7 (1961): 113–26.

SMIRNOFF, V. "The Masochistic Contract." *International Journal of Psychoanalysis* 50 (1969): 665–71.

SNITOW, ANN, CHRISTINE STANSELL, and SHARON THOMPSON, eds. *Powers of Desire: The Politics of Sexuality.* New York: Monthly Review Press, 1983.

SOBO, SIMON. "Narcissism as a Function of Culture." *The Psychoanalytic Study of the Child* 32 (1977): 155–74.

STACEY, JUDITH. "Are Feminists Afraid to Leave Home? The Challenge of Conservative Pro-family Feminism." In Juliet Mitchell and Ann Oakley, eds., *What Is Feminism? A Re-examination.* New York: Pantheon, 1986.

STACK, CAROL. *All Our Kin: Strategies for Survival in a Black Community.* New York: Harper and Row, 1975.

STECHLER, G. and S. KAPLAN. "The Development of the Self: A Psychoanalytic Perspective." *The Psychoanalytic Study of the Child* 35 (1980): 85–106.

STERN, DANIEL. "The Goal and Structure of Mother-Infant Play." *Journal of the American Academy of Child Psychiatry* 13 (1974): 402–21.

———. "A Microanalysis of Mother-Infant Interaction. Behaviors Regulating Social Contact between a Mother and Her Three-and-a-half-month-old Twins." *Journal of the American Academy of Child Psychiatry* 13 (1974): 501–17.

———. "Mother and Infant at Play: The Dyadic Interaction Involving Facial, Vocal and Gaze Behavior." In M. Lewis and L. Rosenblum, eds., *The Effect of the Infant on Its Caregiver.* New York: John Wiley, 1974.

———. *The First Relationship: Infant and Mother.* Cambridge, Mass.: Harvard University Press, 1977.

———. "The Early Development of Schemas of Self, of Other, and of Various Experiences of 'Self with Other.' " In J. Lichtenberg and S. Kaplan, eds., *Reflections on Self Psychology.* Hillsdale, N.J.: The Analytic Press, 1983.

———. *The Interpersonal World of the Infant: A View from Psychoanalysis and Developmental Psychology.* New York: Basic Books, 1985.

STERN, DANIEL, BEATRICE BEEBE, JOSEPH JAFFE, and STEPHEN BENNETT. "The Infant's Stimulus World During Social Interaction: A Study of Caregiver Behaviors with Particular Reference to Repetition and Timing." In H. R. Schaffer, ed., *Studies in Mother-Infant Interaction.* London: Academic Press, 1977.

STOLLER, ROBERT. *Sex and Gender.* New York: Jason Aronson, 1968.

———. "The 'Bedrock' of Masculinity and Femininity: Bisexuality." *Archives of General Psychiatry* 26 (1972): 207–12.

———. "Facts and Fancies: An Examination of Freud's Concept of Bisexuality." (1974) In Jean Strouse, ed., *Women and Analysis.* Boston: G. K. Hall, 1985.

———. *Perversion.* New York: Pantheon, 1975.

———. *Sexual Excitement.* New York: Simon and Schuster, 1980.

STOLOROW, ROBERT, and FRANK LACHMANN. *Psychoanalysis of Developmental Arrests.* New York: International Universities Press, 1980.

STONE CENTER, THE. *Works in Progress.* Wellesley, Mass., 1987.

SULLIVAN, HARRY STACK. *The Interpersonal Theory of Psychiatry.* New York: Norton, 1953.

THEWELEIT, KLAUS. *Male Fantasies,* vols. 1 and 2. Minneapolis: University of Minnesota Press, 1987, 1988.

TOLPIN, MARIE. "On the Beginnings of the Cohesive Self." *The Psychoanalytic Study of the Child* 34 (1971): 316–52.

TOROK, MARIA. "The Significance of Penis Envy in Women." In Janine Chasseguet-Smirgel, ed., *Female Sexuality.* Ann Arbor: University of Michigan Press, 1970.

TREVARTHEN, COLIN. "Descriptive Analyses of Infant Communicative Behavior." In H. R. Schaffer, ed., *Studies in Mother-Infant Interaction.* London: Academic Press, 1977.

———. "Communication and Cooperation in Early Infancy: A Description of Primary Intersubjectivity." In M. Bullowa, ed., *Before Speech: The Beginning of Interpersonal Communication.* New York: Cambridge University Press, 1980.

———. "The Foundations of Intersubjectivity: Development of Interpersonal and Cooperative Understanding in Infants." In D. R. Olson, ed., *The Social Foundation of Language and Thought: Essays in Honor of Jerome Bruner.* New York: Norton, 1980.

TRONICK, E., H. ALS, and L. ADAMSON. "Structure of Early Face-to-Face Communicative Interactions." In M. Bullowa, ed., *Before Speech: The Beginning of Interpersonal Communication.* New York: Cambridge University Press, 1980.

TRONICK, E., H. ALS, and T. B. BRAZELTON. "Mutuality in Mother-Infant Interaction." *Journal of Communication* 27 (1977): 74–79.

WATSON, J. S. "Smiling, Cooing, and 'The Game.' " *Merrill-Palmer Quarterly* 18 (1973): 323–39.

WEBER, MAX. "Science as a Vocation." (1919) In H. Gerth and C. W. Mills, eds., *From Max Weber: Essays in Sociology.* New York: Oxford University Press, 1958.

———. *Economy and Society: An Outline of Interpretive Sociology* (1922), eds. Guenther Roth and Claus Wittich. New York: Bedminster Press, 1968.

WEITZMAN, LENORE. *The Divorce Revolution: The Unexpected Social and Economic Consequences for Women in America.* New York: Free Press, 1985.

WHITE, R. W. "Motivation Reconsidered: The Concept of Competence." *Psychological Review* 66 (1959): 297–333.

WILLIS, ELLEN. "Feminism, Moralism and Pornography." In Ann Snitow, Christine Stansell, and Sharon Thompson, eds., *Powers of Desire: The Politics of Sexuality.* New York: Monthly Review Press, 1983.

WINNICOTT, D. W. "Transitional Objects and Transitional Phenomena." (1951) In *Playing and Reality*. Harmondsworth, U.K.: Penguin Books, 1974.

————. "The Location of Cultural Experience." (1967) In *Playing and Reality*.

————. "The Mirror Role of Mother and Family in Child Development." (1967) In *Playing and Reality*.

————. "Creativity and Its Origins." In *Playing and Reality*.

————. "The Use of an Object and Relating through Identifications." (1971) In *Playing and Reality*.

————. *The Maturational Process and the Facilitating Environment*. New York: International Universities Press, 1965.

————. "The Capacity to Be Alone." (1958) In *The Maturational Process and the Facilitating Environment*.

————. "Ego Distortion in Terms of True and False Self." (1960) In *The Maturational Process and the Facilitating Environment*.

————. *The Child, the Family, and the Outside World*. Harmondsworth, U.K.: Penguin Books, 1964.

————. "Primary Maternal Preoccupation." (1956) In *Through Pediatrics to Psychoanalysis*. London: Hogarth Press, 1978.

WOLFE, TOM, "The 'Me' Decade and the Third Great Awakening." *New York Magazine,* August 10, 1976.

YOGMAN, M. W. "Observations on the Father-Infant Relationship." In S. H. Cath, A. R. Gurwitt, and J. M. Ross, eds., *Father and Child*. Boston: Little, Brown, 1982.

YOUNG, MICHAEL, and PETER WILLMOTT. *Family and Kinship in East London*. (1957) Harmondsworth, U.K.: Penguin Books, 1972.

N O T E S

INTRODUCTION

1. "Truth and Power," p. 119, in *Power/Knowledge: Selected Interviews.* Foucault continues, "What makes power hold good, what makes it accepted, is simply the fact that it doesn't only weigh on us as a force that says no, but that it traverses and produces things, it induces pleasure, forms knowledge, produces discourse." Among the things that a system of power, a discourse, produces is the very character of the revolt against it.

See also *History of Sexuality, Vol. I* for his critique of the psychoanalytic "repressive hypothesis."

2. Freud, *Civilization and Its Discontents,* especially pp. 122–133.

3. Marcuse, *Eros and Civilization,* p. 83.

4. The first important psychoanalytic discussions of the problem of domination occurred in the context of the triumph of fascism in Europe and the consequent failures of left-wing social movements. Wilhelm Reich, known for his work in both the theoretical and the social pedagogy projects of the twenties, had already begun formulating the idea that authority works through the repression of instinct. His writings, *The Mass Psychology of Fascism* and "What Is Class Consciousness," represented the strongest defense of instinct against culture. The alternate point of view, the defense of rational, democratic authority, emerged in the work of the Frankfurt "critical theorists," Max Horkheimer, T. W. Adorno, Herbert Marcuse, and (for a short time) Erich Fromm. (See *Studien über Autorität und Familie.*) The critical theorists affirmed Freud's view of the instincts as dangerous, and gradually assumed the position of defending the old moral authority of the paternal superego over the new "seamless" forms of domination in mass society, fascist or bourgeois (see Horkheimer and Adorno, *Dialectic of Enlightenment;* Horkheimer, "Authority and the Family Today"; Marcuse, "The Obsolescence of the Freudian Concept of Man"). Thus the antinomy of instinct and civilization was reaffirmed, not resolved, by that generation of social psychoanalytic theorists. This antinomy underlies the idea of the "fatherless society" and the defense of paternal authority. See also Alexander Mitscherlich's post-war analysis, *Society Without the Father,* and Russell Jacoby's discussion of the Frankfurt theorists in *Social Amnesia.*

Rejecting instinct theory, but using Freud's notion of the mass leader *(Group Psychology and the Analysis of the Ego)* Erich Fromm developed the idea of the search for the "magic helper" in *Escape from Freedom.* Fromm's emphasis on the avoidance of anxiety rather than on instinct, while useful, lost sight of the erotic nature of submission, and the fact that the primal parental relationship runs on love as well as on anxiety. Two later attempts to break out of the impasse created by the paradigm of instinct versus civilization were N. O. Brown's, in *Life Against Death,* and Marcuse's, in *Eros and Civilization.* Both argue that the instincts need not be destructive, but they were less interested in explaining submission than in showing how civilization is repressive, separating us from our deepest desires.

5. Strictly speaking, we must grant that Reich ("The Imposition of Sexual Morality"), Marcuse *(Eros and Civilization),* and Brown *(Life Against Death)* did not ignore the problem of woman's subordination. However, in both Reich and Marcuse the discussion of the problem was always elided into the discussion of the social relations of production; the feminist analysis gave way to the Marxian one. For Brown, too, male domination was not an independent issue but, instead, a way station in culture's denial of death and the instincts.

6. My analysis shares many common assumptions with, and is indebted to, the theoretical contributions of Nancy Chodorow *(The Reproduction of Mothering* and "Gender, Relation and Difference in Psychoanalytic Perspective"), Evelyn Keller *(Reflections on Gender and Science),* Dorothy Dinnerstein *(The Mermaid and the Minotaur),* and Carol Gilligan *(In a Different Voice* and "Remapping the Moral Domain").

7. De Beauvoir, *The Second Sex.*

CHAPTER 1: THE FIRST BOND

1. There are different currents involved in the psychoanalytic shift toward interest in object relations; some emphasize the internal relationship to the object, while others include the real external object. These currents have fared quite differently in England and America, although both are considered to be about object relations. The British object relations tendency began with Melanie Klein's work on the earliest phases of the mother-child relationship (see, for example, *Envy and Gratitude*) in the thirties and forties, and then took a turn away from instinct theory with the works of Ronald Fairbairn (see *Psychoanalytic Studies of the Personality*), D. W. Winnicott (see *The Maturational Process and the Facilitating Environment*), and Michael Balint, whose work on primary love was the first to clearly posit a social origin to the infant's relationships. (Balint is sometimes treated separately, as part of the Hungarian School; see *The Basic Fault.*) A summary of the development of and differences among object relations theorists, with special emphasis on Fairbairn, can be found in Harry Guntrip, *Personality Structure and Human Interaction.*

In America, object relations theory was eclipsed by ego psychology, the position of mainstream theorists in the post-war period. This school of thought did not focus until significantly later on the inner world of objects; a landmark in this evolution of position was Edith Jacobson's *The Self and the Object World*

(1964). The work of Margaret Mahler et al. on separation-individuation in infancy *(The Psychological Birth of the Human Infant)* also moved ego psychology significantly in the direction of object relations. And important American psychoanalysts have contributed to the development of object relations theory, for example Hans Loewald (e.g., "The Therapeutic Action of Psychoanalysis") and Arnold Modell *(Object Love and Reality)*. Some of the criticisms of instinct theory made by the British object relations theorists were made in this country by Heinz Kohut, who founded self psychology in the seventies (see *The Restoration of the Self*). Harry Stack Sullivan (see *The Interpersonal Theory of Psychiatry*), who concurred with the British School's focus on relationships, did influence, despite his official separation from and rejection by Freudian psychoanalysts in the post-war period, clinical practitioners to pay greater attention to external reality, especially in psychosis. The relations between these different developments is discussed by Jay Greenberg and Stephen Mitchell in *Object Relations in Psychoanalytic Theory*.

2. The focus on differentiation in infancy does not mean that infancy determines later experiences, but that it establishes certain issues and patterns that reappear later, sometimes in other forms.

3. The amount of research being done on neonatal abilities is enormous. Experiments designed to document the infant's early identification of its own mother are becoming increasingly more common. See T. B. Brazelton on the infant's preference for its mother's face and voice in the first week of life in "Neonatal Assessment"; J. MacFarlane's discussion of infant preference for maternal milk in "Olfaction in the Development of Social Preferences in the Human Neonate"; G. Carpenter on two-week-old infants' preference for the mother's face in "Mother's Face and the Newborn"; and A. DeCasper and W. Fifer, "Of Human Bonding: Newborns Prefer Their Mother's Voices."

4. Infancy researchers stress that the infant is an active partner in the relationship. They speak of the "competent" infant who can elicit the kind of behavior from adult caregivers that is optimal for emotional security and development; that is, the infant gives readable cues and is responsive and actively interested in parental stimulation. See S. Goldberg, "Social Competence in Infancy"; M. D. S. Ainsworth and S. Bell, "Mother-Infant Interaction and the Development of Competence"; R. Q. Bell, "The Contribution of Human Infants to Caregiving and Social Interaction"; and Lewis and Rosenblum, eds., *The Effect of the Infant on Its Caregiver.*

5. The idea of infant and parent each mutually influencing the other became prominent especially as a result of the observation of play interaction. My reading of this interaction has been most influenced by the work of Beatrice Beebe (see "Mother-Infant Mutual Influence and Precursors of Self and Object Representations") and Daniel Stern. For an introduction to this research, see Daniel Stern, *The First Relationship.*

6. The drive's indiscriminateness toward the object and the ego's indifference, or hostility, toward the outside world were discussed by Freud in "Formulations on the Two Principles in Mental Functioning" and "Instincts and Their Vicissitudes." Freud's position was criticized by two early influential exponents of the infant's activity and curiosity, Ernst Schachtel *(Metamorphosis)* and R. W. White ("Motivation Reconsidered: The Concept of Competence"). They address the problem of Freud's theory of primary narcissism, which was also critiqued by Balint. Yet another wave of criticism of Freud's view developed later, in response to Mahler's notion of infant autism *(The Psychological Birth of the Human Infant),* and is well summed up by Emanuel Peterfreund ("Some Critical Comments on Psychoanalytic Conceptualizations of Infancy") and Stern *(The Interpersonal World of the Infant).*

7. See Piaget and Inhelder *(The Psychology of the Child)* and Piaget *(The Construction of Reality in the Child).* Psychologists were, of course, influenced by many nonpsychoanalytic trends—not only Piaget, but also G. H. Meade *(Mind, Self, and Society)* and C. H. Cooley *(Human Nature and the Social Order),* whose theories of social psychology asserted the central place of the relationship to the other in the genesis of the self.

8. John Bowlby made use of ethological research on animals as well as children to formulate his highly influential theory of the primacy of attachment. In a study written for the World Health Organization, *Maternal Care and Mental Health,* Bowlby formulated the basic themes of attachment theory. Bowlby's point was that, whereas Freudian theory makes attachment a secondary phenomenon and defines it as "anaclitic" (dependent on the drive for oral gratification), attachment can be observed as a behavior independent of such needs (see

Bowlby, "The Nature of the Child's Tie to His Mother," and Ainsworth, "Object Relations, Dependency and Attachment").

9. Bowlby *(Attachment)* describes how those infants who were separated from their parents but placed in a setting that afforded considerable social interaction were able to form a normal attachment to their parents within two weeks of their return, whereas those who were in a hospital setting without such interaction required eight weeks or more to develop the same attachment. See also H. R. Schaffer, *The Growth of Sociability*.

10. Ainsworth and Bell ("Attachment, Exploration, and Separation") developed an important research technique, the observation of infants in a strange situation, to evaluate a child's attachment to its mother. The test makes use of the infant's anxiety reaction to strangers that develops in the second six months of life, and presumes that normally attached infants cling to the mother when anxious. Ainsworth observed how well the child was able to reunite with the mother after separation and gain reassurance from her presence.

11. Guntrip *(Personality Structure and Human Interaction)* especially emphasized Fairbairn's idea *(Psychoanalytic Studies of the Personality)* that when the drive is directed primarily to one psychosexual aspect rather than the whole object this represents a deterioration of the relationship.

12. Mahler et al., *The Psychological Birth of the Human Infant*.

13. Mahler's idea of hatching has also been challenged by those researchers who have found infant responsiveness and interaction to be a cumulative process. See note 6.

14. Stern, "The Early Development of Schemas of Self, of Other, and of Various Experiences of 'Self with Other.'" See also *The Interpersonal World of the Infant*. Stern, a pioneer in infancy research, argues that emergent structures or capacities are built into the infant and have only to enter into interaction with other people to unfold. For example, since the infant can discriminate between constant and intermittent reinforcement of behavior, this means it quickly learns to discriminate between what it does (voice resonates in chest) and the other does (answer).

15. Winnicott, "Primary Maternal Preoccupation," p. 304.

16. Kohut, *The Restoration of the Self.* Self psychology argues that we need to use other people as "selfobjects" in the service of self-esteem and cohesion throughout life, and criticizes what it sees as psychoanalysis's erroneous inflation of independence as the goal of maturity. As Greenberg and Mitchell point out (*Object Relations*), this critique exaggerates the psychoanalytic disparagement of dependency. It also fails to distinguish between using others as "selfobjects" and recognizing the other as an outside subject, missing the key point of the intersubjective view.

17. See Habermas, "A Theory of Communicative Competence"; Trevarthen, "Communication and Cooperation in Early Infancy: A Description of Primary Intersubjectivity"; and Stern, *The Interpersonal World of the Infant.* Meade's *(Mind, Self, and Society)* theorizing about the creation of shared meaning prefigured Habermas's remarks on intersubjectivity, and his discussion of gestures is relevant to a social theory perspective on infant development. Arnold Modell's distinction *(Psychoanalysis in a New Context)* between one-person psychology and two-person psychology is essentially similar to that I am making between intersubjective and intrapsychic. Lichtenberg's account of intersubjectivity *(Psychoanalysis and Infant Research)* locates it in terms of self-consciousness of doing, in the second year of life, much later than Stern and Trevarthen locate it.

18. The idea of complementarity is useful here, as Michael Eigen has shown in his discussion of Winnicott ("The Area of Faith in Winnicott, Lacan and Bion"). Modell *(Psychoanalysis in a New Context)* also argues that we ought to see them as complementary approaches, and that it is premature to think of synthesizing them.

19. As Emmanuel Ghent points out ("Credo: The Dialectic of One-Person and Two-Person Psychologies"), it is not necessary to make the choice between external and inner reality that Freud posed when he switched from the seduction theory to the idea that his patients were not really seduced but fantasizing.

20. Stern, *The Interpersonal World of the Infant,* pp. 92–93.

21. See J. S. Watson, "Smiling, Cooing, and 'The Game.' " See also M. Lewis and S. Goldberg, "Perceptual-Cognitive Development in Infancy."

22. This phenomenon of checking back with the mother has been documented by Emde and his colleagues in an experiment using the "visual cliff," in which the illusion of a drop is created and the infant either proceeds or stops, depending on maternal response—doubt or encouragement. See Klinnert et al., "Emotions as Behavior Regulators: Social Referencing in Infancy"; and Emde and Sorce, "The Rewards of Infancy: Emotional Availability and Maternal Referencing."

23. On the necessity of the child's recognition of the mother as a subject in her own right, see Dinnerstein *The Mermaid and the Minotaur,* Chodorow, "Gender, Relation and Difference in Psychoanalytic Perspective" and Keller, *Reflections on Gender and Science.*

24. See Chodorow, *The Reproduction of Mothering;* Chodorow and Contratto, "The Fantasy of the Perfect Mother"; and Dinnerstein, *The Mermaid and the Minotaur.*

25. Recognizing the infant as an active, social being who relates to the mother as a person does not entirely remove the problem of psychology's infant-centered perspective, which views the parent as merely the facilitator of the child's development. This perspective tends to make developmental competence an end in itself and has somewhat devalued the emotional relationship of the infant with the parents (perhaps because it ignores the intrapsychic). Some of this emphasis on infant activity and competence, especially on early cognitive abilities, stems more from the dominant tendency to stress performance than from an interest in sociability (see Adrienne Harris, "The Rationalization of Infancy").

26. Chodorow *(The Reproduction of Mothering)* points out that psychoanalysts, with a few important exceptions, ignore the discrepancy between the total nature of the infant's love and the partial nature of the mother's. What psychoanalysis stresses is appropriate to the clinical situation but not to the theoretical one, the child's view, the view of inner, not outer, reality.

27. The use of the concept of maternal mirroring is a common, but problematic, one in psychoanalysis. (See Winnicott on "The Mirror Role of Mother and Family in Child Development" and Kohut's idea of the mirroring object in *The Restoration of the Self.*) The mirror metaphor has been criticized from a feminist viewpoint by Gilligan ("Remapping the Moral Domain") and from the standpoint of infancy research by Stern *(The Interpersonal World of the Infant).*

28. The criticism of separateness as a goal has been made by several feminists, especially the group around Jean Baker Miller (see the *Works in Progress* of the Stone Center), Chodorow, "Gender, Relation and Difference," and Gilligan, "Remapping the Moral Domain."

29. These terms, the figure and the ground, were used somewhat differently by Fred Pine in his illuminating contribution to the debate about the nature of differentiation ("In the Beginning"). Pine, who co-authored the major statement of separation-individuation theory with Mahler and Bergmann *(The Psychological Birth of the Human Infant),* tried to correct the difficulties that arose from the idea of the infant's initial autism. However, he still maintains that play and interaction are the background while drive satisfaction and merging experiences are the intense "magic moments" that form the figure. Thus moments of distress constitute the alternate element in the symbiotic phase to the intensity of merging blissfully in nursing. Stern ("The Early Development of Schemas of Self") criticized Pine's formulation on the grounds that self-other differentiation is a continual process and is not really undone by the intense physical intimacy called merging. Furthermore, exuberant active play in which differentiation is clearly a feature constitutes as intense a high point as merger experiences.

30. Early work on mother-infant interaction in the seventies focused on the structure of reciprocity and how play can be seen as a model of interaction. Research on mother-infant facial play was conducted by several groups, who reached similar conclusions (see Brazelton, Koslowski, and Main, "The Origins of Reciprocity"; Tronick, Als, and Adamson, "Structure of Early Face-to-Face Communicative Interactions"; and Tronick, Als, and Brazelton, "Mutuality in Mother-Infant Interaction"; see also Stern's "The Goal and Structure of Mother-Infant Play," "Mother and Infant at Play: The Dyadic Interaction Involving Facial, Vocal and Gaze Behavior," and *The First Relationship;* and Stern, Beebe, Jaffe, and Bennett, "The Infant's Stimulus World During Social Interaction"; see also Trevarthen, "Descriptive Analyses of Infant Communicative Behavior" and "The Foundations of Intersubjectivity."

31 . Beebe, "Mother-Infant Mutual Influence and Precursors of Self and Object Representations."

32. . Stern, *The First Relationship,* and Beebe, Stern, and Jaffe, "The Kinesic Rhythm of Mother-Infant Interactions."

33 . Stern, *The First Relationship,* p. 116. Stern's formulations emphasize that this is not an instrumental kind of learning; it is bound up with having fun, with excitement, and pleasure.

34 . Discussions of "chase and dodge" interactions can be found in Beebe and Stern, "Engagement-Disengagement"; Stern, *The First Relationship;* and Stern, "A Microanalysis of Mother-Infant Interaction."

35 . Beebe and Stern, "Engagement-Disengagement."

36 . The dynamic patterns of interpersonal interaction coincide with the determinants of inner regulation at this point. The separate sphere—the symbolic unconscious—where the psyche reconstructs and elaborates what has taken place in the exchange with the outside does not yet exist. But representation is already beginning in an earlier form, as Beebe suggests ("Mother-Infant Mutual Influence"), in the interiorization of interaction patterns between self and other, which are the precursors of later representations. She argues that "the very process of reciprocal adjustments, as these create expected patterns," will form early " 'interactive representations.' "

37 . Stern *(The Interpersonal World of the Infant)* defines earlier relatedness not as intersubjectivity but as core relatedness; although he agrees with Trevarthen that intersubjectivity is an innate, emergent human capacity, he argues that it does not exist at three to four months. In my view, intersubjectivity is best used as a theoretical construct encompassing the trajectory of experiences building up to the recognition of separate minds sharing the same state. If this awareness takes a leap forward in attunement at age seven to nine months, then we might say that intersubjectivity takes its first step toward being self-conscious, "intersubjectivity for itself."

38 . Stern, *The Interpersonal World of the Infant,* pp. 138–42.

39. Ibid., p. 127.

40. Mahler et al., *The Psychological Birth of the Human Infant.* See the discussion of refueling, pp. 65–75. Mahler et al. note that children take their first unaided steps away from, not toward, the mother (p. 73). Attachment theory, as formulated by Ainsworth ("Object Relations, Dependency and Attachment"), also sees the main events of development this way, but emphasizes the balance between attachment and exploration. This construction of the tension within the self has begun to influence the proponents of separation-individuation theory. In a response to Stern's critique of Mahler, her research associate Louise Kaplan ("Symposium on *The Interpersonal World of the Infant*") argues for the balance between individuation and attachment, claiming that Stern exaggerates the one-sidedness of separation-individuation theory when he says: "For Mahler, connectedness is the result of a failure in differentiation; for us it is a success of psychic function" (*The Interpersonal World of the Infant,* p. 241). Elsewhere in the book Stern writes—more evenhandedly—that the point is not to reverse the order of development, but that "both separation/individuation and new forms of experiencing union (or being-with) emerge equally out of the same experience of intersubjectivity" (p. 127).

41. As Stern emphasizes, the sharing of affective states is the baseline of intersubjectivity (see *The Interpersonal World of the Infant*).

42. See Modell *(Psychoanalysis in a New Context),* who contends that affects are the central aspect of two-person psychology.

43. See Stechler and Kaplan, "The Development of the Self: A Psychoanalytic Perspective."

44. Hegel, *Phänomenologie des Geistes;* my translation.

45. Ibid.

46. "It is for [consciousness], that it is and is not immediately the other consciousness; and even so, that this other is only for itself, in that it transcends itself as existing for itself; only in existing for the other is it for itself. Each is the medium for the other, through which each is mediated and united with itself;

and each is for itself and the other an immediate being, existing for itself, which simultaneously is only for itself by virtue of this mediation. They *recognize* themselves as *mutually recognizing one another.*" *Phänomenologie,* p. 143.

47. As Hegel continues to elucidate the relationship of the two consciousnesses, he explains that each person must try to prove the certainty of himself or herself in the life-and-death struggle that we all face with one another. This struggle to the death culminates in the master-slave relationship, as one gives in and the other establishes himself over the other. This outcome, rather than mutual recognition, Hegel views as the origin of domination.

48. Mahler et al., *The Psychological Birth of the Human Infant,* pp. 65–75.

49. Ibid., pp. 76–108.

50. Classical psychoanalysis, like Hegel, starts with the individual in a state of omnipotence. Thus Mahler uses omnipotence to characterize the feelings of the child, in the symbiotic union of earliest infancy, who experiences the other's support as an extension of the self. She also uses it in her discussion of the rapprochement toddler who clamors "for omnipotent control." The idea of omnipotence has been criticized with reference to both phases (e.g., Peterfreund, "Some Critical Comments on Psychoanalytic Conceptualizations of Infancy") for projecting an adult state (the belief that you can control others) onto infancy. To this, Mahler's colleague Pine ("In the Beginning") has replied that omnipotence is not about making "impossible demands," but describes an infant's feelings when he or she believes that their cries have "magically" made the mother come to nurse the infant. But one could argue that the infant's subjective feeling when mother answers his cry is probably not one of omnipotence, but simply of effectiveness. The idea of omnipotence, I believe, can only appear in the context of impotence and helplessness. The toddler in rapprochement who encounters the limits of his effectiveness seems to me a better illustration of the idea of omnipotence than the infant who can make no distinction between real and magical accomplishments. Omnipotence is a meaningful idea not as the original state, but as a fantasy that children construct in the face of disappointment, a reaction to loss—indeed, it is usually derived from a perception of the parent's power. It is the sense or threat of loss that leads to "impossible demands," the attempt to get back what we never had but imagine we did. Omnipotence describes a defensive wish, buried in every psyche, that one will have a perfect world, will prevail over time, death, and the other—and that coercion can succeed.

51. Mahler et al., *The Psychological Birth of the Human Infant,* p. 96.

52. Freud, "On Narcissism."

53. Object constancy is ego psychology's term for the ability to maintain a representation of the other as present and good even when the other is absent or there is conflict. Important as this internalization may arguably be, it is not the same as recognizing the other's independence. By conceptualizing the resolution of rapprochement in terms of object constancy, the developmental issue of separation is reduced to being able to tolerate absence or aggression; this leaves out actually appreciating or enjoying the other's separateness, as a mother is supposed to do with her child.

54. Winnicott, "Ego Distortion in Terms of True and False Self."

55. Winnicott, *Playing and Reality.*

56. Ibid., pp. 103–4.

57. Ibid., p. 105.

58. Ibid., p. 106.

59. André Green, "Potential Space in Psychoanalysis: The Object in the Setting."

60. Winnicott, *Playing and Reality,* p. 106.

61. Elsa First, "The Leaving Game: I'll Play You and You Play Me."

62. Eigen, "The Area of Faith in Winnicott, Lacan and Bion."

63. Winnicott, *The Child, the Family and the Outside World,* p. 62.

64. Winnicott, "Transitional Objects and Transitional Phenomena," in *Playing and Reality.*

65. Susan Deri, "Transitional Phenomena: Vicissitudes of Symbolization and Creativity." She explains that when the mother adapts herself to the baby's needs, giving in response to his hungry call, the baby has the "illusion" that he has actually created the breast with his need, that his need is creative; Winnicott called this "the creative illusion."

66. Sander, "Polarity, Paradox, and the Organizing Process in Development."

67. Sander cites Winnicott's article on "The Capacity to Be Alone": " '. . . the basis of the capacity to be alone is a paradox; it is the experience of being alone while someone else is present.' " And further, " 'it is only when alone (that is to say, in the presence of someone) that the infant can discover his own personal life. The pathological alternative is a false life built on reactions to external stimuli.' " (Sander, "Polarity, Paradox, and the Organizing Process in Development," p. 322; Winnicott, "The Capacity to Be Alone," p. 34.)

68. Schachtel's *Metamorphosis* contains one of the earliest descriptions of how the object comes into full view, into focal attention, when there is no pressure from need or anxiety. He writes of the absorption—of becoming lost in contemplation of the object—that can occur in this state when the subject no longer injects himself into the thing. This is obviously the counterpoint to being free from intrusion or impingement by the other.

69. Freud's theory that the ego is the precipitate of abandoned objects has been the basis of ego psychology. Its beginning is usually dated to publication of Freud's "Mourning and Melancholia," and its major formulation was in *The Ego and the Id.* The development of ego psychology continued in the thirties, with Anna Freud's *The Ego and Its Mechanisms of Defense* (1936) and Heinz Hartmann's *Ego Psychology and the Problem of Adaptation* (1939).

70. Marie Tolpin, "On the Beginnings of the Cohesive Self."

71. In this way Tolpin sees the idea of the transitional object as another step

in Freud's notion of ego formation as the "precipitate of abandoned object-cathexes." Tolpin here anticipated the thinking of self psychology, of which she later became an important exponent, which views psychic structure as created by "transmuting internalizations."

72. See André Green, "The Analyst, Symbolization and Absence in the Analytic Setting."

73. T. Field, "Infant Gaze Aversion and Heart Rate During Face-to-Face Interactions." Beebe (in discussion) has suggested a perspective of development in which the infant refines its own capacities for regulation through exercising them, that is, in interaction.

74. Here Stern ("The Early Development of Schemas of Self") is arguing with Pine ("In the Beginning"), who has described the "magic moments" of gratification, like nursing, as the moments of real union. Pine wants to privilege these intense moments of oneness as the figure while still giving importance to the everyday background of distinguishing self from other. Schachtel first introduced this distinction, in a slightly different form.

75. Stern, "The Early Development of Schemas of Self."

76. For example, see Fairbairn, "Steps in the Development of an Object-Relations Theory of the Personality."

77. Freud, *Civilization and Its Discontents.*

78. Keller *(Reflections on Gender and Science),* noting the derogation of oneness in Freudian theory, gives a very good account of a different kind of union that does allow the simultaneous sense of distinctness and of losing self in the other in her discussion of Schachtel and dynamic objectivity.

79. We can trace the desire for difference back to the infant's early interest in the novel, the discrepant, and even the disjunctive. Bahrick and Watson ("Detection of Intermodal and Proprioceptive Visual Contingency") demonstrated that infants preferred looking at a delayed over a simultaneous (mirroring) video

playback of their motions. Recognizing the difference as the complement to sameness or oneness is a major point that distinguishes intersubjective theory from self psychology.

80. Following Stern's taxonomy (in "The Early Development of Schemas of Self") we can say that both having one's state transformed by the other, as in drive theory, and the complementarity of being held, as in object-relations theory, focus on the individually conceived subject and his complementary relationship to the object. Both stand in contrast to the mutuality posited by intersubjective theory.

81. Kundera, *The Unbearable Lightness of Being.*

82. Freud, *Civilization and Its Discontents.*

CHAPTER 2: MASTER AND SLAVE

1. See Freud's remarks on omnipotence in "On Narcissism" and in *Civilization and Its Discontents.*

2. De Beauvoir, following Hegel, begins *The Second Sex* with the argument that the question is not why men want to dominate, but why they are able to do so. This approach, comparable in a way to Freud's assumption that man is a wolf to man unless restrained by civilization, might make submission seem unproblematic, but, in fact, de Beauvoir explores woman's psychology in detail.

3. See Andrea Dworkin, "Woman as Victim: *Story of O,*" and Susan Griffin, *Pornography and Silence.*" Part of the failure of such analyses, which are endemic to the feminist movement against pornography, is the denial of the difference between voluntary, ritual acts of submission that are subjectively considered pleasurable and acts of battery or violation that are terrifying and involuntary although they may occur within a theoretically voluntary contract like marriage.

4. Regine Deforges, *Confessions of O: Conversations with Pauline Réage.*

5. Réage, *Story of O,* pp. 15–17.

6. Ibid., p. 82.

7. Ibid., p. 81.

8. Ibid., p. 93.

9. Freud, "The Economic Problem of Masochism." The idea of masochism as pleasure in pain was perhaps an overly influential condensation of Freud's thinking (in "Instincts and Their Vicissitudes" he distinguishes between the "pain itself" and "the accompanying sexual excitement"). It has been amended by many contemporary psychoanalysts, who interpret masochism in terms of the ego or the self and its object relations; they see masochism as a desire for submission to an idealized other in order to protect against overwhelming feelings of psychic pain, object loss, and fragmentation. See my review of the problem in "The Alienation of Desire"; see also Masud Khan, *Alienation in Perversions;* Robert Stoller, *Sexual Excitement* and *Perversion;* Esther Menaker, *Masochism and the Emerging Ego;* and V. Smirnoff, "The Masochistic Contract." These writings point to the underlying narcissistic dilemmas that are "solved" by the infliction of pain administered by an idealized authority. These explanations do have a precedent in Freud's original idea of "moral masochism," which he defined as "the ego's own masochism" (see "The Economic Problem of Masochism") and which Karen Horney subsequently related to low self-esteem and difficulty in separation ("The Problem of Feminine Masochism").

10. Réage, *Story of O,* p. 152.

11. Khan, *Alienation in Perversions.*

12. Freud's point ("The Economic Problem of Masochism") is that eroticization allows unmanageable, negative stimuli to be managed.

13. See Leo Bersani, *Baudelaire and Freud,* for a discussion of this.

14. Freud not only used the term "repression" to refer to a specific defense, but also as the fundamental pillar *(Grundpfeil)* of psychoanalysis *(An Outline of Psychoanalysis).* Splitting was originally used by Freud in a narrower sense (see "The Splitting of the Ego"), but was made a key concept by Melanie Klein (see

Envy and Gratitude, pp. 324–25) and those influenced by her. Here splitting refers variously to the process of separating the object into good and bad to keep the bad from contaminating the good, to the early division between love and hate, to splitting off part of the self and projecting it onto the object, and related mechanisms. Freud did refer to the splitting of bad and good object in just this sense in a footnote to "The 'Uncanny.'" Kernberg *(Borderline Conditions and Pathological Narcissism)* has claimed splitting (especially idealization and devaluation) is the crucial defense in borderline disorders, thus giving it a function parallel to that of repression in neurosis. I prefer Fairbairn's view *(Psychoanalytic Studies)* which insists on the defensive character of splitting— however ubiquitous—to Klein's view, which makes it a developmental phase.

15. Georges Bataille, *Death and Sensuality,* pp. 11–25, especially p. 24.

16. In the view of self psychology, it is the fear of losing the self, fragmenting, and falling apart that is a primary motive in masochism (see Stolorow and Lachmann, *Psychoanalysis of Developmental Arrests*).

17. Elizabeth Harris, "Sadomasochism: A Personal Experience." The psychoanalytic interpretation of masochism shows how the masochist is the hidden director of the experience, as Stoller *(Sexual Excitement)* points out. Those who write about sadomasochism from personal experience concur. See Susan Farr, "The Art of Discipline."

18. Georges Bataille, "Hemingway in the Light of Hegel," p. 12. See also Richard Sennett, *Authority*, for a reading of Hegel in terms of power and obedience.

19. Freud, *Civilization and Its Discontents;* see also *Beyond the Pleasure Principle* on the death drive.

20. Freud, *Civilization and Its Discontents,* p. 119. Freud concludes this passage with his famous remark that aggression is "the greatest impediment to civilization," threatening us with the "hostility of each against all and of all against each"; that the evolution of civilization depends upon "the struggle between Eros and Death" (p. 122).

21. Freud, *Civilization and Its Discontents,* p. 121. I am suggesting here that we see instinctual tension as a metaphor for the experience of the self, for the

condition of stasis between self and other represented in the mind as a condition
of the self. This representation has a real appearance—what began as something
between subjects winds up being experienced as the fantasy life of the single
subject, appearing as instinctual or primary, as purely internal and self-generated.

22. Descriptions of sadomasochistic experiences by women participants emphasize such emotions. Susan Farr ("The Art of Discipline") argues that for the
sadist, who enjoys the "illusion of complete powerfulness" and the other's
survival, the sense of reality is enhanced: "In the process, lovers become real to
each other . . . like the process of becoming Real described in the children's
book, *The Velveteen Rabbit*. . . ."

23. My position here is a modification of Winnicott's which postulates a kind
of early omnipotence. The outcome of failed destruction is splitting. Norbert
Freedman ("On Splitting") gives a good account of this sequence: Splitting
"comes from a point in time at which the infant faces the total randomness of
the environment vis-à-vis his or her own actions, so that it no longer seems
possible to affect the environment (the 'not-me') strictly through the action of
the self. The rage that ensues from this confrontation with helplessness forms
the genesis of splitting. The key to the resolution of splitting is the establishment
of externality" (p. 244).

24. Freud, "Instincts and Their Vicissitudes."

25. Laplanche, *Life and Death in Psychoanalysis,* p. 124. Laplanche writes: "Eros
. . . differs from sexuality, the first discovery of psychoanalysis. Eros is what
seeks to maintain, preserve, and even augment the cohesion and the synthetic
tendency of living beings and of psychical life. . . . [W]hat appears with Eros
is the *bound and binding* form of sexuality. . . . In the face of this triumph of
the vital and the homeostatic, it remained for Freud . . . to reaffirm . . . a kind
of antilife as sexuality, frenetic enjoyment [*jouissance*], the negative, the repetition compulsion. . . . For the death drive does not possess its own energy. Its
energy is libido. Or better put, the death drive is the very soul, the constitutive
principle of libidinal circulation" (p. 123). Thus Laplanche argues, rightly I
think, that sexuality can be alloyed either with Eros or with death and destruction, but the great discovery of psychoanalysis was this latter, negative form of
sexuality, which opens up to us the peculiar attraction of death and destruction.

26. Sheldon Bach, "Self-Love and Object-Love."

27. Emmanuel Ghent, "Masochism, Submission, and Surrender."

28. Ibid.

29. In *Metamorphosis,* Ernst Schachtel developed the idea of becoming creatively absorbed in the other as a kind of transcendent experience of losing the
self.

30. Chodorow, *The Reproduction of Mothering.* See also Miller, *Toward a New
Psychology of Women.*

31. Stoller, *Perversion,* p. 99.

32. Ralph Greenson, "Dis-identifying from Mother."

33. Chodorow, "Gender, Relation and Difference in Psychoanalytic Perspective."

34. Keller *(Reflections on Gender and Science)* has discussed the consequences of
disidentification from the mother for a certain kind of rationality, a static
objectivity, that distances from the object.

35. Stoller *(Perversion)* speculates that "perversion is that ultimate in separa-
tions, mother murder" (p. 150). Stoller perceives in perversion both the undoing
and the promotion of separation. I agree with this paradox. I think it offers a
better explanation than Chasseguet-Smirgel's view that violation is simply an
effort at dedifferentiation, a transgression against the paternal law (see "Reflections on the Connections between Perversion and Sadism" and "Perversion and
the Universal Law"). The contradictory intentions of sadism should be kept in
mind, since they express the dark side of paternal separation.

36. Chasseguet-Smirgel ("Perversion and the Universal Law") demonstrates
how de Sade's main object of attack is the maternal body, for the mother is
perceived as poisoning the child, using him for her own purposes. I believe that
the crucial motivation in this attack is envy of the mother's perceived power,

or, in Klein's sense, envy of the breast; mother is able to provide or withhold the goodness she alone contains. This envy has a double consequence, which forms the essence of male sadism: to simultaneously deny mother's goodness and declare it bad, and to become oneself the powerful figure who can withhold or grant satisfaction.

37. I am supposing that de Beauvoir's woman as other is fundamentally the mother.

38. Chodorow *(The Reproduction of Mothering)* emphasizes not only that the girl maintains her identification with the mother, but that this identification is from the outset different than the boy's, and based on a different kind of object relationship between daughter and mother.

39. Hegel, *Phänomenologie.* Hegel states that without servitude, the fear of death remains "inward and mute," but service gives it objective form.

40. Freud developed the idea of feminine masochism "as an expression of feminine nature" and the form of masochism "most accessible to our observation" in his 1924 essay, "The Economic Problem of Masochism." However, his reference was to the femininity in men, to the fantasies of male homosexuals. It remained for Marie Bonaparte *(Female Sexuality)* and Helene Deutsch to actually apply the concept in a more elaborate way to women. Deutsch *(The Psychology of Women)* went so far as to posit that women not only seek masochistic satisfaction in sexual relations with men, when they relinquish their aspiration to activity along with the wish for a penis, but also in motherhood and in the pain of childbearing. Despite Horney's ("The Problem of Feminine Masochism") excellent critique of the concept, it remained popular in psychoanalytic circles until the late sixties. It has since fallen into disrepute, as one can see in the criticism by such mainstream psychoanalysts as Harold Blum ("Masochism, the Ego Ideal, and the Psychology of Women").

41. See Susan Griffin's *Woman and Nature* for an illustration of this equation.

42. Paula Caplan, "The Myth of Woman's Masochism," p. 137. Interestingly, Catherine MacKinnon, in *Feminism Unmodified,* argues that feminists should

accept women's submission as a fact, indeed, as the basic element of their heterosexual experience.

43. Caplan rightly points out that the sacrifice of motherhood is confused by Deutsch with a desire for pain, rather than the ability to bear it in the interests of a higher goal, and in support cites de Beauvoir and Blum, among others. Caplan's critique of the early theorists is good ideologically, but does not offer a particularly useful psychoanalytic exploration.

44. Excerpted from *Coming to Power,* an anthology of writings on lesbian sadomasochism. Note the book's alternate subtitle: *S/M: A Form of Eroticism Based on a Consensual Exchange of Power.*

CHAPTER 3: WOMAN'S DESIRE

1. Freud, "The Dissolution of the Oedipus Complex," "Some Psychical Consequences of the Anatomical Distinction Between the Sexes," "Female Sexuality," and the lecture on "Femininity" in *New Introductory Lectures.*

2. See Ethel Person's discussion of women's sexual difficulties in "Sexuality as the Mainstay of Identity."

3. See Juliet Mitchell, *Psychoanalysis and Feminism.* From the viewpoint of the child, psychoanalysis argues that the preoedipal mother whose power has not yet been surrendered to the father is phallic (see Freud, "Femininity"). It is the "phallic" mother who is loved and powerful in the preoedipal era and the "castrated" mother who is repudiated by the child in the oedipal era.

4. Lazarre, *On Loving Men,* page 17.

5. See Muriel Dimen, *Surviving Sexual Contradictions,* on woman as object of desire.

6. This is true not only of explicitly feminist writing, like that of Chodorow, but of a wide range of psychoanalytic discussion. A prominent example is Irene Fast's *Gender Identity: A Differentiation Model.*

7. The most important formulation of gender identity theory was initially put forth by Robert Stoller in *Sex and Gender.* The work of Money and Erhardt, *Man and Woman, Boy and Girl,* was also important. All based their arguments on cases of ambiguous sexual development in which physiological gender identity was uncertain and psychological gender identity had to be attributed. See also Stoller's discussion, "Facts and Fancies: An Examination of Freud's Concept of Bisexuality" and "The 'Bedrock' of Masculinity and Femininity: Bisexuality"; and Money, "Gender Role, Gender Identity, Core Gender Identity: Usage and Definition of Terms." For a current evaluation of the theory of gender identity, see Person and Ovesey, "Psychoanalytic Theories of Gender Identity."

8. The work of Jean Baker Miller is a good example of this reevaluation of the mother. Since writing *Toward a New Psychology of Women,* Miller has developed a position that reevaluates women's relational self and the values, such as empathy, that go along with it *(Works in Progress* of the Stone Center).

9. The problem of woman's desire is more likely to be addressed by those who have stayed within the Freudian terms, by those influenced by Jacques Lacan, who begin with the phallus as the representative of desire; they are highly sensitive to the lacuna in the representation of woman's desire, and there is a wide spectrum of positions here, from Luce Irigaray ("This Sex Which Is Not One") and Jane Gallop *(The Daughter's Seduction),* who are critical of Lacan, to Juliet Mitchell *(Psychoanalysis and Feminism)* and Jacqueline Rose (see Rose and Mitchell's introductions to *Feminine Sexuality*), who expound him.

10. Catherine MacKinnon, in *Feminism Unmodified,* thus excoriates all heterosexuality as domination. A number of feminist critics have discussed how the original feminist advocacy of emancipating sexuality has been pushed aside in favor of a moralizing stance. See Ellen Willis, "Feminism, Moralism and Pornography," and the introduction to Snitow, Stansell, and Thompson's anthology, *Powers of Desire.*

11. See Echols's critique of the idealization of the mother-daughter relationship in cultural feminism in "The New Feminism of Yin and Yang."

12. See Ellen Dubois and Linda Gordon's "Seeking Ecstasy on the Battlefield," and Linda Gordon's "Why Nineteenth-Century Feminists Did Not Support Birth Control."

13. The idea of the little girl as "little man" was put forth by Jeanne Lampl–de Groot ("The Evolution of the Oedipus Complex in Women"), who adopted and elaborated Freud's view of the feminine Oedipus complex. Freud expounded on the significance of a girl's lack of a penis in "The Dissolution of the Oedipus Complex" and "Some Psychical Consequences of the Anatomical Distinction Between the Sexes"; he took up the issue of the girl's shift from mother to father in "Female Sexuality" and "Femininity."

14. See Horney's "The Flight from Womanhood" for her discussion of the impulse toward heterosexuality and "The Denial of the Vagina" on the girl's knowledge of her own genital. A useful review of the psychoanalytic debate on femininity in the twenties can be found in Zenia Fliegel's "Feminine Psychosexual Development in Freudian Theory: A Historical Reconstruction" and "Women's Development in Analytic Theory."

15. Mitchell's *(Psychoanalysis and Feminism)* judgment is somewhat one-sided on this issue. As Fliegel ("Women's Development in Analytic Theory") has pointed out, there is much more to Horney's position than biology; it also offers a sophisticated psychoanalytic notion of how the girl uses penis envy as a defense against oedipal wishes toward the father. And while Mitchell cites Freud's criticism of Jones and Horney in which he claimed they were too biological, Freud himself made many a statement honoring biology, which Mitchell ignores.

16. Of course it would be more precise to say that Mitchell is trying to be faithful to Freud as read by Lacan.

17. Mitchell, *Psychoanalysis and Feminism,* p. 96.

18. Ibid., p. 97. Mitchell does refer to the girl's preoedipal attachment to her mother, but gives it an oedipal meaning, as does Freud.

19. The focus on the mother in preoedipal life can be found in Mahler's ego psychology, object relations theory, Kleinian theory, self psychology, and non-Lacanian French psychoanalysis.

20. Chasseguet-Smirgel, "Freud and Female Sexuality."

21. Ibid., p. 285.

22. See Chasseguet-Smirgel's anthology, *Female Sexuality,* especially the contribution of Maria Torok, "The Significance of Penis Envy in Women." The child's defense of her own bodily integrity and pleasure, the anal battle, imbues the phallus symbol with its character, both its intrusive penetrating aspect and its unacceptable dirty aspect, its magic and its forbiddenness. The girl who is absorbed in such a battle with the mother, according to Torok, says, "This Thing—I want it, I must have it." In a sense she is grabbing at straws as she struggles with her own feelings of helplessness that are induced by maternal control. The anal battle is also a paradox—the mother exerts force to make the child become more independent, she denies it the freedom to do as it will with its products in the name of becoming more grown up and free of her. Thus the child seeks to break out of the paradox by finding another way to assert independence, including holding on to a body product, the penis. But the penis that derives all its power from the feces and none from the father, with his "real" independence, does not help the child to separate, only to remain in embattled opposition. See also Marion Oliner, "The Anal Phase."

23. As Chodorow puts it, "When an omnipotent mother perpetuates primary love and primary identification in relation to her daughter . . . a girl's father is likely to become a symbol of freedom from this dependence and merging" (*The Reproduction of Mothering,* p. 121).

24. Separation is not just a "beating back" but a move *toward* the world, implying an ability to extend the love felt for primary others to the world at large. Mahler's separation-individuation theory has the advantage of including the child's love affair with the world and emphasizing how painful it is when that love comes into conflict with love of the mother. See Chodorow's comments in *The Reproduction of Mothering.*

25. See sociologist Jessie Bernard's *The Future of Motherhood,* Chodorow and Contratto, "The Fantasy of the Perfect Mother," Dinnerstein, *The Mermaid and the Minotaur,* and Keller, *Reflections on Gender and Science.*

26. Woolf, *To the Lighthouse* (New York: Harcourt Brace Jovanovich, 1955).

27. Stoller, *Sex and Gender*. See also Fast, *Gender Identity: A Differentiation Model.*

28. Ernest Abelin's suggestive article, "Triangulation, the Role of the Father, and the Origins of Core Gender Identity During the Rapprochement Subphase," has been crucial in my formulation of this idea. I think that this role of the father lies unrecognized behind Lacan's well-known concept of the mirror phase ("The Mirror-Stage as Formative of the Function of the I"). The thing Lacan explains in terms of the child's use of the mirror as a projection of an imaginary coherent self (the first constitution of the self in alienation) strikes me as more accurately represented in the relationship of identification with the idealized father as mirror of desire, with all its grandiosity.

29. It is not referred to by Mahler or others as ambivalence, but ambitendency, because strict Freudian theory reserves the term ambivalence for instinctual opposites—love and hate.

30. M. W. Yogman, "Observations on the Father-Infant Relationship."

31. J. Kestenberg et al., "The Development of Paternal Attitudes."

32. This is a quotation from Kyle Pruett, cited in Anita Shreve's "The Working Mother as Role Model." See also Pruett's *The Nurturing Father*. In addition to learning from the observation of nontraditional heterosexual couples, we will also learn a great deal from observing children raised by homosexual couples.

33. These notable exceptions have been women analysts: for example, Doris Bernstein, "The Female Superego: A Different Perspective"; V. L. Clower, "Theoretical Implications in Current Views of Masturbation in Latency Girls"; Esther Menaker, "Some Inner Conflicts of Women in a Changing Society"; and Ricki Levenson, "Intimacy, Autonomy and Gender: Developmental Differences and Their Reflection in Adult Relationships."

34 . Mahler, Pine, and Bergmann, *The Psychological Birth of the Human Infant*, p. 75. See also Wendy Olesker, "Sex Differences in Two- and Three-Year-Olds."

35 . See Chodorow, *The Reproduction of Mothering*, and Flax, "Mother-Daughter Relationships."

36 . Abelin, "Triangulation, the Role of the Father, and the Origins of Core Gender Identity During the Rapprochement Subphase."

37 . In Abelin's formulation, the boy toddler develops "the first symbolic representation of the object and the separate self, desperately yearning for that object" (p. 154). The idea of the separate self and its object is taken for granted as the basic relationship of desire. In defining "I want Mommy" as the central wish of rapprochement, Abelin diminishes the desire *for* the father even though, following Mahler, he notes what makes the father attractive: his externality to ambivalence and his representation of the one who desires, who acts in the world.

38 . Abelin suggests that the shift in the child's interest toward being the subject of desire coincides with the child's transition from Piaget's sensory-motor stage to one where the child is capable of a symbolic perception of the world. This transition allows the development of consciousness of desire, which is felt to emanate from one's own subjectivity.

39 . While it is important to recognize the disjunction between cultural ideal types and actual life, further inquiry about the cultural forms that develop in the space this disjunction creates should be explored. Familial metaphors often flourish precisely where the individual and collective experiences differ radically from the relationships that gave rise to them. Kinship terms can create a familial bond where one is lacking. Hines and Boyd-Franklin ("Black Families") have remarked how an aunt or grandmother who raises a child in the black community will be called "mother," and Carol Stack has noted similar usages in *All Our Kin*. These studies show that the endowment of significance to a certain role is independent of its biological role, but not of the cultural models the role simultaneously relates to and differs from.

40 . See Freud, *Group Psychology and the Analysis of the Ego*, on the "emotional tie" of identification.

41. This declaration was made by a twenty-six-month-old toddler at the dinner table with his mother. I suggest that the distinction between source of goodness and identificatory love corresponds to Freud's distinction between the two kinds of object choices, narcissistic (seeking "the subject's own ego and find[ing] it again in other people") versus anaclitic ("attachment to early infantile proto-types"). (See, for example, Freud, *Three Essays on the Theory of Sexuality,* p. 222, *fn*). Freud's argument that women are more likely to have narcissistic object choice (in "On Narcissism") might be reconstructed as: boys love their mothers, the object of attachment, whereas girls love their fathers, the narcissistic object choice of both sexes. Freud recognized that a woman is apt to choose an object "in accordance with the narcissistic ideal of the man whom the girl had wished to become" ("Femininity," p. 132).

42. See Fiedler's famous description of homoerotic relationships in American literature, "Come Back to the Raft, Huck Honey."

43. Freud clearly stated that early identificatory love of the father prepares the way for the positive Oedipus complex; only when the child loses this identifica-tory love does it reappear as the negative oedipal form of object love for the father. Thus the passivity of the negative oedipal stance is the opposite of what I have been describing. The ego ideal has been mistakenly associated with the negative Oedipus and with a passive sexual stance toward the father because the early ideal love of the father has been ignored. An example of this conflation appears in the work of Peter Blos ("The Genealogy of the Ego Ideal"), the influential psychoanalytic theorist of adolescence.

44. Mahler et al., *The Psychological Birth of the Human Infant,* p. 216.

45. Doris Bernstein pointed out at a recent symposium that there are five pages of entries on fathers and sons in the *Chicago Psychoanalytic Literature Index* and only a handful of articles on fathers and daughters.

46. Whereas the girl's development is made to hinge on the *organ,* the absence of the penis, the boy's is made contingent on his *object relations* with his father: "Paradoxically, the father seems to occupy a much more important place in the psychosexual development of the boy than of the girl, be it as a love object or as a rival" (Chasseguet-Smirgel, "Feminine Guilt and the Oedipus Complex," p. 95).

47. Herman Roiphe and Eleanor Galenson, *Infantile Origins of Sexual Identity;* and Galenson and Roiphe, "Some Suggested Revisions Concerning Early Female Development" and "The Preoedipal Relationship of a Mother, Father and Daughter."

48. See Galenson and Roiphe, "Some Suggested Revisions Concerning Early Female Development," and Roiphe and Galenson, *Infantile Origins of Sexual Identity.*

49. Horney, in "On the Genesis of the Castration Complex in Women," conceded as a starting point that girls display a narcissistic interest in the penis that predates the oedipal phase. But she rightly argued that this was not actually "penis envy." The toddler penis is not yet invested with the meanings of genital sexuality, that is, a means of penetrating the mother. It is only narcissistically invested as an organ that allows mastery, especially in urination.

50. In my observation, the focus on the penis (and its symbols) in boys and girls is much more prominent if there has been a prior focus on the breast (or an equivalent intensity of mother-infant symbiosis). In general, the more the mother has been represented as the good, all-giving breast, the more useful is another organ—the penis—in beating her back. This association of maternal power with the organ is intensified when the mother wishes to hold on to the nursing bond, having derived from it not only the feeling of closeness, but also the sense of power in being the (only) source of sustenance. My interpretation intentionally focuses only on the preoedipal meaning of penis envy. I wish to distinguish between the early identification with the father and the oedipal idea of having the penis in order to woo the mother.

51. See M. Lamb, "The Development of Parental Preferences in the First Two Years of Life." Linda Gunsberg reviews some literature on this in "Selected Critical Review of Psychological Investigations of the Early Father-Infant Relationship."

52. See Doris Bernstein ("The Female Superego: A Different Perspective"): "To the extent that the father's individuation rests on the biological base of difference from mother, to the extent that he mobilized, or continues to mobilize the 'no, I am unlike' to maintain his autonomy, the more *unable* he is to permit or welcome his daughter's identification with him as he is his son's" (p. 196).

53. See Roiphe and Galenson *(Infantile Origins of Sexual Identity)* and Abelin ("Triangulation") on girls' social maturity and maternal identification.

54. Galenson and Roiphe, "The Preoedipal Relationship of a Mother, Father and Daughter," p. 162.

55. Chodorow *(The Reproduction of Mothering),* following Philip Slater ("Toward a Dualistic Theory of Identification"), argues that the identification with the father is "positional" and abstract compared to that with the mother, because the father is seldom physically present. What I find significant is the relationship between abstract/distant and a feeling of excitement.

56. Fast, *Gender Identity: A Differentiation Model.* In recognizing this early phase of homoerotic identification with the opposite-sex parent as the basis for later heterosexual love, I do not mean to argue that heterosexual object choice necessarily or "normally" follows from identification, for many factors play a role in object choice. I do wish to argue that this process of identification is a necessary stage in coming to love what is different, and it explains the girl's love of the father, which mystified Freud.

57. Freud, "A Child Is Being Beaten."

58. Miriam Johnson discusses the literature on this issue in "Fathers and 'Femininity' in Daughters: A Review of the Research."

59. For small children, this is the "normal" narcissism of wishing to be every-thing; see Fast, *Gender Identity: A Differentiation Model.*

60. Of course women, especially adolescents, have traditionally sought in intimate friendship with a woman a figure of identification, a homoerotic love that facilitates separation from one's own mother. The theme of identification with a female ideal has become highly significant within the women's move-ment, central to feminist literary creativity and criticism. Nancy Miller ("Changing the Subject: Authorship, Writing and the Reader"), referring to Barthes's idea that the text contains a "subject to love," suggests that the woman writer who is looking for " 'somebody to love' . . . would have to find someone somehow *like her* in her desire for a place in the discourse of art and identity, from which to imagine and image a writing self."

61. This is the burden of all the arguments for equal parenting (see Chod-orow's *The Reproduction of Mothering* and Dinnerstein's *The Mermaid and the Minotaur*).

62. See Freud's "Some Psychical Consequences of the Anatomical Distinction Between the Sexes" (p. 253) and "Femininity" (pp. 129–30).

63. De Beauvoir, *The Second Sex,* pp. 716–17.

64. Ibid., p. 717.

65. Eliot, *Middlemarch,* Penguin, 1965 ed., p. 243.

66. Ibid., pp. 25–26.

67. The ideal love of the father differs from the later love of the oedipal authority figure. The latter figure demands prohibition, conscience, and self-control, whereas the preoedipal ideal fits in with the rapprochement phase in which the father is seen as powerful but playful, more a figure of liberation than of discipline.

68. See Dinnerstein, *The Mermaid and the Minotaur.*

69. Thus the correct labeling and open discussion of the female genitals in childhood, however important, is not the key to changing the unconscious perception of women. Nor do I agree with positions like the one put forth by Luce Irigaray in "This Sex Which Is Not One," which valorizes the female genitals as a starting point for a different desire, although I am in sympathy with other aspects of her critique of Freud. A great deal of feminist art is also dependent on such reversal, which certainly has a redemptive moment, and is in any case scarcely avoidable in the historical process of change. Nonetheless, it is theoretically necessary to criticize this position, especially insofar as it becomes dominant and static.

70. Julia Kristeva has made some attempts to base the early role of space ("Women's Time"), as well as a possible preoedipal relationship to language ("About Chinese Women"), on "maternal rhythms," corresponding to "an intense echolalia." Although not further elaborated, her thinking has the advantage of simultaneously acknowledging the problematic aspects both of idealizing motherhood or rejecting the symbolic.

71. See Winnicott, "The Location of Cultural Experience": "From the beginning the baby has maximally intense experiences in the potential space between the subjective object and the object objectively perceived . . ." (p. 118).

72. Quoted in Winnicott's "The Location of Cultural Experience." According to Marion Milner, in "D. W. Winnicott and the Two-way Journey," Winnicott said the aphorism was "to aid speculation upon the question, If play is neither inside, nor outside, where is it?" (p. 39).

73. Erik H. Erikson, "Womanhood and the Inner Space."

74. Winnicott, "Creativity and Its Origins," p. 97.

75. Donna Bassin, "Woman's Images of Inner Space." Bassin demonstrates how the theme of self-discovery runs through women's poetry. The view of psychoanalysis as a space in which to explore one's own inner life and share it with an other contrasts with Freud's archaeological metaphor in which the analyst is the phallic explorer uncovering the patient's relics and delivering the mutative interpretation. It suggests how psychoanalysis may, at times, step out of the discourse of knowledge as power. For the feminist critique of knowledge as power in psychoanalysis, see the essays in Bernheimer and Kahane (eds.), *In Dora's Case,* and Jane Gallop, *Reading Lacan.*

76. Carol Gilligan and Eve Stern, "The Riddle of Femininity and the Psychology of Love."

77. Montgrain, "On the Vicissitudes of Female Sexuality: The Difficult Path from 'Anatomical Destiny' to Psychic Representation."

78. Ghent, "Masochism, Submission, and Surrender."

CHAPTER 4: THE OEDIPAL RIDDLE

1. Freud, *Civilization and Its Discontents,* p. 72.

2. Much of the groundwork for Lasch's position had already evolved in his earlier book, *Haven in a Heartless World.* Lasch's work gave intellectual respectability to what might more properly be called the "popular" critiques of narcissism (e.g., Tom Wolfe, "The 'Me' Decade and the Third Great Awakening") and public exposure to the psychoanalytic critiques (e.g., Simon Sobo, "Narcissism as a Function of Culture"). His arguments also differed, by his own account, from serious sociological critiques of this period in that he saw not individualism but "lack of privacy" as the problem. Here Lasch polarizes the issues: one either criticizes the invasion of public life by inappropriate forms of intimacy, as does Richard Sennett in *The Fall of Public Man,* or one correctly recognizes that "personal life has almost ceased to exist." Thus he dismisses Sennett's defense of bourgeois civility as a valid basis for public political life, while he himself clamors for the same bourgeois values in private life.

3. The interest in narcissistic pathology, in problems of regulating self-esteem and establishing a cohesive self or self-representation, began to take shape in the sixties (see Annie Reich, "Pathological Forms of Self-Esteem Regulation," and Edith Jacobson, *The Self and the Object World*) and was flourishing by the time of Kohut's publication of *The Analysis of the Self* in 1971.

4. Kohut's *The Restoration of the Self,* Kernberg's *Borderline Conditions and Pathological Narcissism,* and more recently Modell's *Psychoanalysis in a New Context.*

5. Kohut, *The Restoration of the Self.*

6. Freud elaborates this in *The Ego and the Id.*

7. Lasch, *The Culture of Narcissism,* p. 41.

8. In formulating his position, Lasch drew heavily on the more sophisticated arguments of the Frankfurt School which had been presented anew in the seventies by Russell Jacoby (see *Social Amnesia*). The main outlines of the thesis relating declining parental authority to loss of oedipal autonomy had been formulated by Horkheimer in his 1949 "Authority and the Family Today," and amplified by Marcuse in "The Obsolescence of the Freudian Concept of Man."

9. Lasch, *The Culture of Narcissism,* pp. 300–305. See also Rogow, *The Dying of the Light,* and Sobo, "Narcissism as a Function of Culture."

10. See Lasch, *Haven in a Heartless World,* and Jacques Donzelot, *The Policing of Families.*

11. Joel Kovel suggests how the same intellectual tradition can lead to a different analysis of the family. He recognizes that capitalist development, particularly expanding commodity consumption, has not vitiated but stimulated the growth of personal life, so that the individual is frustrated in the home and confronts a depersonalized public world, which "is nowhere enriched . . . to the level of demand created by the development of the personal sphere" (Kovel, *The Age of Desire,* p. 117). See also M. Barret and M. McIntosh, *The Anti-Social Family.*

12. The oedipal model is an internalization theory, in the sense that I discussed earlier, stressing identification with parental functions and ideals. Some psychoanalysts, like Otto Kernberg (see *Borderline Conditions and Pathological Narcissism*), do give the superego an important role. But the formation of the superego is not the only aspect of internalization, and the force that controls insatiable desire and infantile wishes is a less popular concept than the ego that oversees differentiation between self and other. Lasch himself later criticized (see *The Minimal Self*) the overemphasis on the superego (while not specifically disavowing his position in *The Culture of Narcissism*) as he came to see that the issue takes a back seat to that of separation.

13. Juliet Mitchell, in *Psychoanalysis and Feminism,* states that the father is the necessary intermediary "if any relationship is to move out of a vicious circle," and his phallus "breaks up . . . the dyadic trap" (p. 397). The idea that the child remains trapped in the maternal dyad, a closed circle of the imaginary, unless the symbolic father (who can be presented mediately by the mother) intervenes, means that mutual recognition is not possible within the dyad.

14. Freud, *Civilization and Its Discontents,* p. 73.

15. Freud, *The Future of an Illusion,* p. 24: "The mother, who satisfies the child's hunger, becomes its first love-object and certainly also its first protection against all the undefined dangers which threaten it in the external world—its first protection against anxiety, we may say. In this function the mother is soon replaced by the stronger father, who retains that position for the rest of childhood."

16. In *The Culture of Narcissism,* Lasch states: "The most convincing explanations of the psychic origins of this borderline syndrome draw on the theoretical tradition established by Melanie Klein. In her psychoanalytic investigations of children, Klein discovered that early feelings of overpowering rage, directed especially against the mother and secondarily against the internalized image of the mother as a ravenous monster, make it impossible for the child to synthesize 'good' and 'bad' parental images" (p. 83). Klein's theory has been used by Michael Rustin ("A Socialist Consideration of Kleinian Analysis") to make the opposite argument—namely, that good object relations generally enable the child to integrate destructive emotions. Lasch often moves in one breath from a reference to the image of the archaic mother to real "narcissistic" mothers: "Behind this image of the phallic father stands an even earlier attachment to the primitive mother, equally untempered by experiences that might reduce early fantasies to human scale. Narcissistic women seek to replace the absent father, whom the mother has castrated, and thus to reunite themselves with the mother of earliest infancy" (p. 299). Both the archaic mother image and the narcissistic ideal of an all-powerful father arise because of what the castrating mother does when the father is gone.

17. See George Devereux, in "Why Oedipus Killed Laius: A Note on the Complementary Oedipus Complex in Greek Drama," and Marie Balmary, *Psychoanalyzing Psychoanalysis.*

18. The firstborn son, unseated by the next sibling, also identifies with the father. Freud's own guilt at his murderous wishes toward his younger brother, which seemed to have been fulfilled when that brother died in infancy, may have led to his identification with Laius's infanticide, as his mix-up of fathers and brothers in *The Interpretation of Dreams* (see note below) suggests.

19. Freud, *The Interpretation of Dreams,* pp. 256–57. Donna Bassin called my attention to the Kronos myth.

20. Freud, *The Psychopathology of Everyday Life,* pp. 218–19.

21. Freud, *Civilization and Its Discontents,* pp. 131–32: "This remorse was the result of the primordial ambivalence of feeling towards the father. His sons hated him, but they loved him, too. After their hatred had been satisfied by their act of aggression, their love came to the fore in their remorse for the deed. It set up the super-ego by identification with father; it gave that agency the father's power, as though as a punishment for the deed of aggression they had carried out against him, and it created the restrictions which were intended to prevent a repetition of the deed."

22. Fairbairn, *Psychoanalytic Studies of the Personality,* pp. 65–67.

23. Freud, *Group Psychology and the Analysis of the Ego,* pp. 122–28. The idea of a dreaded primal father is rather undeveloped in psychoanalytic theory; it plays its largest role under a different name, the fear of homosexuality, which is a reaction to the unconscious fantasy of being the father's passive victim. This fantasy is not a function of the early preoedipal phase of identification but of an early oedipal phase involving the "negative Oedipus complex" with an anal-phallic father.

24. Freud, *Group Psychology and the Analysis of the Ego,* p. 105. Freud states that it is only later, in the Oedipus complex, that the boy "notices that his father stands in his way with his mother. His identification with his father then takes on hostile coloring." As I shall point out, it is only with this hostile coloring that all the feelings ascribed to the son regarding the preoedipal father properly begin—the murderousness, the rivalry, the rebellion against authority.

25. Freud, *Group Psychology and the Analysis of the Ego,* pp. 112 and 113. What distinguishes ordinary identification from submission, Freud says, is whether we identify with the other in our ego or *take the other as our ideal.* But "with many people this differentiation within the ego does not go further than with children" (p. 110). For children the identification with the parent as ego and as ego ideal are not so different, and that is why childhood ideal love, if affirmed, can serve to build the ego, whereas in adulthood it generally only exacerbates the distance between ego and ideal.

26. T. W. Adorno, "Freudian Theory and the Pattern of Fascist Propaganda." This analysis was applied to American mass culture in Horkheimer and Adorno, *Dialectic of Enlightenment.*

27. The Frankfurt theorists' own study of authoritarianism, *The Authoritarian Personality* (Adorno et al.), did not confirm the "fatherless" thesis about disappointment in a weak father: the liberal subjects were more critical of their parents; the authoritarian ones were uncritically idealizing of their parents.

28. Epigraph to Chasseguet-Smirgel's *Sexuality and Mind* from Thomas Mann's 1930 story, "The Trees in the Garden."

29. For example, Hans Loewald writes in "Ego and Reality": "Against this threat of the maternal engulfment, the paternal position is not another threat or danger, but a powerful force" (p. 14).

30. Chasseguet-Smirgel, "Freud and Female Sexuality."

31. Freud, "On Narcissism" and *The Ego and the Id.* See also Chasseguet-Smirgel, *The Ego Ideal.*

32. Chasseguet-Smirgel, *The Ego Ideal.*

33. Chasseguet-Smirgel, "Some Thoughts on the Ego Ideal," p. 357.

34. Ibid., pp. 358–59; and Chasseguet-Smirgel, *The Ego Ideal,* p. 76. In her later formulation in the book, Chasseguet-Smirgel stresses the "progressive" function of the ego ideal as a compromise between primary narcissism and object relations, since the child's projection of his narcissism on to the parental ideal draws him closer to reality and encourages his development.

35. Chasseguet-Smirgel, "Some Thoughts on the Ego Ideal," p. 359.

36. Ken Corbett, in "Illness, Variation, Liberation: Psychoanalytic Interpretations of Male Homosexual Development," shows how Chassseguet-Smirgel reduces the erotic relationship to the narcissistic tie.

37. Honey and Broughton, "Feminine Sexuality: An Interview with Janine Chasseguet-Smirgel." Chasseguet-Smirgel makes this point about Lacan when suggesting how problematic is the use of Lacan by feminists.

38. Chasseguet-Smirgel, *The Ego Ideal*. She points out that the threat of castration is simply a reflection of the concrete recognition that, for both boys *and* girls, "compared with father I am too small, too impotent, I do not have what is required to satisfy mother"—a point also made by Horney in "The Dread of Woman." This idea of the narcissistic injury was originally developed by her colleague, Bela Grunberger, in *Narcissism*. Yet another way to look at this is that since the father's phallus is the object of the mother's desire, it represents the fact that the mother needs something outside of herself; thus she is not perfect, not omnipotent, and not the realization of the narcissistic ideal of self-completion.

39. Kernberg, *Internal World and External Reality*, pp. 288–91.

40. The contradiction between external reality and unconscious fantasy cannot be ignored, or simply dissolved by saying that psychoanalysis deals only with fantasy. Rather we must try to account for the contradiction, to explain the inability to represent the mother in a more differentiated way.

41. Gilligan, *In a Different Voice*. See also Doris Bernstein, "The Female Superego: A Different Perspective," and J. Alpert and J. Spencer, "Morality, Gender and Analysis."

42. Chasseguet-Smirgel, *The Ego Ideal*, p. 31.

43. Ibid., p. 30: "In fact it falls principally to the mother—at least in the early stages of life—to encourage her child to project his ego ideal onto successively more evolved models." The idea that our narcissism develops, and what conditions foster that development, was highlighted in Kohut's work (see *The Restoration of the Self*). By emphasizing the parent not only as ideal object, onto whom we project our narcissism, but also as mirroring object, who confirms our own sense of agency and self-esteem, Kohut contributed decisively to the idea of an evolving narcissism.

44. Chodorow *(The Reproduction of Mothering)* points out that the abstractness of paternal "positional" identification is also a source of idealization.

45. Chasseguet-Smirgel, "Some Thoughts on the Ego Ideal," p. 362. She reiterates this point in each of her later works, *The Ego Ideal* and *Sexuality and Mind.*

46. Chasseguet-Smirgel, *Sexuality and Mind,* pp. 87–89. Her assumption that this kind of perversion is the key to understanding fascism strikes me as problematic. By contrast, Klaus Theweleit, in his exhaustive study of early fascist militants, *Male Fantasies,* argues that the fascist has no experience of primary gratification or narcissistic fusion with the mother, nor does he seek such reunion by circumventing the father.

47. Chasseguet-Smirgel, "Freud and Female Sexuality" (p. 286) and "Some Thoughts on the Ego Ideal" (p. 371).

48. Chasseguet-Smirgel, "Freud and Female Sexuality," p. 284.

49. Freud, "Female Sexuality," p. 226.

50. Stephanie Engel, "Femininity as Tragedy."

51. Ibid., p. 101.

52. Lasch, *The Minimal Self,* see especially pp. 178–85.

53. Ibid., pp. 245–46.

54. Ibid., p. 192. In this regard Lasch did not alter his original position as presented in *The Culture of Narcissism*. For example, see pp. 299–301.

55. Chasseguet-Smirgel, "Perversion and the Universal Law."

56. Lasch, *The Minimal Self*, p. 246. In a reply to his critics, "The Freudian Left and the Cultural Revolution," Lasch claims that I propose as an alternative to patriarchy such values as " 'women's kinship and friendship networks,' 'sisterhood,' 'mutual recognition and nurturant activity,' " values that could only be "institutionalized in a totalitarian setting . . ." (p. 30). In fact, I did not claim women's solidarity and networks as an alternative but as the real basis of nineteenth-century family and socialization—what the fatherless-society critics regard as a "lost utopia" and mistakenly attribute to paternal authority; see my "Authority and the Family Revisited."

57. Freud, "Analysis Terminable and Interminable," p. 252.

58. Freud, "Some Psychical Consequences of the Anatomical Distinction Between the Sexes."

59. Freud, *The Ego and the Id*, p. 34.

60. See Freud's discussion of homosexual libido, the ego ideal, and love of someone like the self, in "On Narcissism."

61. Hans Loewald ("The Waning of the Oedipus Complex") has also argued that the point of the oedipal prohibitions is to establish a "barrier between identification and object cathexis." The important thing, in regard to a mother who can draw one back, is to make sure that one loves her only in one way, inside or outside, as it were.

62. Horney, "The Flight from Womanhood." See also Dinnerstein's discussion of this point in *The Mermaid and the Minotaur*.

63. Dinnerstein, in *The Mermaid and the Minotaur* (p. 43), speaks of "the mother-raised boy's sense that the original, most primitive source of life will always lie outside himself."

64. Chasseguet-Smirgel, "Freud and Female Sexuality."

65. Freud, "Female Sexuality" and "Femininity." See Horney's disagreement, "The Denial of the Vagina."

66. Chasseguet-Smirgel, "Freud and Female Sexuality," p. 281.

67. Honey and Broughton, "Feminine Sexuality: An Interview with Janine Chasseguet-Smirgel," p. 542.

68. Gallop, *The Daughter's Seduction,* p. 58. This is a reading of Irigaray's essay from *Speculum of the Other Woman.* The blind spot is the vagina, obscured by the phallus; it is the blindness of Oedipus, who remains embedded in the phallic phase.

69. Chasseguet-Smirgel, "Freud and Female Sexuality," p. 283.

70. Chasseguet-Smirgel ("Freud and Female Sexuality," p. 282) cites an argument of Joyce McDougall to the effect that the sight of castration would require the child to recognize "the role of the father's penis and to accept the primal scene," again referring us back to the primary importance of the father's phallus rather than accepting the vagina for its own sake.

71. Chasseguet-Smirgel, "Freud and Female Sexuality." I suggest that the best position regarding the Oedipus complex (as now theorized, it is the male complex) in the phallic phase is to consider it only one step toward accepting "reality," for it only recognizes the rights of the father. A critical psychoanalytic view would find the phallic phase's insistence on the exclusive rights of the male sex as a makeshift and defensive resolution to the dilemma of difference, which ought to be superseded in a later phase. It is evident that the failure of psychoanalysis thus far to delineate another equally important phase—the true "genital phase," which Freud located in adolescence but never elaborated—implies a powerful statement about the limits of theory (and probably of development itself) under male supremacy.

72. Fast, *Gender Identity: A Differentiation Model,* pp. 97–98.

73. Ibid., p. 106.

74. The loss of capacities associated with these identifications is more severe in those whose identity is more rigidly defined by gender. See Ricki Levenson, "Boundaries, Autonomy and Aggression."

75. The consequence of repressing this sense of bodily continuity may be, as Bataille implies, that the desire for it becomes tied to erotized images of death and murder. One might be justified in arguing that in male fantasy, love of death takes the place of primal continuity with others. On this, see Theweleit *(Male Fantasies)*, who emphasizes the role played by denial of the body.

76. N. O. Brown, *Life Against Death,* p. 51. The upshot of this position is that all striving is Faustian restlessness and all sociability is repressive. In essence, this position represents a refusal to accept ambivalence, as accepting disillusionment along with hope. Brown, like Marcuse in *Eros and Civilization,* juxtaposes a repressive reality principle to the connection to the world achieved through primary narcissism. And so man's ultimate desire is, like the final salvation of Faust by "Das ewig weibliche," (the eternal feminine), the image of the virgin mother.

77. Loewald, "The Waning of the Oedipus Complex," pp. 772–73.

78. Ibid., p. 757

79. This phrase from Braunschweig and Fain's *Eros et Anteros* is cited and discussed by Kernberg in *Internal World and External Reality,* p. 286.

80. Freud, *The Interpretation of Dreams,* pp. 256–57.

81. Loewald, "The Waning of the Oedipus Complex."

82. Descartes, *Discourse on Method,* p. 47.

CHAPTER 5: GENDER AND DOMINATION

1. See Sandra Harding and Meryl Hintikka, *Discovering Reality,* and Seyla Benhabib and Drusilla Cornell, eds., *Feminism as Critique.*

2. See Michele Rosaldo, "Women, Culture, and Society," and the historical discussion of the separation of male and female spheres in Nancy Cott, *The Bonds of Womanhood*.

3. Weber, *Economy and Society*.

4. Weber, *Economy and Society*, pp. 85–87. This problem was further elaborated by other social theorists, such as Karl Mannheim in *Man and Society in an Age of Reconstruction*.

5. For example, Max Horkheimer, "Traditional and Critical Theory," p. 226. Lukacs's discussion of the penetration of culture and society by the commodity form is in his *History and Class Consciousness*.

6. Marx, in *Capital I,* shows how the commodity form, based on the exchange of equivalent value, serves to obscure the relation of domination—the fetishism of commodities.

7. Foucault's idea of discourse or "discursive practice" is developed in *The Archaeology of Knowledge and The Discourse on Language*. A discourse is not ideology, not a result of some deeper structure; it is, itself, a system of power.

8. See Adorno's critique of the concept in "Sociology and Psychology," and the Frankfurt Institute for Social Research's *Aspects of Sociology*.

9. Marcuse, "Philosophy and Critical Theory," p. 138.

10. Keller, *Reflections on Gender and Science*, pp. 33–42.

11. Keller, "Making Gender Visible in the Pursuit of Nature's Secrets," p. 74.

12. Ibid.

13. Keller, *Reflections on Gender and Science*, p. 87.

14. Ibid., pp. 75–94.

15. See Lukacs, "The Antinomies of Bourgeois Thought" in *History and Class Consciousness*, Horkheimer and Adorno, *Dialectic of Enlightenment*, and Horkheimer's "Authority and the Family." This idea is comparable to Freud's notion (in "Mourning and Melancholia") that the ego takes into itself the lost object, building itself through identification, but this depletes the subject of his connection to the outside world.

16. Lacking an intersubjective theory, the critical theorists were confined to the Freudian concept of the ego. In *Dialectic of Enlightenment,* Horkheimer and Adorno put forth the slim hope that the act of reflection that consumed the world might now restore it by reflecting on and limiting itself. See Benjamin, "The End of Internalization."

17. Marcuse (in *Eros and Civilization*) sought a solution to the impasse of reason with a notion of Eros that was able to infuse mind and spill over to the world, a sensuous perception of and play with the world that was friendly toward living things, a notion of "the reunion of all that has been separated." However, this notion does not address the problems of omnipotence and the subject-object split, which Marcuse had already understood in his philosophical writings. In "Technology and Science as Ideology," Habermas criticized Marcuse's solution and proposed that the Marxian concept of the social as given through labor stayed within the terms of instrumental reason. He proposed an additional dimension of the social as symbolic interaction, and the idea of intersubjective discourse as illustrated by the psychoanalytic dialogue *(Knowledge and Human Interests)*. However, in adopting this perspective Habermas lost interest in the *psychological* question of what makes rationality instrumental and an agency of domination.

18. Keller, *Reflections on Gender and Science.*

19. See Ernst Schachtel, *Metamorphosis.*

20. Keller, *Reflections on Gender and Science,* p. 165. See also *A Feeling for the Organism,* a study of the life and work of Barbara McClintock.

21. Gilligan, *In a Different Voice.* See also Erik H. Erikson, *Childhood and Society.*

22. See L. Kohlberg, *The Philosophy of Moral Development,* and L. Kohlberg and R. Kramer, "Continuities and Discontinuities in Childhood and Adult Moral Development." See J. M. Murphy and C. Gilligan, "Moral Development in Late Adolescence and Adulthood: A Critique and Reconstruction of Kohlberg's Theory."

23. Benhabib, "The Generalized and the Concrete Other." (I have quoted from an earlier version of this article; see published version in Benhabib and Cornell, *Feminism as Critique,* in bibliography.) It is not Gilligan's intention to explain the *origins* of sexual difference and inequality, but to chart its *consequences* in the biased view of femininity, especially in psychology, that excludes and invalidates feminine experience. (The question is, would an analysis of the origins significantly change the consequences?) In correcting that bias she does not intend to equate care with passivity or self-sacrifice, but instead to challenge that equation. See her response to critics in "On *In a Different Voice:* An Interdisciplinary Forum."

24. Gilligan, "Remapping the Moral Domain." She argues that the mirror metaphor does not include the subjectivity of the other as does the notion of dialogue.

25. Gilligan, "Remapping the Moral Domain," p. 240.

26. Lawrence Kohlberg, "Reply to Owen Flanagan." See Benhabib, "The Generalized and the Concrete Other," for a discussion of Gilligan's critics, including Kohlberg and Habermas. Benhabib criticizes their formalism in separating moral development from ego development, and argues that, according to Habermas's own theory ("Moral Development and Ego Identity"), it should be possible to construct an intersubjective dialogue about moral values that does take account of particular needs. In my view, to ground intersubjectivity in demonstrable psychological capacities of self development is crucial; the theory itself has to specify the capacities that allow us to sustain the necessary tension between protecting universal morality from relativism and protecting particularity from universality.

27. Benhabib, "The Generalized and the Concrete Other" (see n. 23, above).

28. Weber, "Science as a Vocation," p. 155.

29. Bellah et al., *Habits of the Heart.*

30. Brigitte and Peter Berger, *The War over the Family;* Christopher Lasch, *Haven in a Heartless World* and *The Culture of Narcissism;* Jean Bethke Elshtain, *Public Man, Private Woman.* For a critical discussion of this position, see Michele Barret and Mary McIntosh, *The Anti-Social Family.*

31. Berger and Berger, *The War over the Family,* pp. 102, 117, 172.

32. Ibid., pp. 118–24.

33. Ibid., p. 120.

34. Lasch, "Why the Left Has No Future"; Elshtain, "Feminism, Family, and Community." Lasch blames feminists and socialists for upholding individual rather than communitarian values. He conflates the left with liberalism, which indeed espouses the ideal of the individual, even though the critique of that liberal ideal always came from the left. He also suggests that the sexual liberation espoused by feminists means that they repudiate the need for binding commitments in personal life—ignoring feminist criticism of the masculine rejection of intimacy and abrogation of parenting responsibility.

35. Berger and Berger, *The War over the Family,* p. 120.

36. Ibid., p. 205.

37. Ibid., p. 210: "In terms of family policy, it seems to us that high on the agenda should be measures to arrest the rampant interventionism by the state and to restore the autonomy of the family." For example, they believe all families should receive education vouchers so that they could choose whatever type of schooling they prefer for their children. However, the funds to build and maintain schools come not from tuition, but from the state or from private endowments. Furthermore, their opposition to public childcare flies in the face of economic reality: while they argue that only intellectuals and feminists think that women should work outside the home, and that the working class esteems the traditional family and sex roles, it is, in fact, working-class families that are hardest hit by unstable and inadequate childcare (see the Census Bureau's 1982 report, "Childcare Arrangements of Working Mothers"). In 1986, the Bureau of Labor Statistics reported that 48 percent of mothers with children under one year old worked outside the home (*New York Times,* March 16, 1986). The percentage of working mothers of preschool children increased from 29 in 1970, to 42 in 1980 (see Clarke-Stewart, *Daycare*), to about 50 percent in 1987 (see Children's Defense Fund, "U.S. Work Force in the Year 2000").

38. Elshtain's *Public Man, Private Woman* strongly upholds this position.

39. *The Minimal Self,* p. 243. There is much valuable thinking in Lasch's book. But there appears to be a dreamlike blind spot in his presentation of mothers and fathers. When he cites the discussion of instrumental rationality in my article "Authority and the Family Revisited; or, A World Without Fathers?" (a commentary on Horkheimer's "Authority and the Family"), he drops the first part of the title and leaves out the question mark, which leaves it "A World Without Fathers." What does this slip mean? After all, Lasch is the one who believes that our society is fatherless—I agree with those who argue that men are more interested in parenting than in the past. The blind spot is the inability to see that "what Freudian feminists want" is not to abolish fathers, but for men to give up abstract authority in favor of the active nurturing of children.

40. Elshstain, *Public Man, Private Woman,* pp. 291–96.

41. Winnicott, *The Child, the Family, and the Outside World,* p. 10.

42. On the decline of interfamilial, especially female, networks in the post-war period and the difficulty of replacing them with conjugal solidarity, see Young and Willmott, *Family and Kinship in East London,* and Elizabeth Bott, *Families and Social Networks.* The nineteenth-century family form which gave rise to the specific vision of motherhood and marital balance that gender conservatives refer to relied on a world outside the family that no longer exists. According to Mary Ryan *(Cradle of the Middle Class),* the separation of male and female spheres was not tantamount to women's privatization in the individual home. Instead, her study of Oneida, New York, in the early nineteenth century showed that all the functions of emotional support, physical care, socialization, and sexual regulation extended beyond "the walls of a single dwelling unit and the bonds of kinship . . . [into] a larger social universe."

43. See Lenore Weitzman's study, *The Divorce Revolution,* on female poverty after divorce.

44. See Barbara Ehrenreich, *The Hearts of Men.*

45. Elshtain, *Public Man, Private Woman,* p. 305. Elshtain asks: "Why should a personalized, localized, particular female subject be brought into the more abstract rationalized, universal mode?" Having posed the question, one might expect Elshtain to affirm or dispute the obvious answer—to get power over the conditions that affect her particular existence. But instead she offers some evocative rhetoric about women's world: "who would tend to the little world, keeping alive its life-redeeming joys and tragedies?" Elshtain entirely ignores the major point of the feminist critique of sexual relations: that men must assume their share of responsibility for personal relations, even as women join the public world. The conclusion is to repudiate sexual politics and deny the problem of male domination, as Judith Stacey points out in "Are Feminists Afraid to Leave Home?"

46. See Jessie Bernard's critique of isolated motherhood in *The Future of Mother-hood.*

47. Fraiberg, *Every Child's Birthright,* p. 94.

48. Ibid., p. 100.

49. Berger and Berger, *The War over the Family,* p. 155.

50. Bowlby's position on daycare, cited in Clarke-Stewart, *Daycare.* The revision of his theory of monotropic attachment in favor of multiple attachments is discussed in H. R. Schaffer's *The Growth of Sociability* and *Mothering.* Schaffer and Emerson ("The Development of Social Attachments in Infancy") found in their study of infant attachment that within three months of the onset of attachment behavior, a minority of 41 percent of the infants had only one attachment figure, and by eighteen months of age only 13 percent had one attachment figure. Within one month of onset, 27 percent also chose their father as an attachment figure, and by eighteen months of age, 75 percent did.

51. See Clarke-Stewart, *Daycare.* In 1982, as of Clarke-Stewart's writing, there were only two million daycare places for eight million preschool children.

52. Rosalind Petchesky, "Fetal Images: The Power of Visual Culture in the Politics of Reproduction."

53. Lasch, *The Minimal Self,* p. 169.

54. Chodorow and Contratto, "The Fantasy of the Perfect Mother."

55. Winnicott, *The Child, the Family, and the Outside World,* p. 62.

56. The lack of opportunity for successful destruction is significantly related to the problem of the regressive uses of reenchantment. The issue here is the "malady of the ideal," which has informed symbolic politics of both right and left. The cataclysmic outcome of the revolutionary tradition in our century has been diagnosed, with some justice, as a kind of "unbearable lightness" of idealism, a loss of reality in the headiness of power or the euphoria of righteousness. I would put it this way: the idealistic lightness is a breakdown of tension between self and other, the flying off into space that happens when destruction wins out and the other does not survive. The revolutionary ideal of just violence, unchecked by the sense of limits or the connection to the real other, becomes a case in failed destruction. By idealizing the cause and putting all badness on the enemy, a field of mental omnipotence is created in which everything is permitted. Inevitably, the self-idealization of political movements has been followed by disillusionment, which repudiates what it once idealized. This should be understood in terms of the breakdown of the tension between idealization and destruction. It is the inability to tolerate the questioning of the ideal and the turning of all destruction away from it which finally results in such disillusionment. The counterpoint to idealism is the opportunity to creatively destroy, in other words, to challenge and criticize authority, the very persons, ideas, and institutions that have been idealized.

57. Freud, "Femininity," p. 133: "A mother is only brought unlimited satisfaction by her relation to a son; this is altogether the most perfect, the most free from ambivalence of all human relationships." See also *Civilization and Its Discontents,* p. 113.

58. Dworkin, "Pornography and Grief," p. 289.

59. MacKinnon, *Feminism Unmodified,* p. 7.

60. I have not tried to name the origin of this structure, to locate it in a specific set of social relations. The issue of the relationship between culture, representation, and language on the one side, and object relationships and individual development on the other has rightly been controversial in feminist theory. Feminist psychoanalytic theory has taken two different approaches to understanding the reproduction of the gender system and its manifestation in a culture. As the editors of a volume of feminist psychoanalytic criticism (S. N. Garner, C. Kahane, and M. Sprengnether, *The (M)other Tongue,* p. 20) put it, one side, represented especially by Chodorow, has assumed the perspective of the individual child and parental object relations, which in turn mediate social structure; the other, influenced by French psychoanalytic theory, has emphasized "the effect of a preexisting system of representation on the emergence of gender." But despite (or because?) of its focus on culture and its roots in literary criticism, the latter approach defines gender as a less mutable, symbolic structure; it becomes constitutive of the psyche, rather than a function of historically constructed relationships. The object relations theory thus takes the more historical approach, anchored in social science. From my point of view, these approaches need not be mutually exclusive. The object relations approach, while not itself a theory of representation, has offered a theory of the splitting, of the relationship between male subject and female object, at the heart of gender representation. Where the two approaches intersect is precisely at this crucial point, the critique of splitting.

INDEX

ABOUT THE AUTHOR

Jessica Benjamin is a practicing psychoanalyst in New York City and a fellow of the New York Institute of the Humanities at New York University. Her highly acclaimed articles have been published in feminist and psychoanalytic journals and are widely anthologized.